601 West 26th Street, 18th Floor
New York, NY 10001, USA
www.assouline.com
ISBN: 9781614282594
Printed in China.
Design by Jihyun Kim.

BY KATE YOUNG

DRESSING FOR THE DARK

FROM THE SILVER SCREEN TO THE RED CARPET

ASSOULINE

“Dressing up for a party is good manners, as important as thanking your host or making conversation with the other guests. When I see a film where the characters dress up, even for dinner, I wish we still did. Clothes have incredible transformative powers.”

Kate Young

Contents

Introduction

My first job as a stylist was working with up-and-coming actresses for the "People Are Talking About" section of *Vogue.* At the time, in the early 2000s, no one in fashion got overly excited about celebrities. Models ruled; celebrities were not shadowed in the way they are today, having their every outfit and coffee break tracked by *Us Weekly.* But for me, the assignment brought together two of my passions: the way real people dress and the movies. It was when I started styling shoots for Herb Ritts—encouraged, I am very grateful to say, by Anna Wintour and *Vogue* fashion director Tonne Goodman, whom I was assisting at the time—that everything changed for me. Herb had the ability to make actresses look like screen goddesses. Consequently, every star in Hollywood wanted to be photographed by him, and I was outfitting the biggest names in film.

But whether I'm finding a dress for a newcomer or someone with a career's worth of major films to her credit, I love working with actresses because they're real people. I know that might sound strange, but compared with models, they are. Yes, they have access to more glamour than most women do. But unlike models, they have real bodies and real personalities. I think that's why women find actresses so inspiring, both in life and on the screen. They're characters who you care about and can identify with. If you're a petite brunette from Long Island, you probably think you have something in common with Natalie Portman and may recognize a bit of yourself in her. It's natural to want to re-create her aesthetic in your life. I think this ability to be a bit of an everywoman is what makes Sofia Vergara so successful. She's beautiful, with an amazing body, but she's also playful and approachable.

This desire to emulate and identify is often especially potent when watching films, because it's such an intrinsically voyeuristic experience. When you watch *Dirty Dancing,* even if you've never been to a Catskills resort, you know what it's like to be on a family holiday, or to be treated like a child, or to have failed at something important. You don't have to be exactly like Baby to identify with her. I'm a sucker for a sweeping storyline, beautiful scenery, and characters you want to be friends with.

And, of course, I obsess over the clothes on-screen, especially the gowns, because they're the ones associated with the big, emotional moments. I could watch *Marie Antoinette* on mute and just look at what the actors are wearing. And when I see a film where the characters dress up, even for dinner, like in *Atonement,* I wish we still did. Clothes have incredible transformative powers. When Julia Roberts puts on that red dress and those white gloves in *Pretty Woman,* everything has changed. That's true in real life, too, especially with gowns, because we wear them for the major events in our lives—weddings, romantic dinners, when we're honored for our work. We look to them to both bolster our confidence in these moments and to help us enjoy them. This is why I always say that context is the most important thing when choosing a dress. Will it be worn in the city or the country? Will you be the center of attention or a supporting player? Is it a family or work event? I would not, for example, suggest wearing the same dress to a friend's wedding as I would for the red carpet. They're both important events, but they have completely different needs. You can be fairly secure in your ability to put yourself together for the office and still not have a clue what to put on for a big night.

That's where this book comes in—to provide inspiration, ideas, and practical tips. Film is an endless source of sartorial inspiration for me. Who wouldn't want to look as sexy as Eva Green in *Casino Royale* in her cutout dress, or as elegant as Grace Kelly in *To Catch a Thief*? When I start working with a client on a project—for example, dressing her for a series of movie premieres—I begin by making a mood board. One of my main sources of imagery is film. I can show an actress a runway shot from a designer's latest collection, but that won't rev up her imagination. However, if I present her with an image of Elizabeth Taylor in *Cat on a Hot Tin Roof*, she can immediately think, *I loved that film. I want to look like her.* I believe most women would feel the same way. And so, what you're holding in your hands grew out of the research that I've done for clients.

This book is structured with chapters on the cocktail dress, the sexy dress, the statement dress, the black dress, and the formal dress, reflecting the way, in my experience, women approach dressing for the evening. The cocktail dress is probably the most common form of special-event dressing. Similarly, almost everyone finds a black dress indispensable. The other categories are ones I've noticed that women gravitate toward. A sexy woman will always want to wear a sexy dress, just as a fashion woman will always want a statement dress. In each chapter, I've explained how I see the category, which I've illustrated with examples from films and from actresses I've dressed. I've also included inspirational still lifes—if you're wondering, for example, what the ideal pair of black pumps look like or what a good update of a 1950s cocktail gown would be, they're here.

Lastly, I would like to say that the key to evening dressing up is to enjoy yourself. Choose the dress that makes you smile. If you're a person who wears black, have a black dress in your closet. It's worth its weight in gold lamé. If you're a potter and you live in Woodstock, a black dress may not have any place in your life, so make it a color you love. The bottom line is, every woman should have a dress that makes her feel beautiful.

Dressing up for a party is good manners, as important as thanking your host or making conversation with the other guests. As with so many things about etiquette, Emily Post put it best: "In the world of smart society...clothes not only represent our ticket of admission, but our contribution to the effect of a party. What makes a brilliant party? Clothes. Good clothes."

It's Always Five O'Clock Somewhere: The Cocktail Dress

I like to say that it's always five o'clock somewhere. For me, cocktail is the most fun of all the dressing-up categories. It's relaxed enough that you don't have to worry about managing a formal gown, but dressy enough that you get to indulge in girlie flourishes like red lipstick, high heels, and fun accessories. I love the allure of cocktails, the feeling that the night is young, that you can leave your workday self behind and slip into a glamorous world where it's all martinis and witty banter. It makes you feel like your life is a scene from a movie.

Cocktail culture, and cocktail dresses, originated in the 1920s, when social codes loosened, allowing the sexes to mingle for predinner imbibing. Before that, ladies and gentlemen did not drink together; ladies had wine with dinner and the occasional sherry. So in a sense, the cocktail dress is a symbol of emancipation. It may not be as historic as women getting the vote, which happened in 1920, but it was part of the same process. In a similar vein, though cocktail parties were an international phenomenon, there's something very American about their informality and inclusiveness, which is perhaps what Christian Dior was referring to when he said, "The real masterpieces of American design are the cocktail dresses, the cocktail being the symbol par excellence of the American way of life." I'll drink to that!

In the movies, the ultimate cocktail party has to be the one depicted in *Breakfast at Tiffany's,* where Audrey Hepburn as Holly Golightly accidentally sets a woman's hat on fire and just as accidentally puts it out—and no one in her completely packed apartment notices because they're having such a good time. Holly's the ultimate cocktail girl; it's definitely always five o'clock in her world! You can see it in the way she dresses: 90 percent of the time we see her, she's in a well-fitted sheath with a matching shoe,

A glass of champagne, a sparkly dress, a mix of jewelry—Mia Farrow as Daisy Buchanan in *The Great Gatsby* really conveys the fun and optimism of cocktail dressing. She looks as if she has rummaged through her jewelry box and put on her favorite pieces.

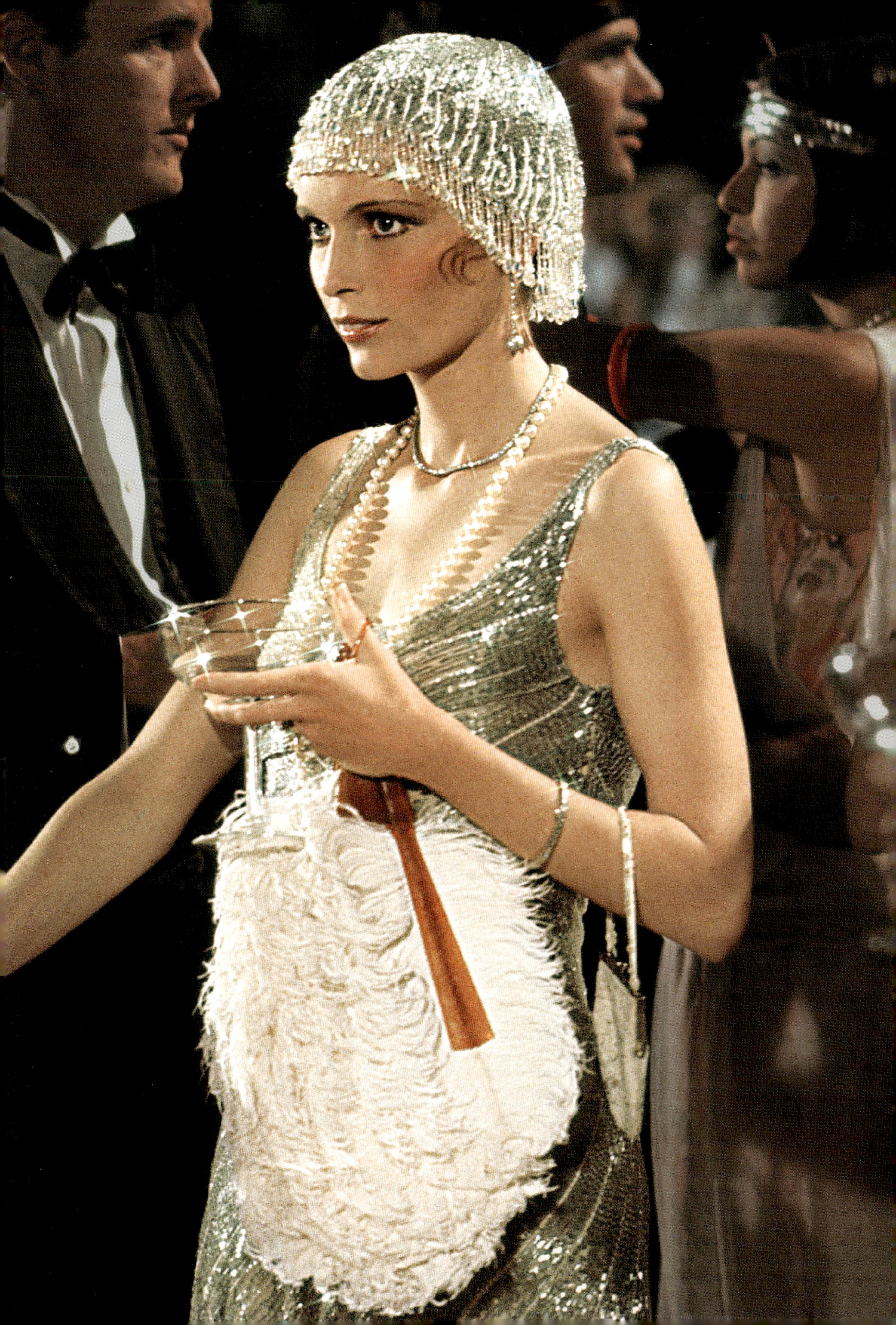

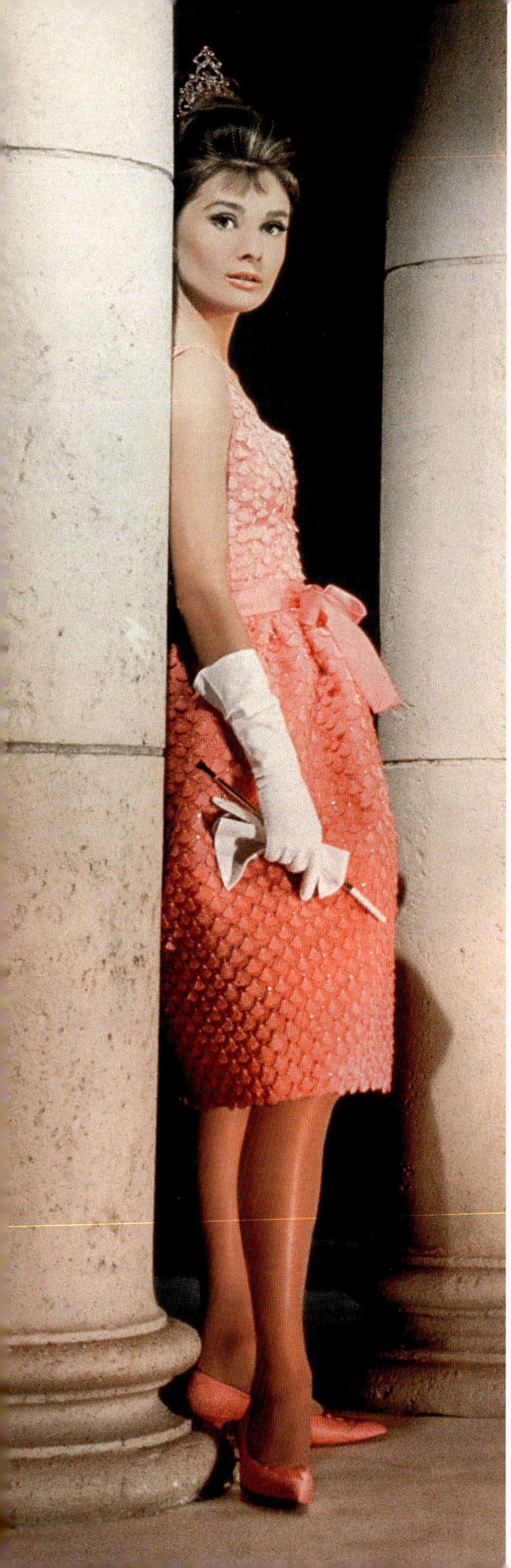

accessorized with whimsical jewelry. This is the classic cocktail look. I don't think any girl can see this film, and this outfit, and not want to move to New York and be fabulous. Yet take away the accessories, and the look is pretty conservative. But—and this is why I think accessories are so important for cocktails—the accessories make it playful. You know Holly's not a stuffy lady by the blonde streaks in her hair and the fact that she's carrying a cigarette holder that's about a foot long. Part of your obligation as a guest is to contribute to the mood and the sociability—it's bad manners to just stand around. A quirky accessory helps you out because it's a great conversation starter. It shows that you've put some effort into your look and are ready to be social. In another Audrey Hepburn cocktail look, from *How to Steal a Million,* she wears a black lace mask cut from the same fabric as her dress. This may sound kind of outlandish, but you could wear that sort of thing into a room, laugh, take it off, look completely normal, *and* have something to talk about.

No one exemplifies classic cocktail dressing like Audrey Hepburn, seen here in *Breakfast at Tiffany's* (wearing another of the fabulous ensembles that appear in the film) and *How to Steal a Million* (*opposite*). A chic little dress paired with fun accessories works every time.

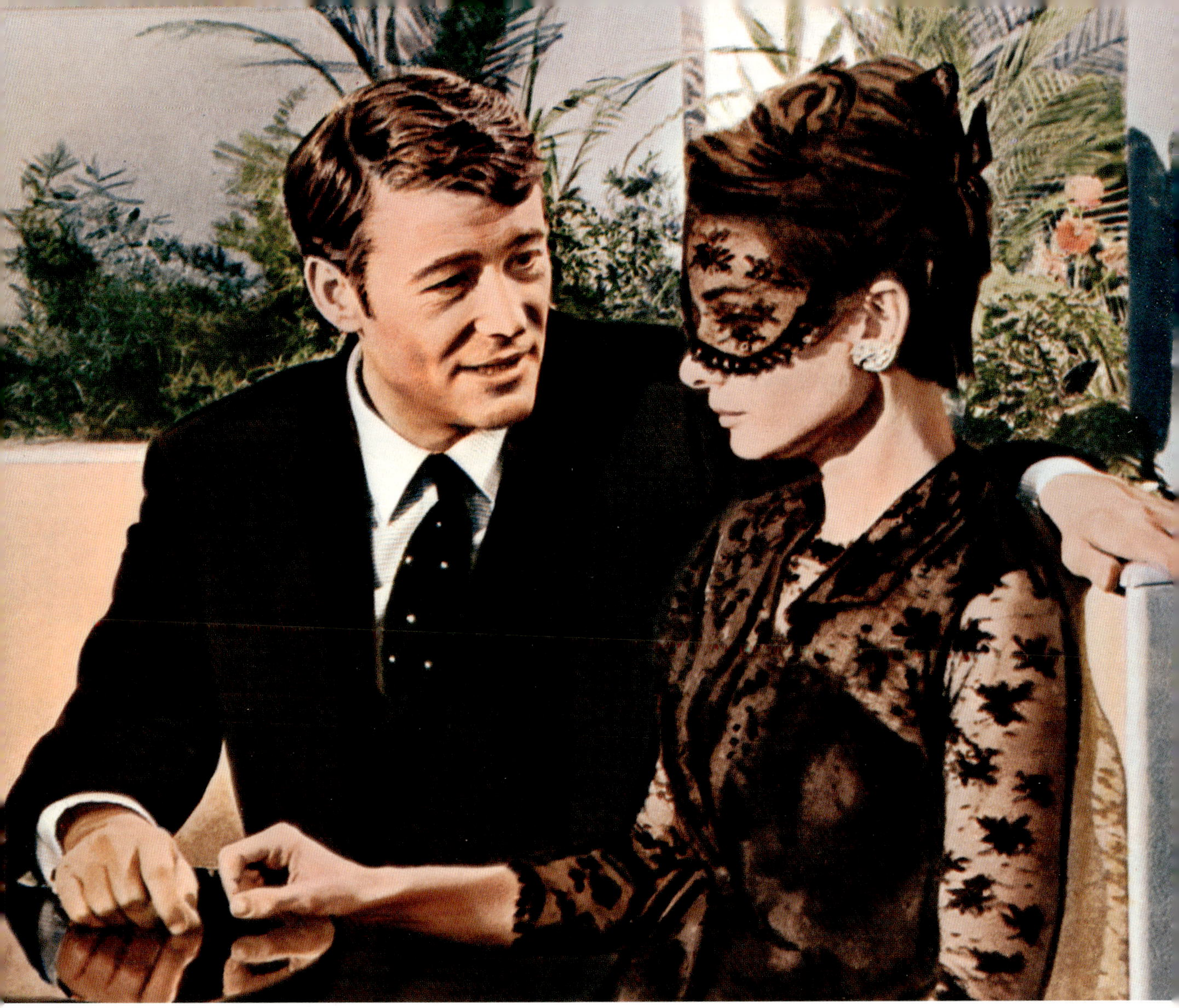

“I believe in manicures.
I believe in overdressing.
I believe in primping at leisure
and wearing lipstick.”

Audrey Hepburn

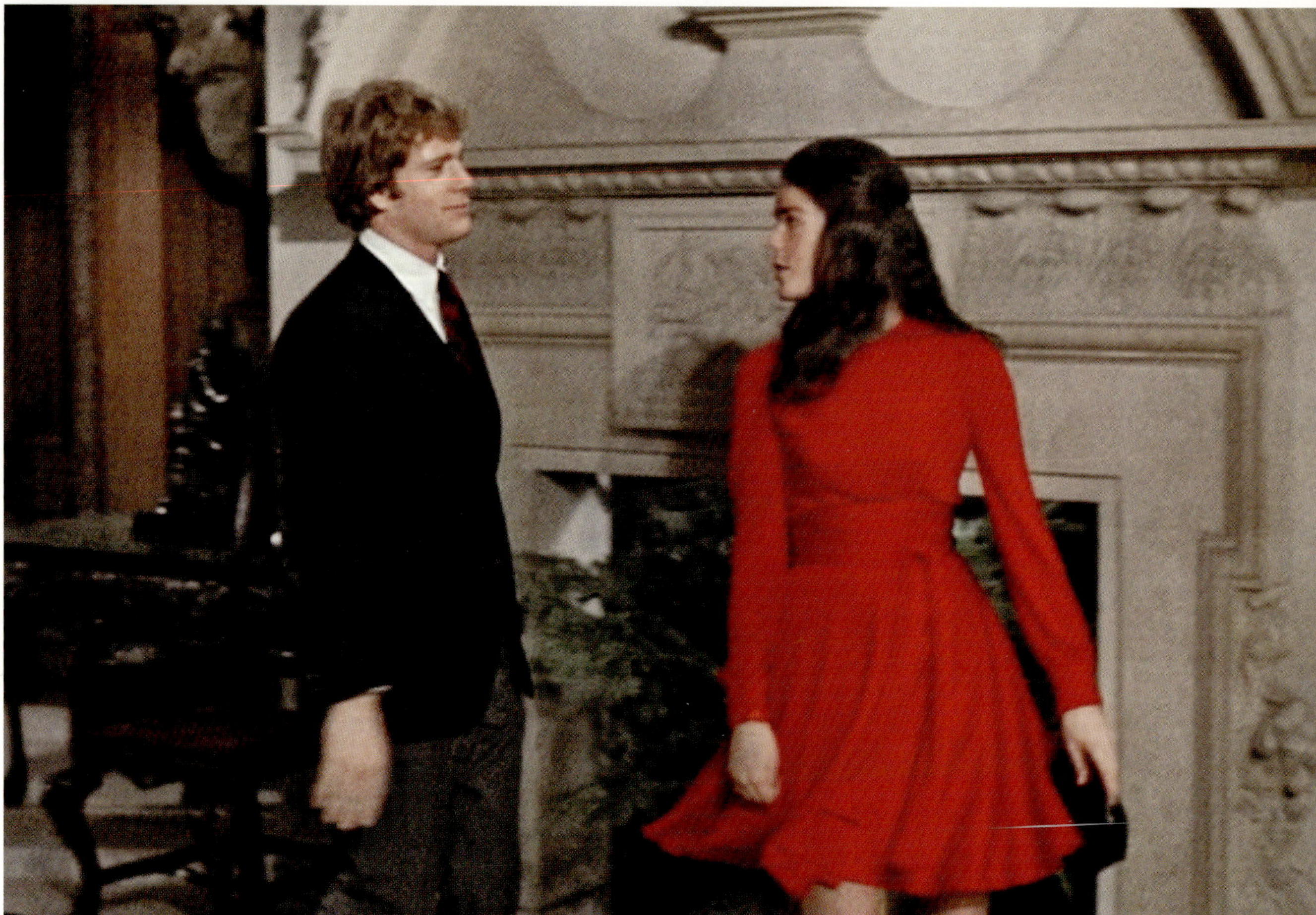

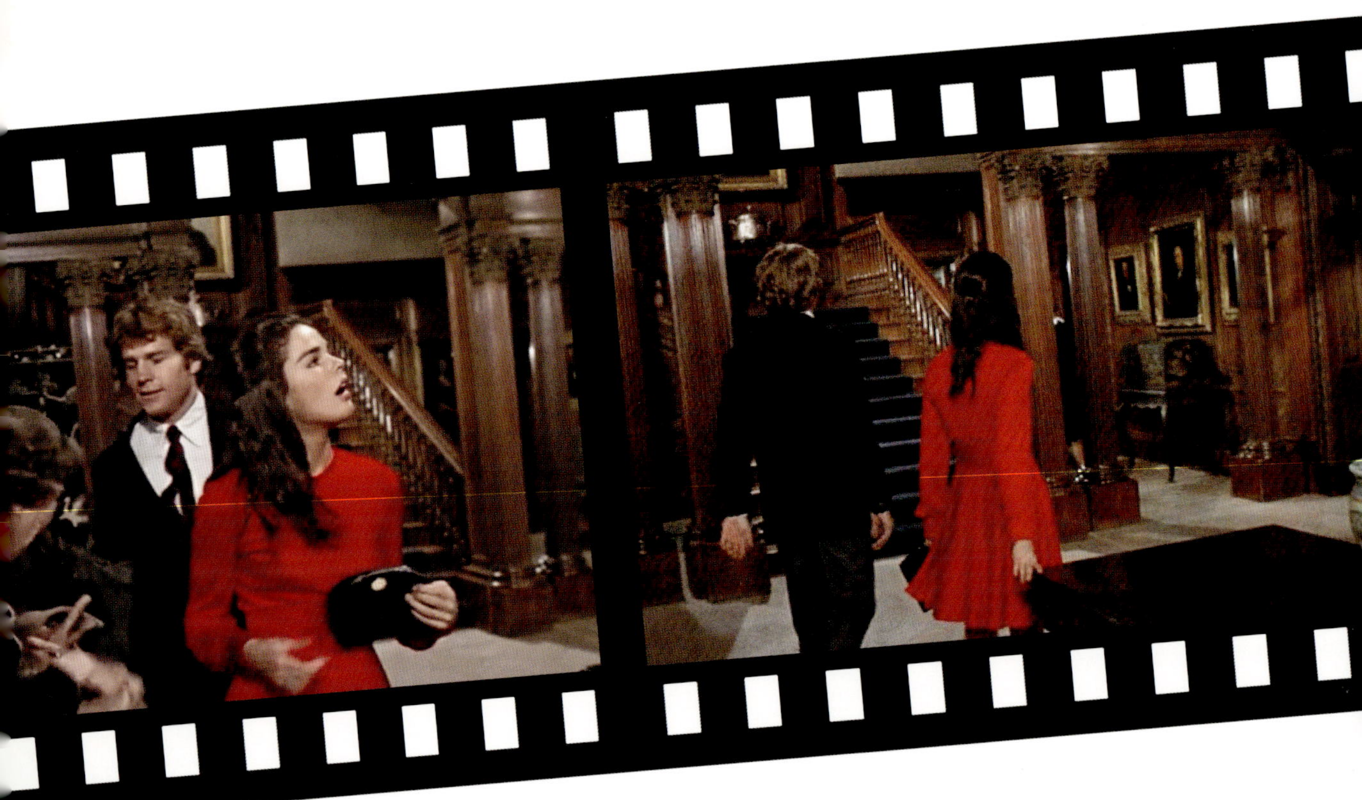

> “The dress must not hang on the body but follow its lines. It must accompany its wearer and when a woman smiles the dress must smile with her.”

Madeleine Vionnet

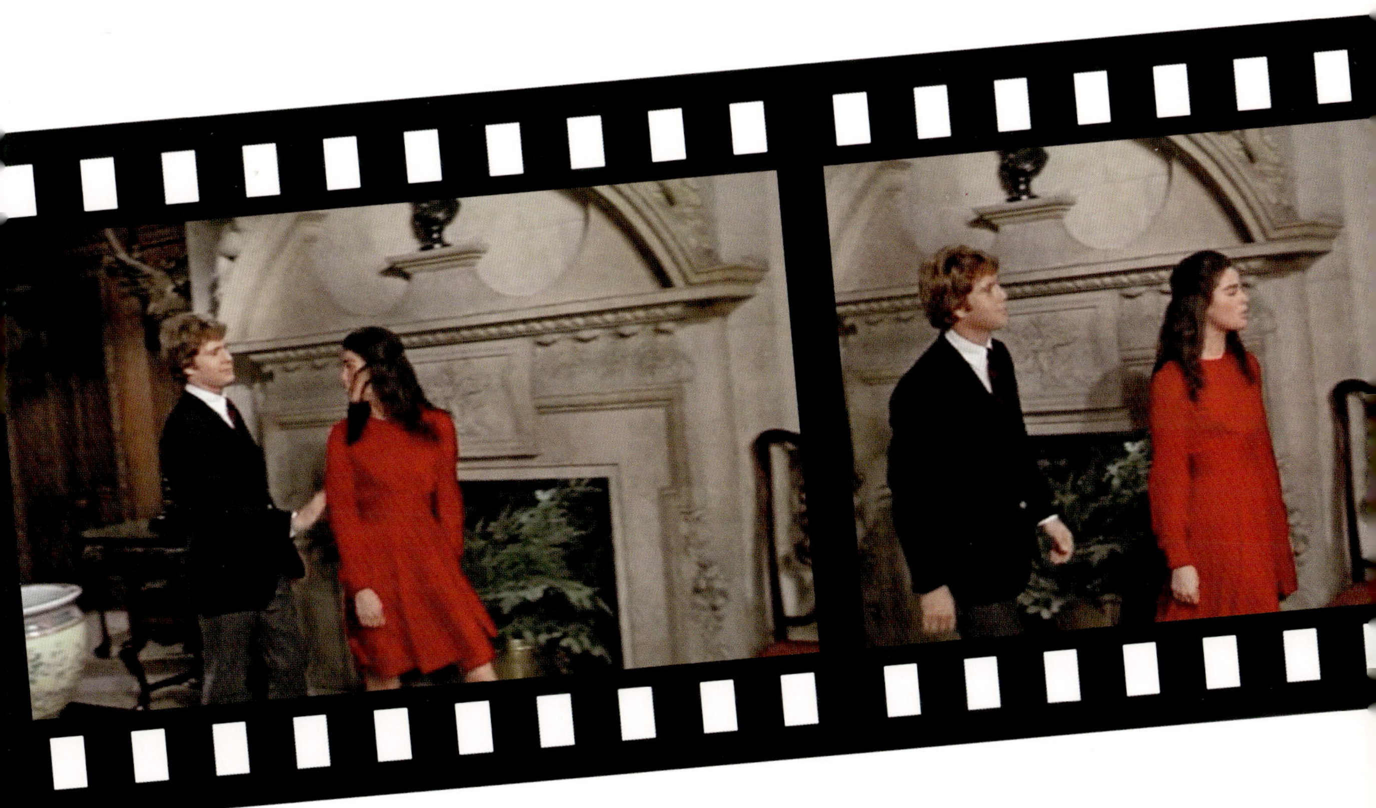

Don’t be afraid to embrace color. The simple red fit-and-flare dress Ali MacGraw wears in *Love Story* makes a powerful—but still sweet and flirty—statement.

This gold dress by Lanvin makes you want to twirl around. Even though it's metallic, it looks as light as meringue thanks to the raw edges and the slightly dull finish—the exact opposite of the usual tight gold-beaded cocktail dress. *Opposite:* Cocktail dressing is a great time to embrace vintage. Whether you go with a flapper frock à la Kirsten Dunst in *The Cat's Meow,* a 1940s tea dress, or a 1980s stretchy mini, you can get away with a costume-y feel.

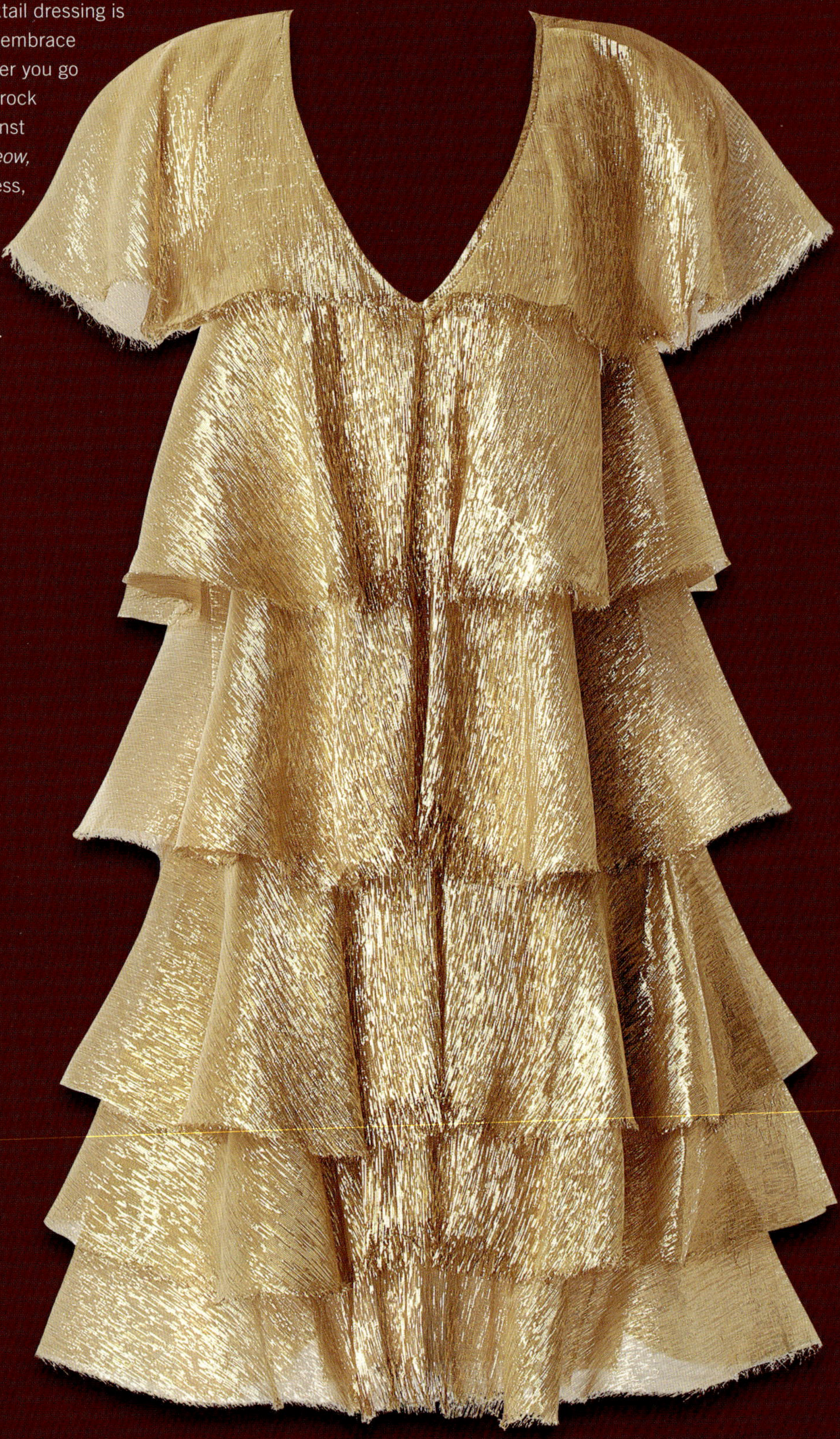

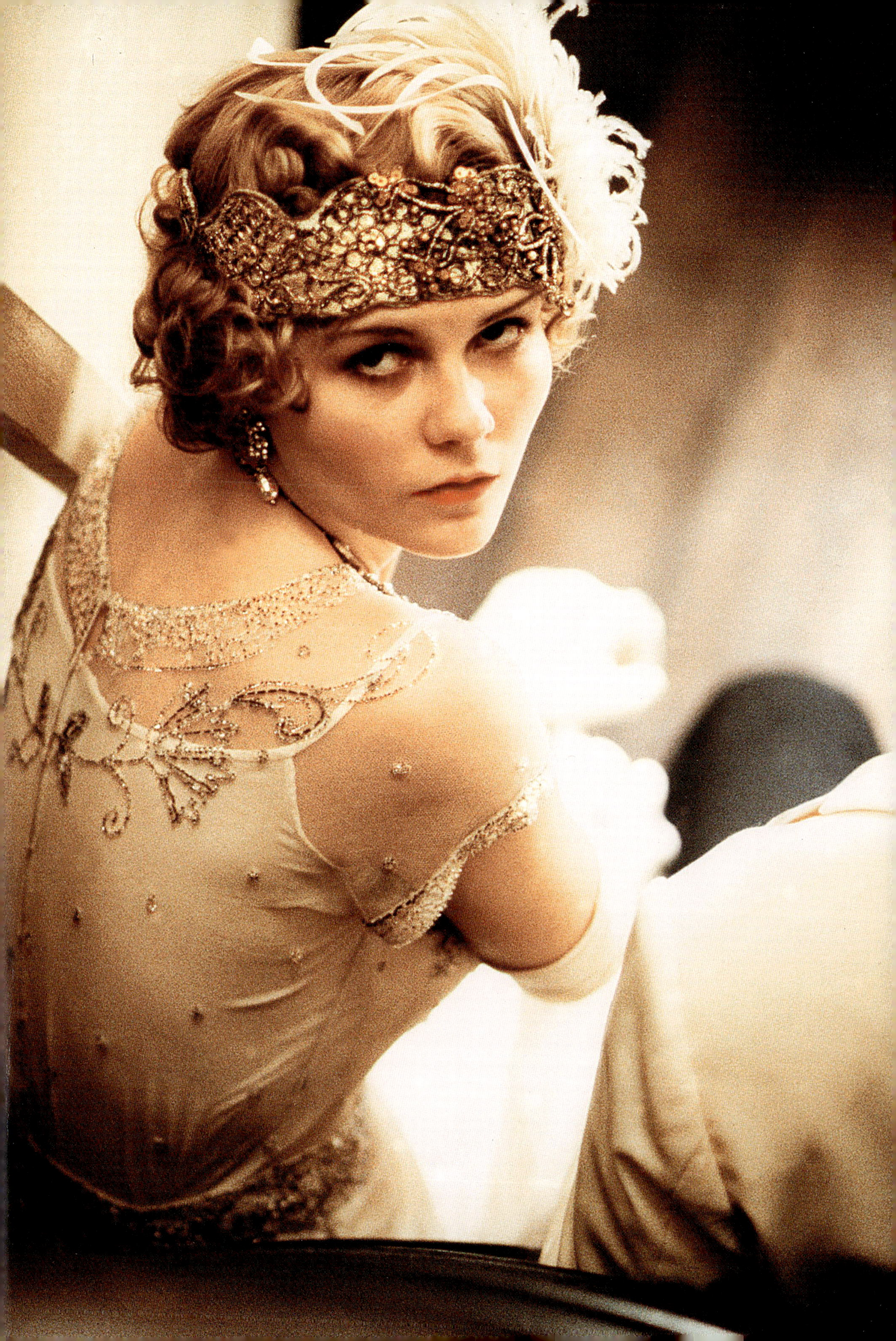

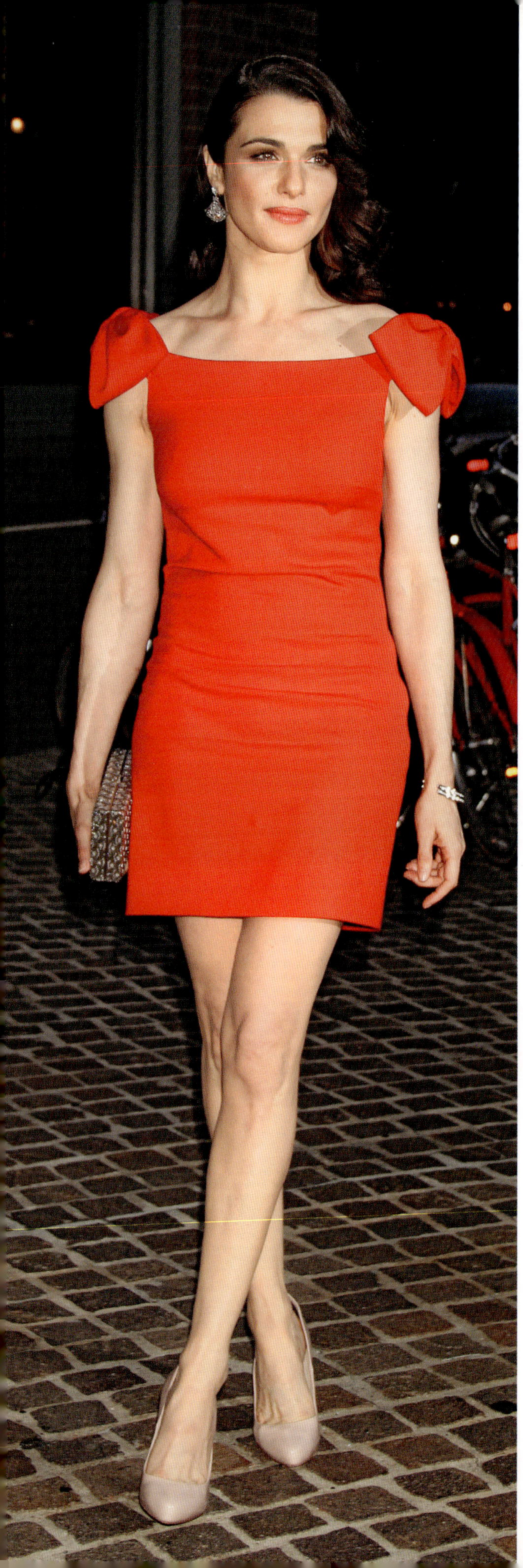

“Beauty, to me, is about being comfortable in your own skin. That or a kick-ass red lipstick.”

Gwyneth Paltrow

Whimsy + color + sparkle = the perfect cocktail look. The bows on Rachel Weisz’s dress for this screening of *The Whistleblower* make it feel feminine and festive; the jewels and minaudière add some sparkle; and the nude heels elongate her legs. *Opposite:* I love a body-conscious dress with a flirty detail, like the flutter hem on this beaded Azzedine Alaïa number. A tight dress needs a lighthearted touch to keep it from seeming heavy-handed and female predator-ish.

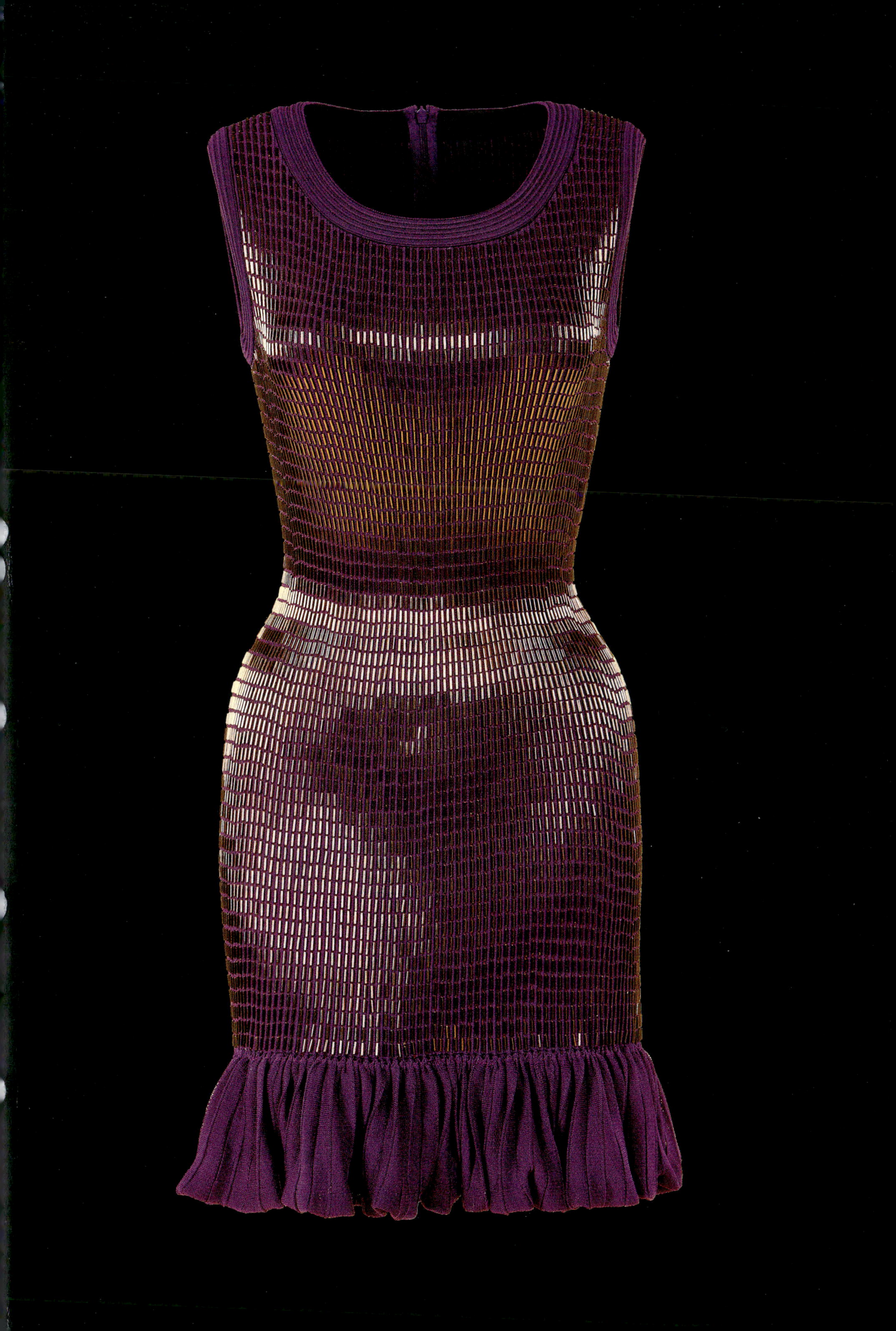

It's good to step outside your comfort zone a little when it comes to a cocktail party. I would never wear a bright green pants suit, but I would wear a bright green cocktail dress—or even a bright green evening suit. In that context, it feels right. It's always a bold statement to commit to wearing all one color, like the white suit, hat, and heels Michelle Pfeiffer wears in *Scarface.* This may be my favorite look in this chapter. It's so pulled together in an Old Hollywood way, yet totally modern—you could put a silk blouse under that suit and go to work. If you don't want to make color the focus of your outfit, consider a little sparkle. Nothing says I'm ready to have a good time like sparkle. It's why I love Mia Farrow's shiny green party dress in *The Great Gatsby.* Everything about it, from her simple frock to the way she has casually layered on different necklaces, says that she's relaxed and happy. Maybe you won't go as far as wearing a full-on beaded cap like Mia does, but cocktail hour is the perfect time to wear hair jewelry. A little tulle headband or a simple gold barrette takes your look out of the ordinary and feminizes even the most minimal outfit. Wear a big print.

"I wear my sort of clothes to save me the trouble of deciding which clothes to wear."

Katharine Hepburn

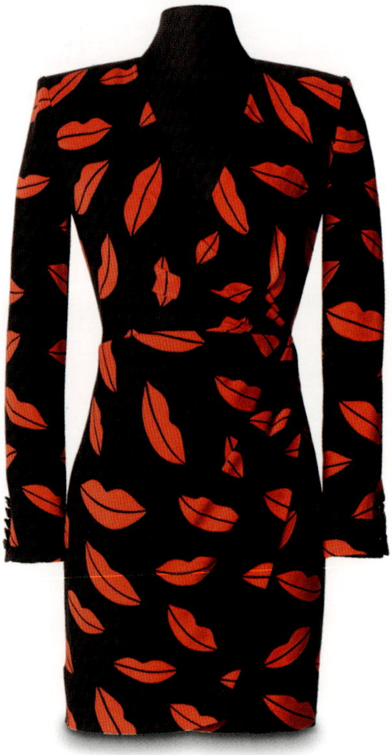

A lip print like the one on this Saint Laurent dress allows the clothes to flirt for you. A fun print is a conversation starter, which, combined with the always flattering wrap shape, makes this dress a cocktail hour winner. *Opposite:* Sometimes you just have to decide on one note and carry it through, as Michelle Pfeiffer does in this chic all-white ensemble in *Scarface.* If this outfit had been styled with red shoes and a black bag, it would have lost its power.

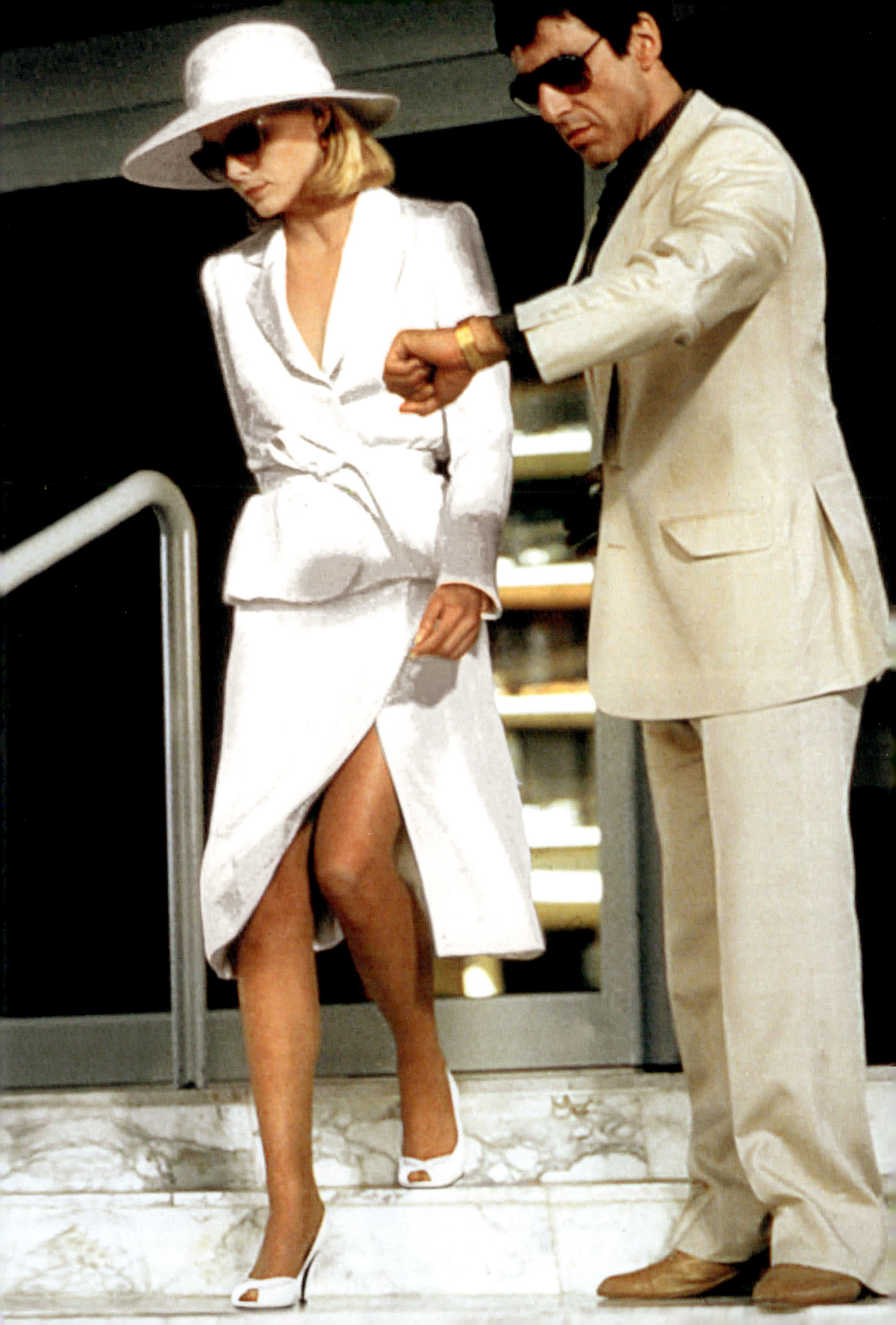

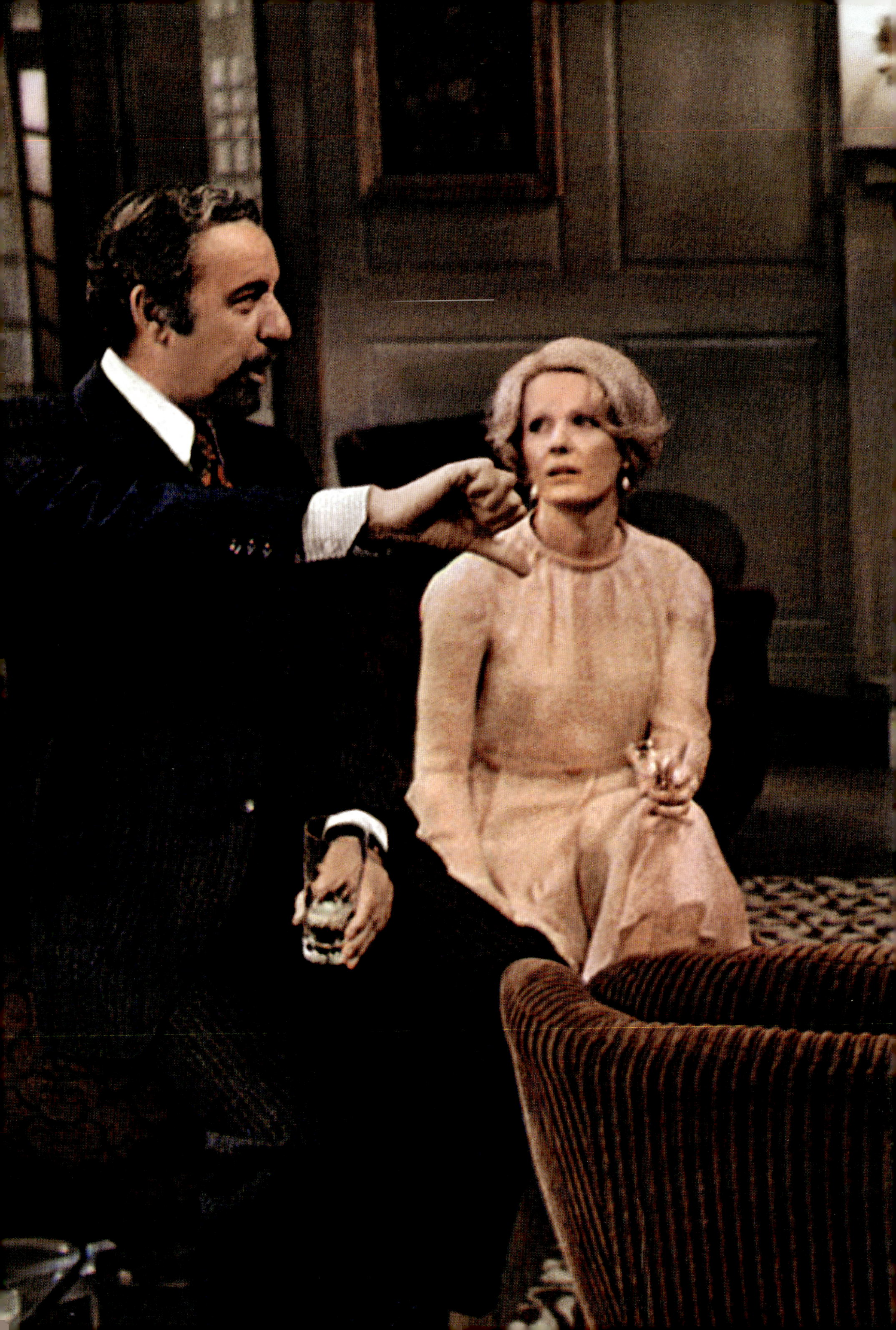

“When I went to Hollywood in 1927, the girls were wearing lumpy sweaters and skirts... I was wearing sleek suits and half-naked beaded gowns and piles and piles of furs.”

Louise Brooks

Mingling and chatting, as shown in this scene from *The Discreet Charm of the Bourgeoisie,* are prerequisites for cocktail party guests. It's bad manners not to, just as it's bad manners not to dress up for the occasion.

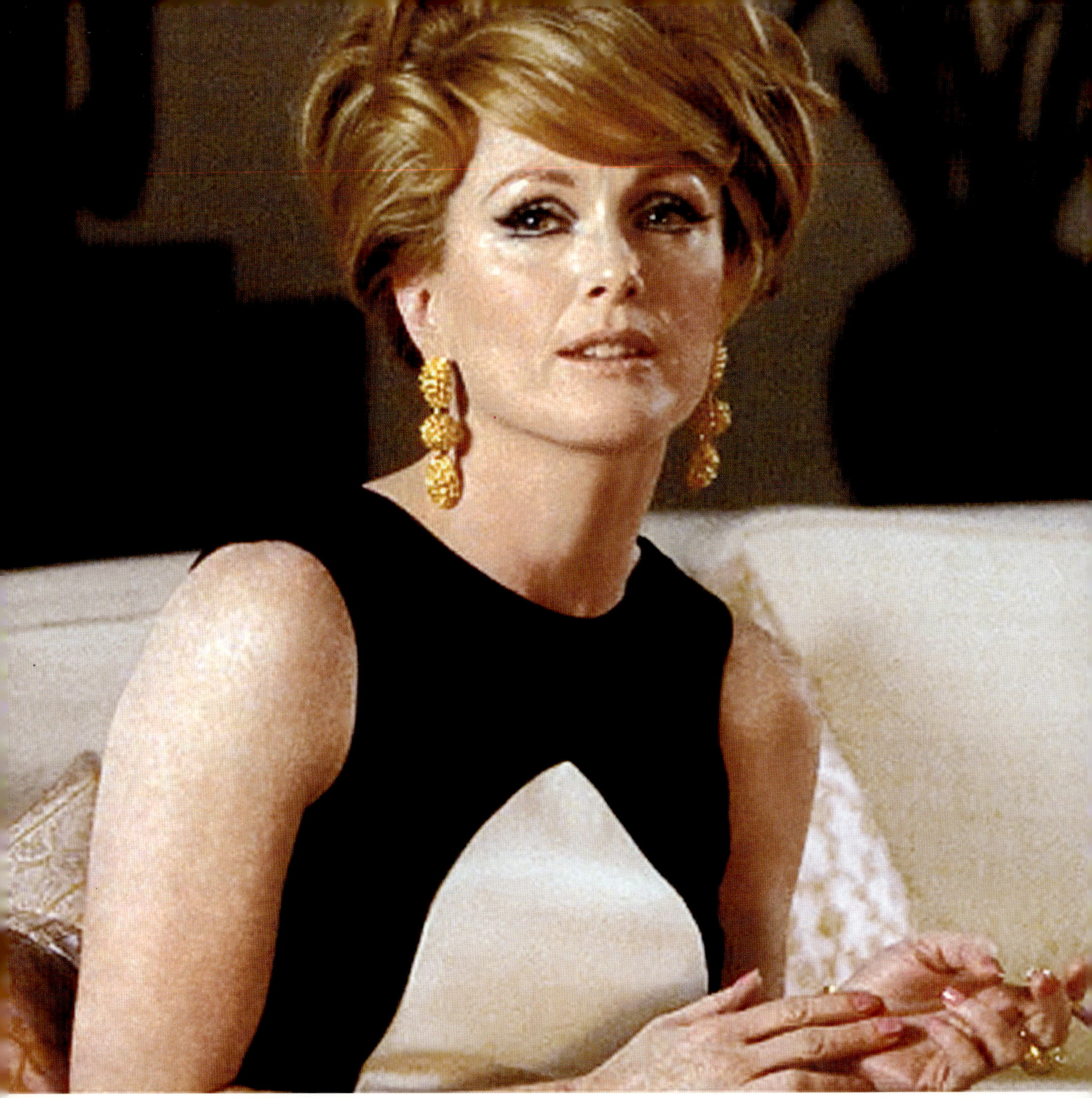

When your dress is as graphic as the one Julianne Moore wears in *A Single Man,* keep your look balanced with more-organic accessories and hair. *Opposite:* Cocktail hour gives you a chance to be more feminine than you can be at work, which is why I love the scalloped hem and white rose at the waist of this Valentino dress—they're simple but effective.

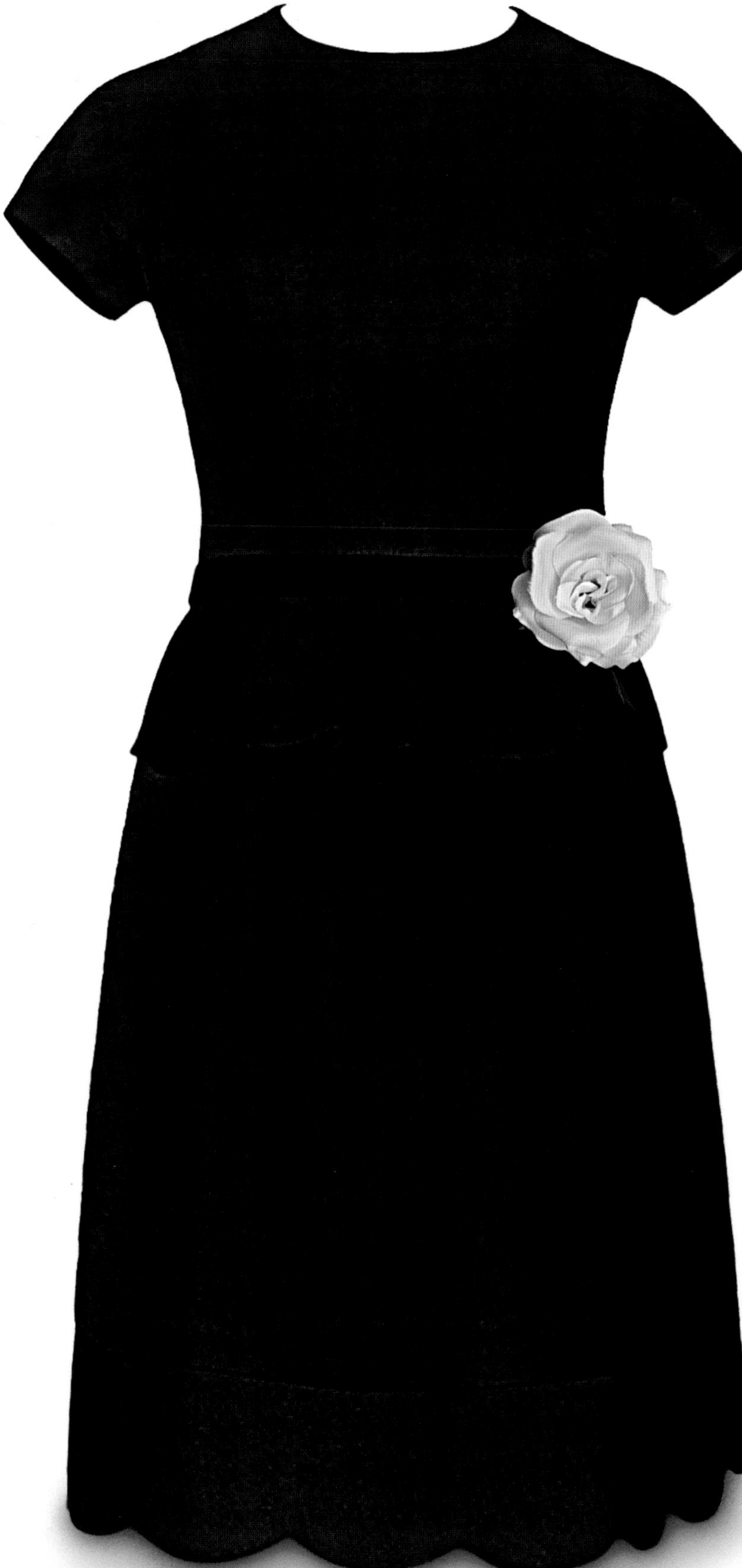

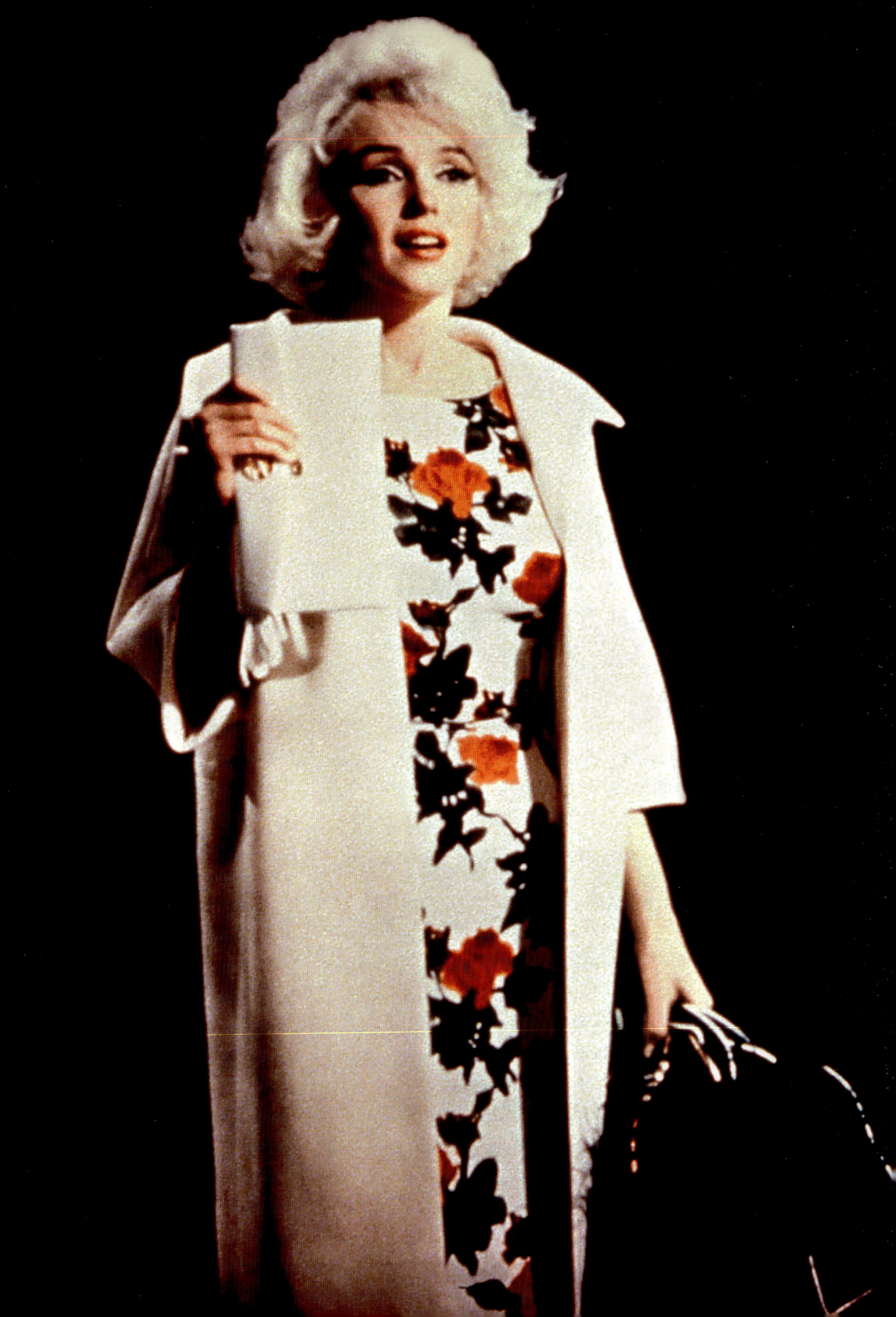

Experiment with vintage, like a 1940s tea dress or a stretchy 1980s dress—this is one time when it's okay to look a little costume-y. And wearing vintage lets you tap into feminine details such as silky fabrics, which have largely disappeared from daywear.

If you're coming from work, you have to plan ahead a little. You don't want to look like you're wearing a day dress to a party. What a wasted opportunity! I know a lot of women prefer to wear a dress for a party, but my go-to for postwork cocktails is a jumpsuit. During the day, I'll pair it with a jacket or a button-down shirt. For evening, I'll take off the jacket or the button-down, exchange flats for heels, put on red lipstick, pick up a fun clutch, and I'm ready to go anywhere. In fact, I keep sexy heels and lipstick at the office exactly for this reason.

Maggie Cheung's shoes and bag in *In the Mood for Love* say "daytime," but her perfectly tailored dress is all evening. The print gives it an old-fashioned charm. *Opposite:* If you find a print you love and that works for you, don't be afraid to wear it in a big way, like Marilyn Monroe did in her last, never-completed film, *Something's Got to Give. Following pages, left:* This knit dress by Azzedine Alaïa is the modern equivalent of the deceptively simple but totally right dress Elizabeth Taylor wears (*right*) in *Cat on a Hot Tin Roof.* Alaïa's clothes cinch you in for a sexy fit but have a whimsical quality—for example, the ruching in the skirt—that makes them smart and cool. The fit of the white chiffon dress Taylor wears as Maggie the Cat is perfection—flattering neckline, trim waist, high armhole. Sometimes the plainest dress makes the biggest impact.

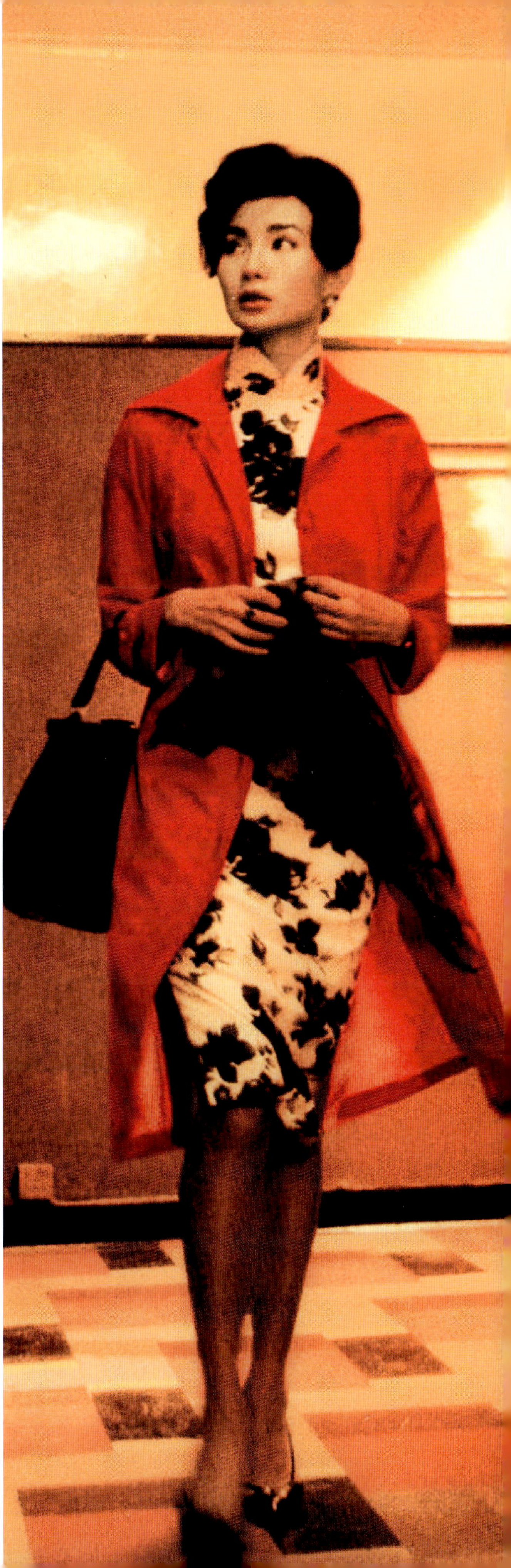

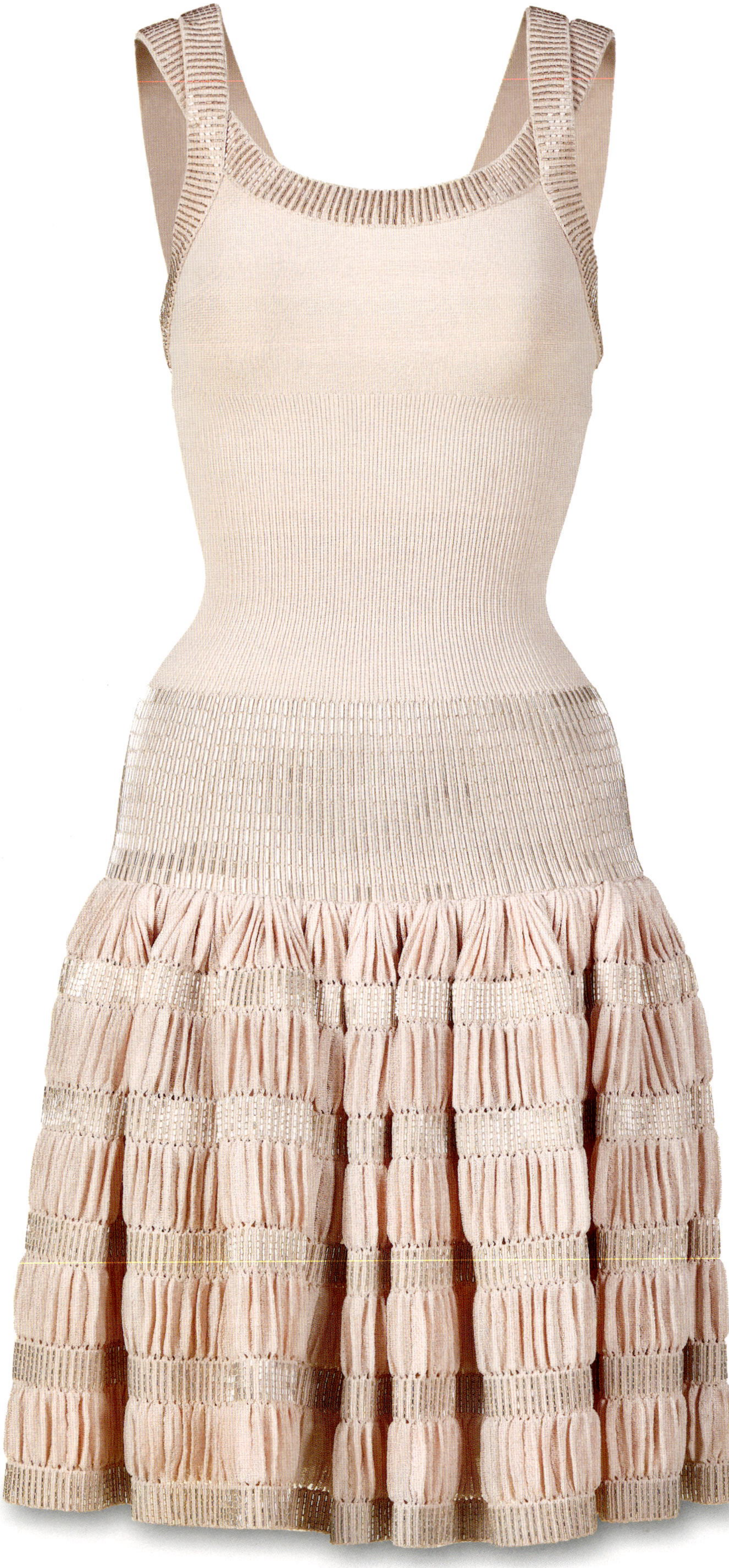

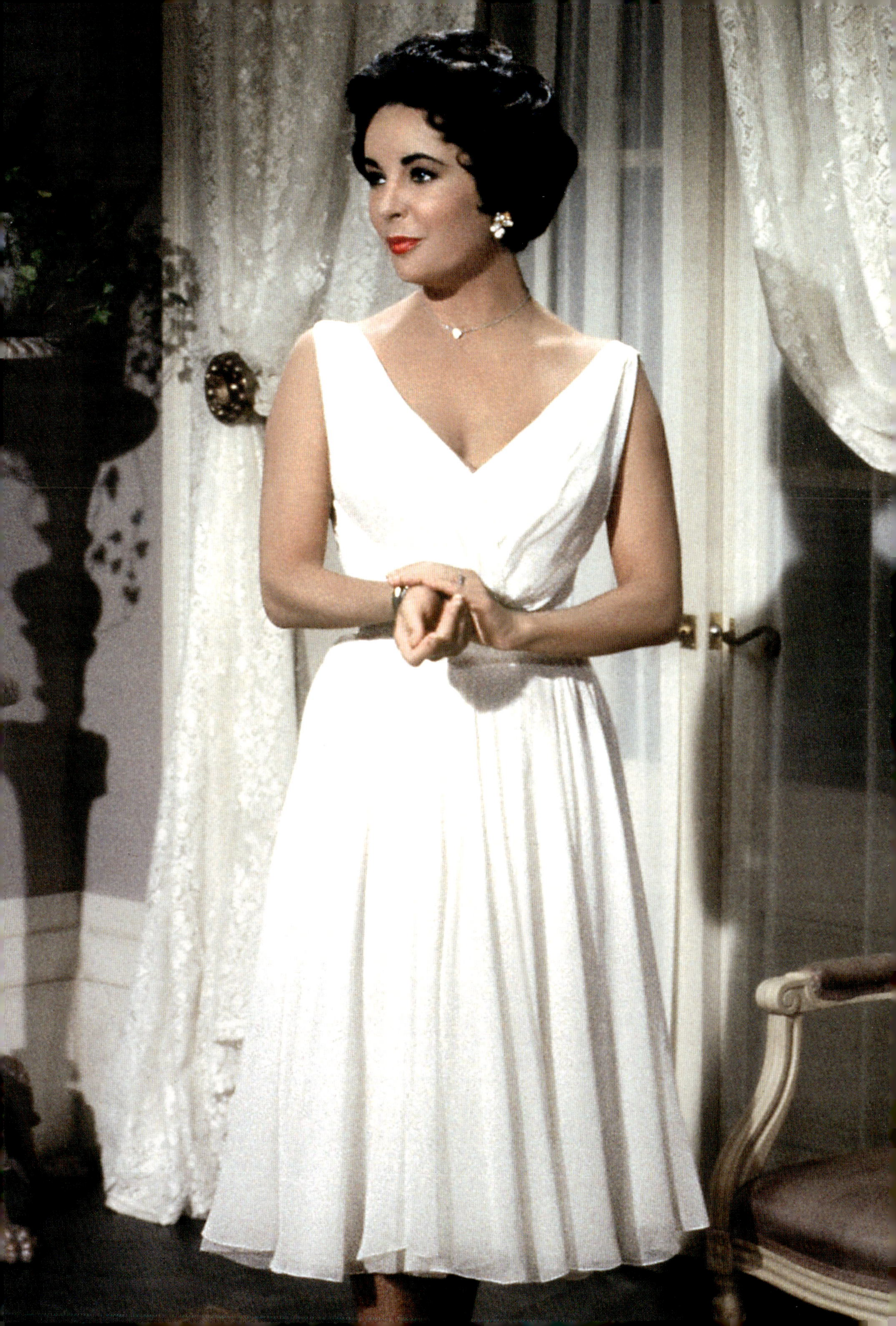

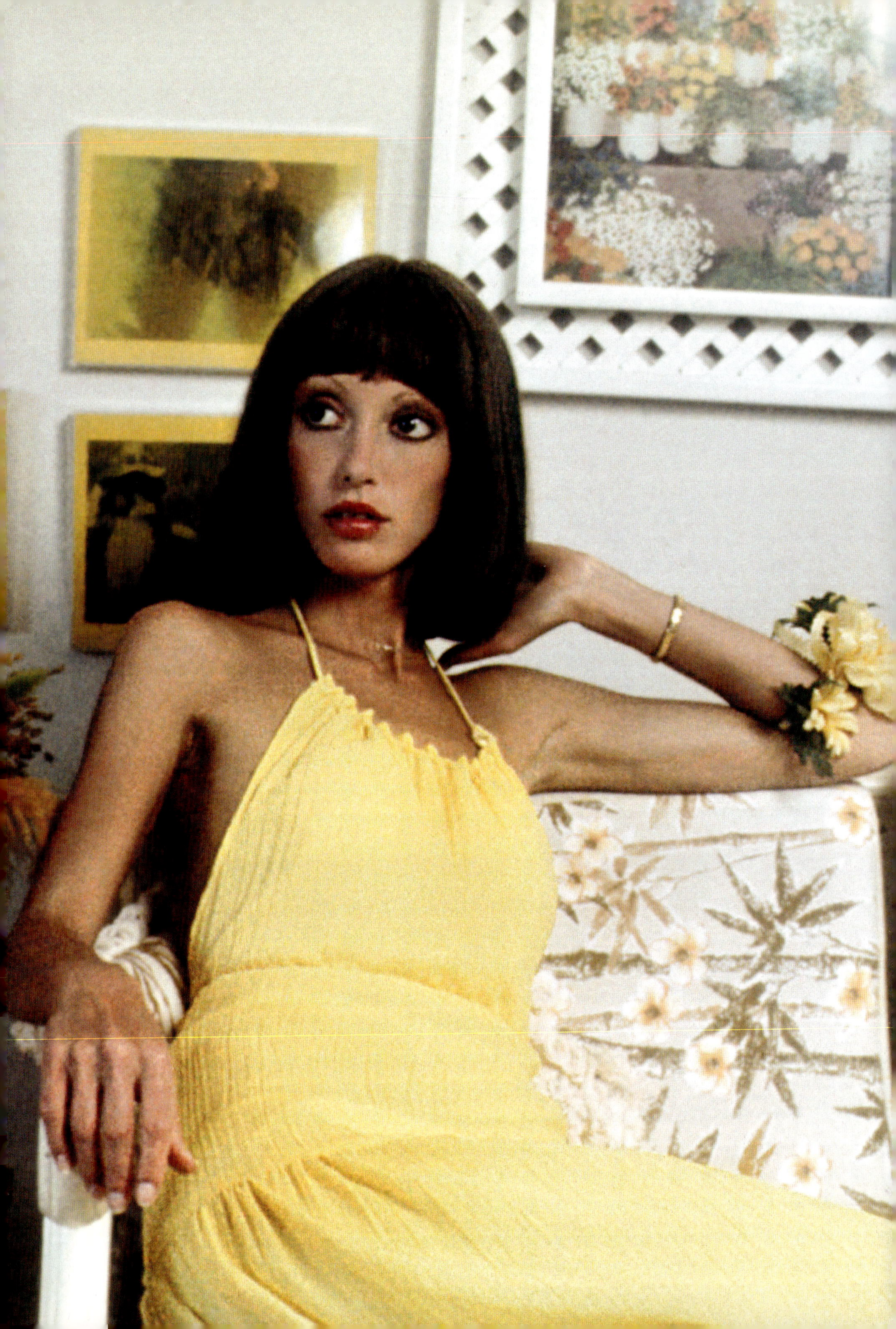

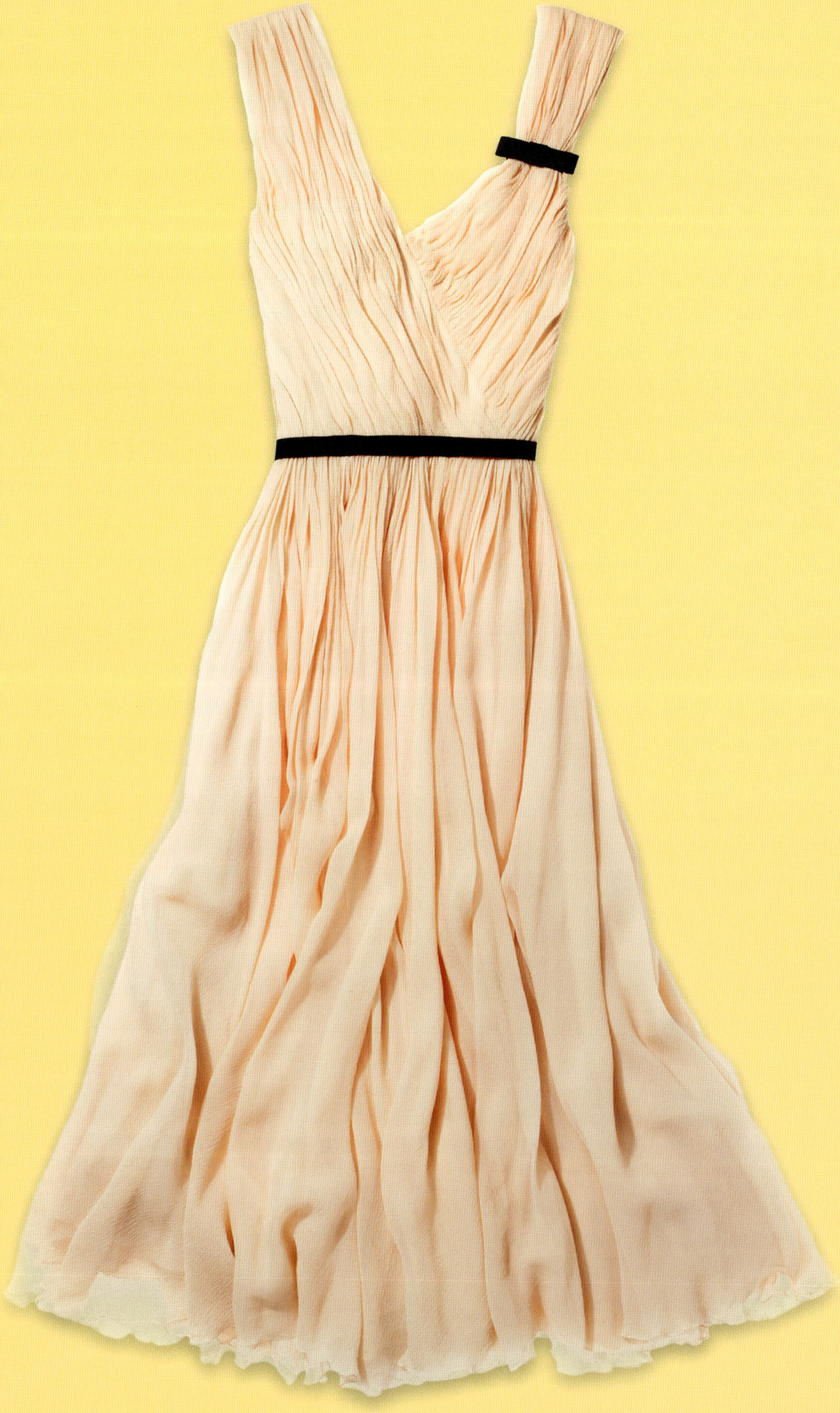

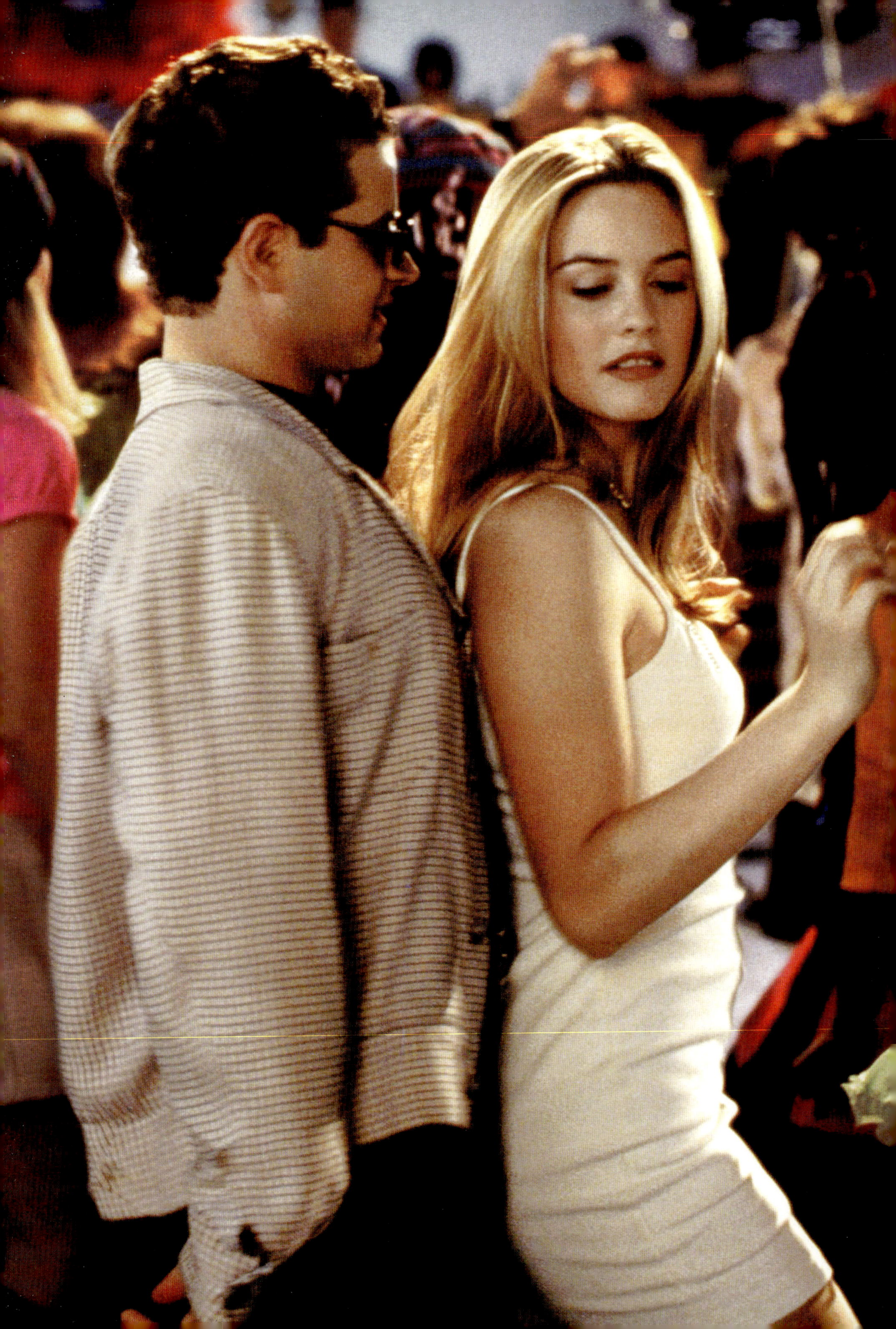

Whatever you wear, you want to make sure it flatters your body. If you're curvy, try a fit-and-flare silhouette. If you're boyish, a shift looks fantastic. A dress doesn't need to be ornate or intricate; it just needs to make you look your best. One of the most flattering cocktail dresses of all time is the white silk chiffon one Elizabeth Taylor wore in *Cat on a Hot Tin Roof.* It's a little nothing of a dress made for her by the Hollywood costume designer Helen Rose—low V-neck, cinched waist, full skirt. But the perfect fit puts the dress in another category altogether. The deep neckline makes the ideal frame for Taylor's décolletage and face, and the silhouette makes her waist look tiny and her bust and hips look lush. Rose even cut the dress so that her underarms are hidden. Because the jewelry is minimal, the emphasis is all on Taylor. Sometimes it's not about an amazing dress, but a dress that is the perfect foil for you.

This image from *The Stepford Wives* is a textbook example of how there's a cocktail dress for every body type, from the classic sheath to the strapless fit-and-flare. *Opposite:* Never underestimate the slip dress. Seen here on Alicia Silverstone in *Clueless,* it's both basic and sexy. Just be sure to stick to one type of jewelry—a ring or a bracelet or a necklace, not all three—or it looks too sultry. *Previous pages, left:* You can go sexy for cocktails if you balance the amount of skin shown with the amount that's under wraps, as Shelley Duvall does in *3 Women.* I love how her flowy dress bares her neck and shoulders but doesn't display any décolletage. *Right:* This lovely chiffon dress from Chloé—which bears a striking resemblance to the one Elizabeth Taylor wears in *Cat on a Hot Tin Roof*—is very charming. Asymmetrical dresses are flattering because we're all asymmetrical. Conversely, wearing one makes you look balanced.

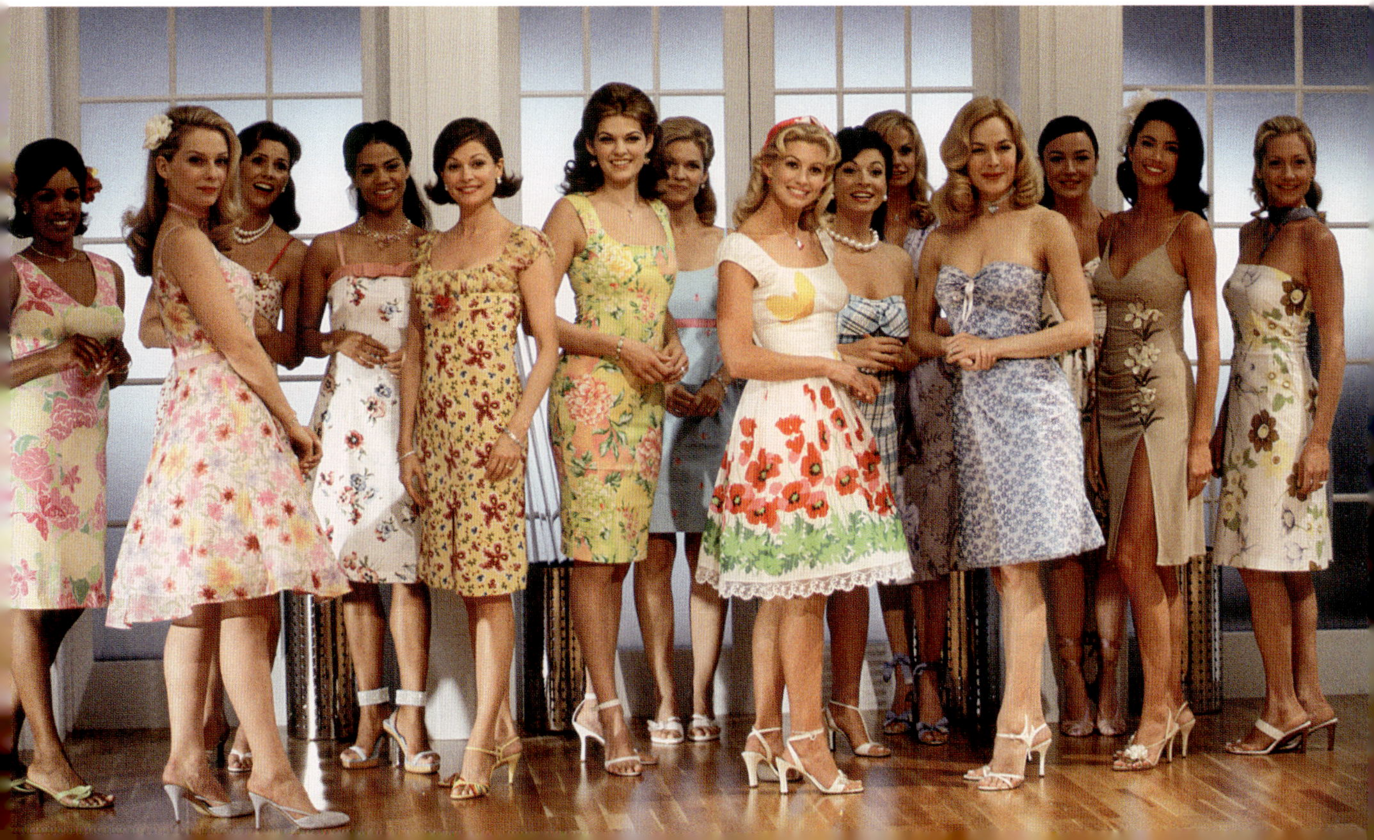

Sartorial Seduction: The Sexy Dress

Is there a sexier moment in cinema than when Sharon Stone uncrosses and crosses her legs in *Basic Instinct?* She has total control of the situation, from her cool announcement that she has nothing to hide (talk about an understatement!) to the way she's dressed. She's wearing a *turtleneck,* and she makes it look hot. Granted, it's a turtleneck that's cut off to micromini proportions, but still. You look at her legs and her slicked-back dominatrix hair, and you just know this woman's thinking naughty thoughts, turtleneck be damned. This dress is a monument to the first rule of sexy dressing, which is that your body is as powerful as your face, your hair, or your makeup.

All the dresses I chose for this chapter have one thing in common: They're simple. Because when you're talking about sexy, you're talking about the woman, not what she's wearing. The negative space—what you see of her skin—is as important as what's covering it. Skin is *lush.* When Sharon Stone walks into that interrogation room, she's completely covered up except for those bare legs, which she uses to supreme effect. If her dress had also been backless and had a plunging neckline, the effect would have been altogether different and not nearly as memorable. She reeks of sex, but she doesn't look cheap.

The navy blue jersey Guy Laroche dress that Hilary Swank wore (see page 50) to collect her Academy Award for *Million Dollar Baby* in 2005 played off a similar theme: It had long sleeves and came up to her neck in front, then the back was cut down to *there.* She looked like a lady—except for that unexpectedly, unforgettably naked back. There's a fine line between sexy and desperate. To stay on the right side of it, you have to think about balance. Don't show everything at once. If a dress is short, it should have sleeves. If it's super-low-cut, it should be long. If it's backless, it should have a high

The point of sexy dressing is to show off your best feature—in the case of Sharon Stone in *Basic Instinct,* her legs. But only show off one body part at a time or it cheapens the look.

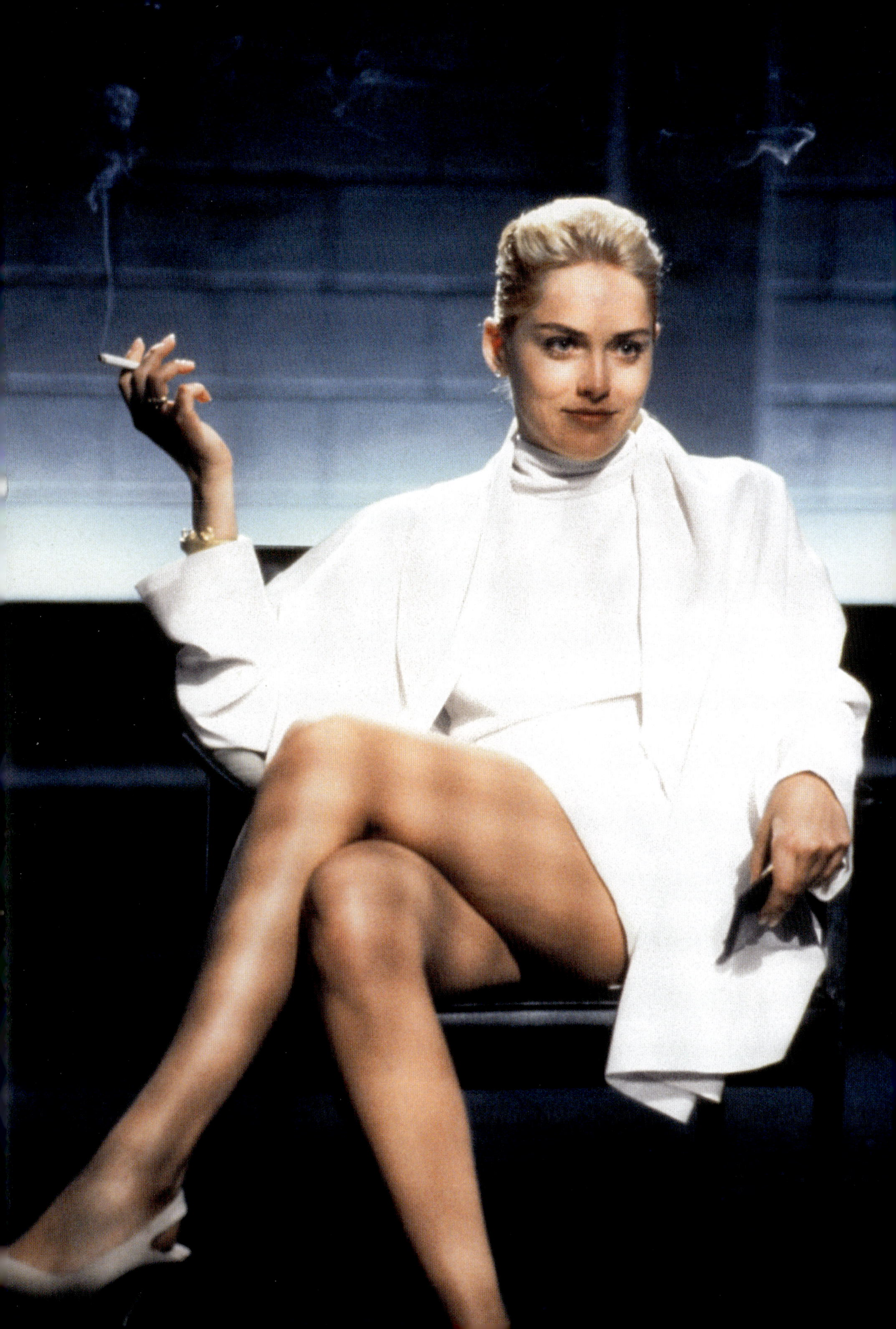

"I think all women have a certain elegance about them which is destroyed when they take off their clothes."

Rita Hayworth

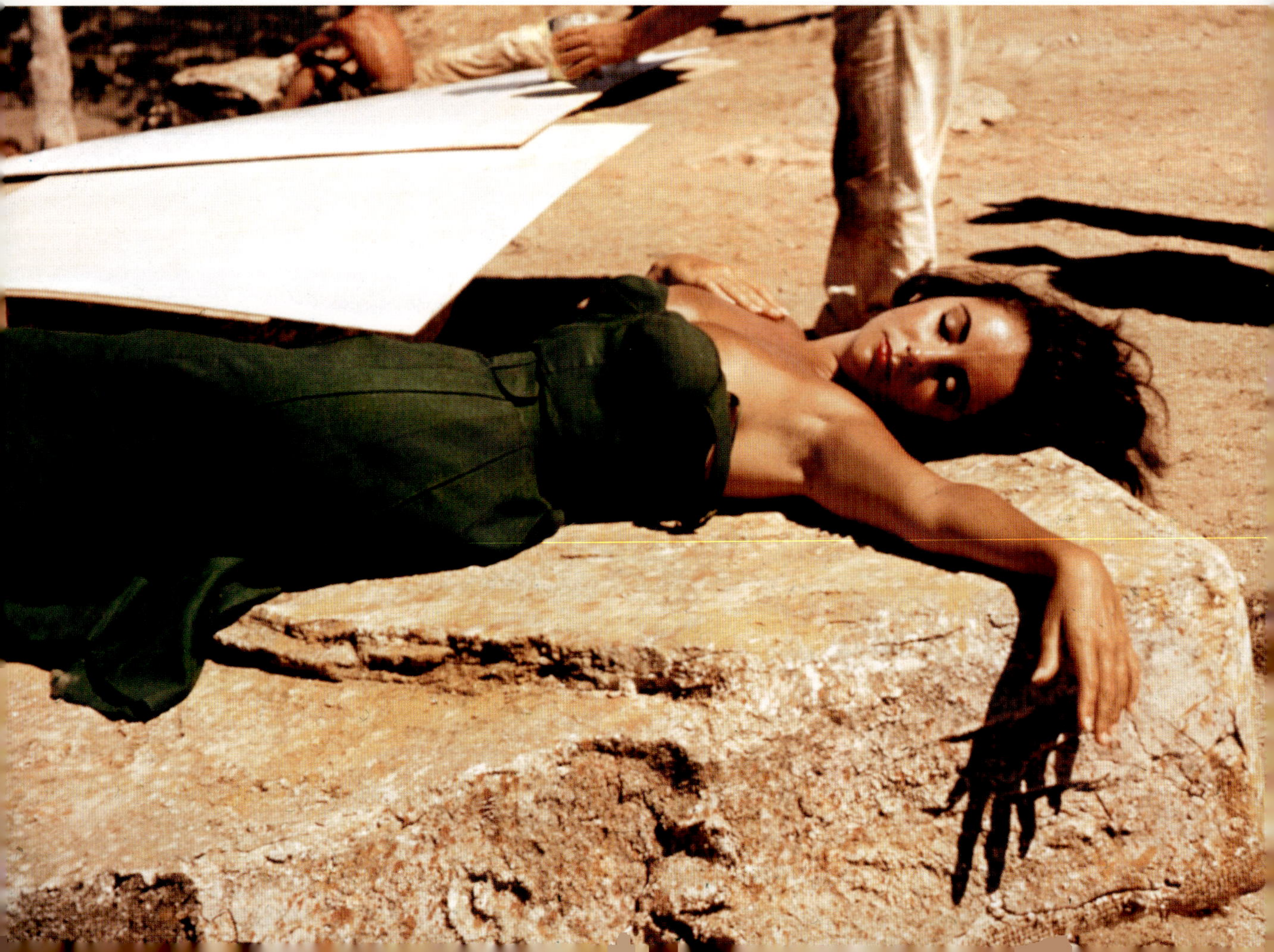

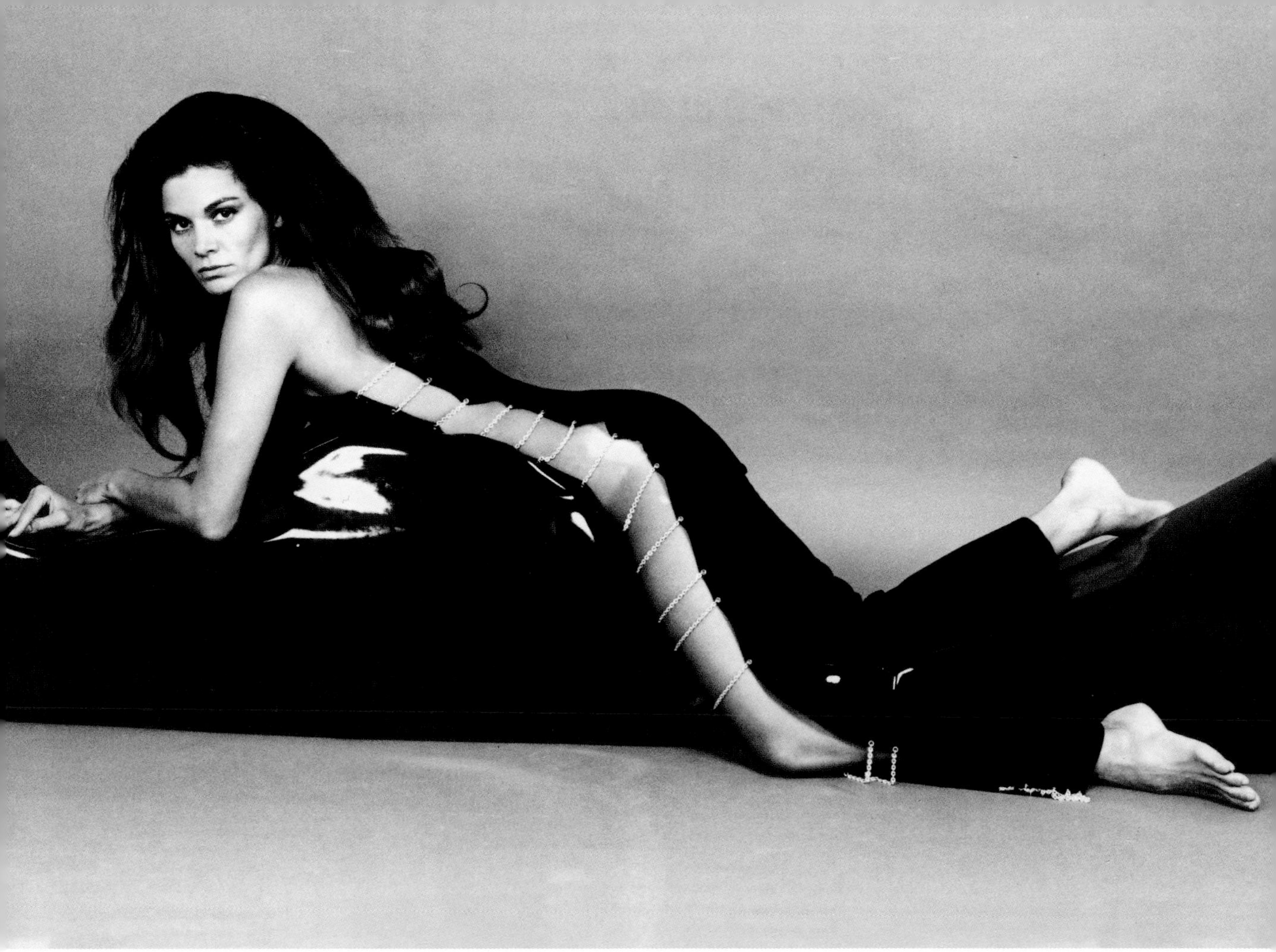

front. Another way to think of this is that you should only have one asset on display at a time. Whatever the cut of your dress, it should fit perfectly. I'll tuck some double-sided tape into an actress's bag at the start of the evening as an emergency backup, but it's too unreliable to work on its own. Instead, I prefer to have something tailored within a millimeter of its life. Which is not to say that it should leave nothing to the imagination. The great Hollywood costume designer Edith Head said it best: "Your dress should be tight enough to show you're a woman but loose enough to show you're a lady."

It's much sexier to suggest than to reveal. Take the black dress Eva Green wears in *Casino Royale.* The harness detail covers more skin than a backless dress would, but that detail makes the exposed skin all the more enticing. And the bondage-style straps inevitably lead to thoughts of what happens when the dress comes off: You can't see a strap without thinking of undoing it. A corset top has the same effect, with the added advantage of giving you a little costume drama thrill. It also feels incredible to wear—

Sometimes you just need to pull out all the stops: From the lush, untamed hair to the sultry outfit—surely the precursor to the Elizabeth Hurley safety-pin Versace dress—Florinda Bolkan in *Metti, una sera a cena* oozes sex appeal. *Opposite:* It's the contrast between prim and sensual that makes this photo of Elizabeth Taylor in *Suddenly, Last Summer* so sizzling. She's wearing a superstructured sundress, but her skin is sun-kissed, and her hair looks like she just got out of the water.

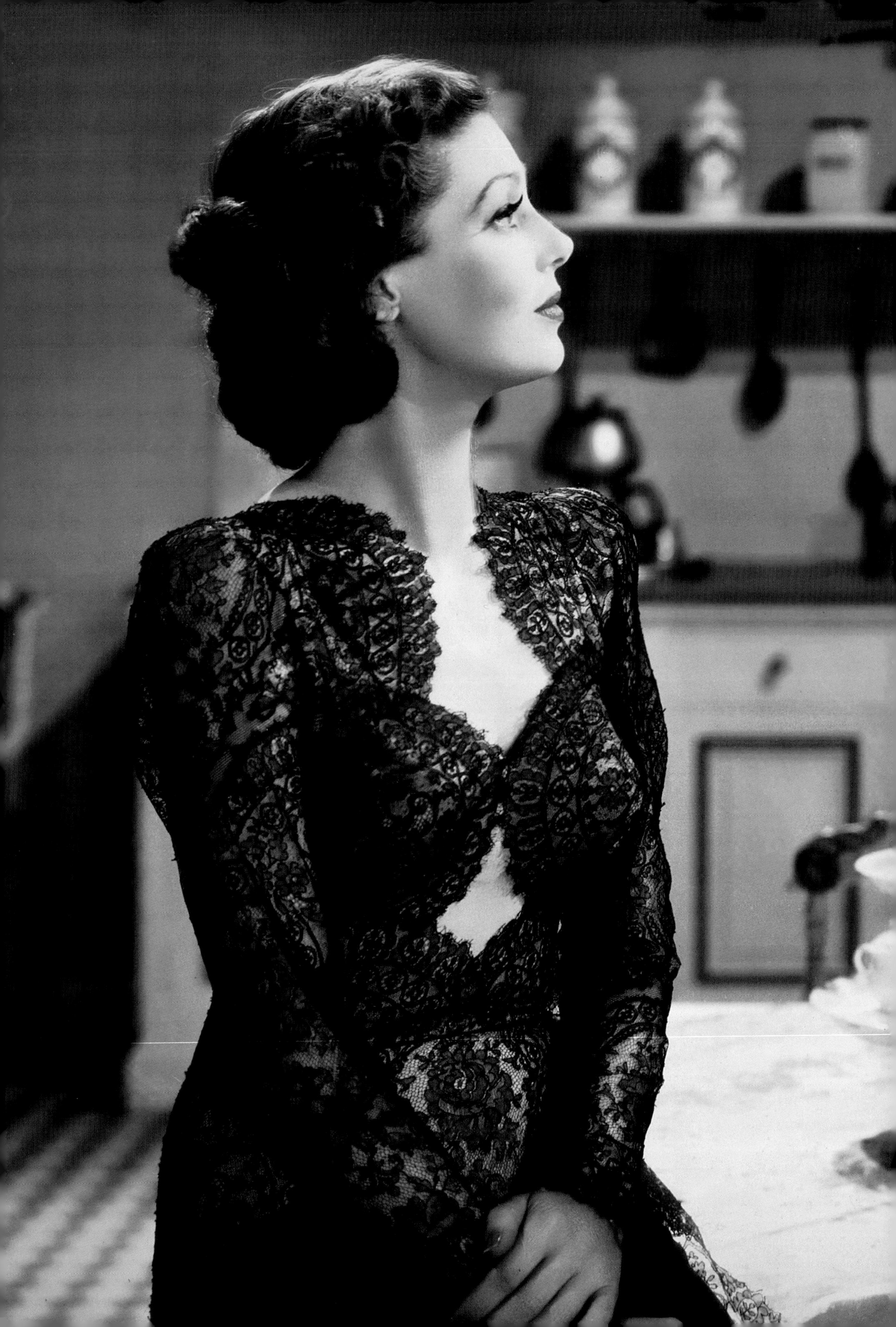

your waist is tiny, your spine is straight, and your bust is high. It's empowering to feel that sexy, just as it's empowering to wear strong colors. Pastels are lovely, but a dress with a sexy cut is going to have its impact seriously undermined if it's a sweet shade. It's like ordering a whiskey neat versus a piña colada. I like a cocktail umbrella in my drink as much as the next girl, but there are times when you just have to serve it straight up.

Every sexy look I style starts with the undergarments. If you want to smolder, it's absolutely crucial to have the right bra on—and that goes for when you're buying the dress, too. Always try on the dress with the bra. The minute the bust is lifted up and inside the rib cage, you look five pounds lighter. It's like zipping the silhouette in. And while we're on the subject, consider silicone nipple pads. When you see nipple through a dress, it takes it to a rude place. Overkill is not sexy.

You can see the power of a good bra at work in the image of Jane Russell from *The Outlaw,* a film so sexy that it took

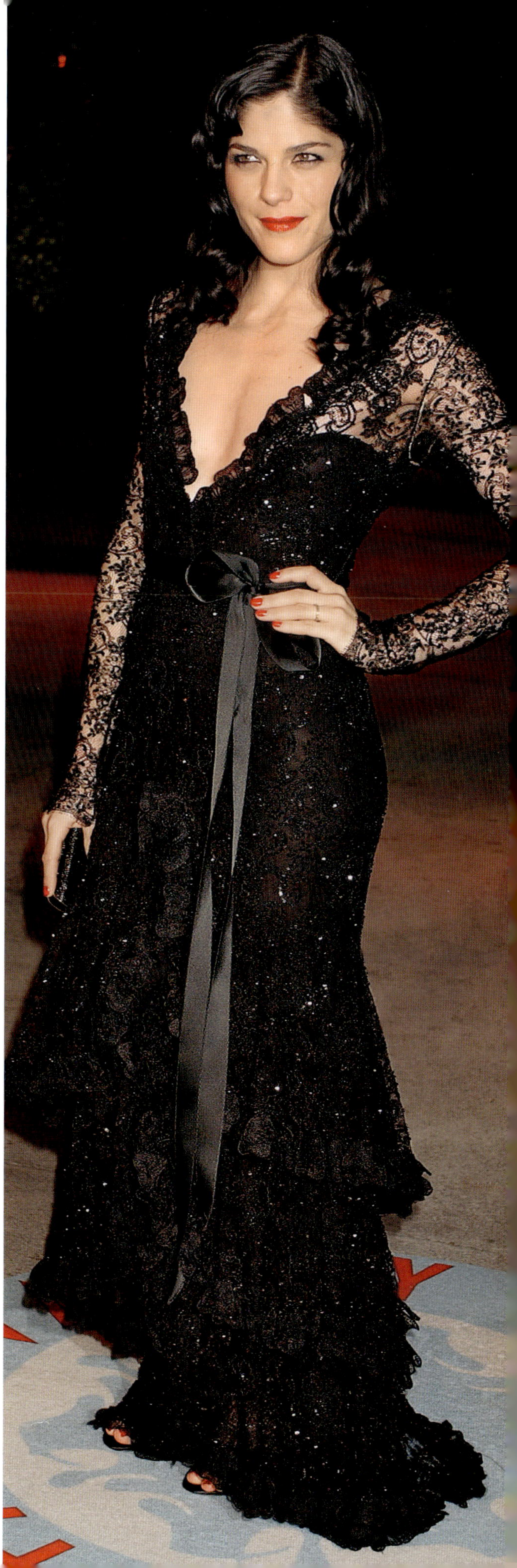

Lace can be sweet, but in black it's supersexy and a little mysterious—it gives the illusion of nakedness without actually showing anything. Because of its demure connotations, you can get away with revealing a little more, as in the cutouts on Loretta Young's dress in *He Stayed for Breakfast* (*opposite*) and the plunging neckline of the gown Selma Blair wore for the Oscars in 2006 (*right*).

two years to get Hollywood censors to approve its release. This photo is just beyond (see page 46). She's practically naked but totally supported. Russell was supposedly wearing a special cantilevered underwire bra designed by Howard Hughes, the film's director. More than forty years later, when she wrote her autobiography, she revealed that Hughes's bra was so uncomfortable, she just wore her own.

Today, women are more likely to complain that their shoes are uncomfortable. Nothing ruins a look like not being able to walk in your shoes. Everyone has their threshold; with each of my clients, I know exactly how high I can go. (Hint: If you can't straighten your knee, that's your limit.) To make shoes more comfortable, I like those gel pads that you wear under the ball of your foot. You can also get ones that can be placed on the inside of an ankle strap.

Some stylists insist that you have to wear Spanx under a red carpet look. Personally, I think there's nothing sexier on a woman than a jiggly behind. I remember Oscar de le Renta once sent his models down the runway with

"A woman's dress should be like a barbed wire fence: serving its purpose without obstructing the view."

Sophia Loren

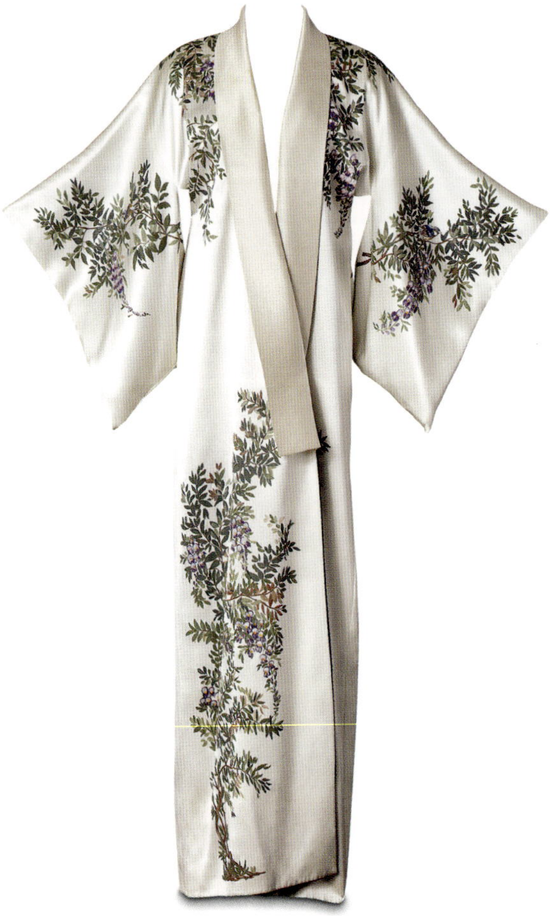

My pet peeve for evening is the pashmina. If you think you may be chilly, wear something more original, like this kimono from Dolce & Gabbana. Plus, kimonos make you think of geishas, always a sexy reminder. *Opposite:* A dress doesn't have to be tight or revealing to be sexy. Sometimes suggesting is more sexy than revealing, as with Eva Green's bondage-inspired dress in *Casino Royale*.

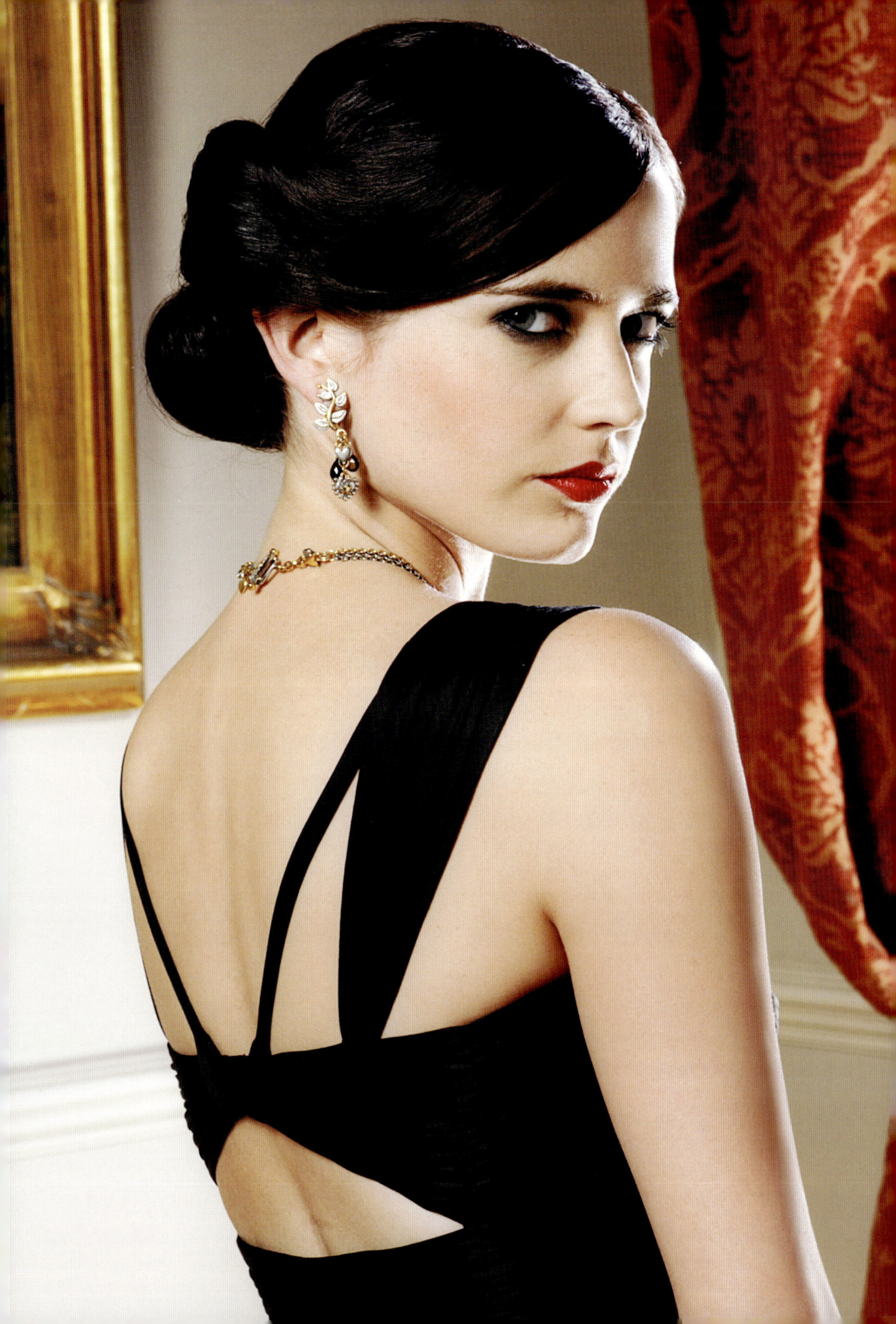

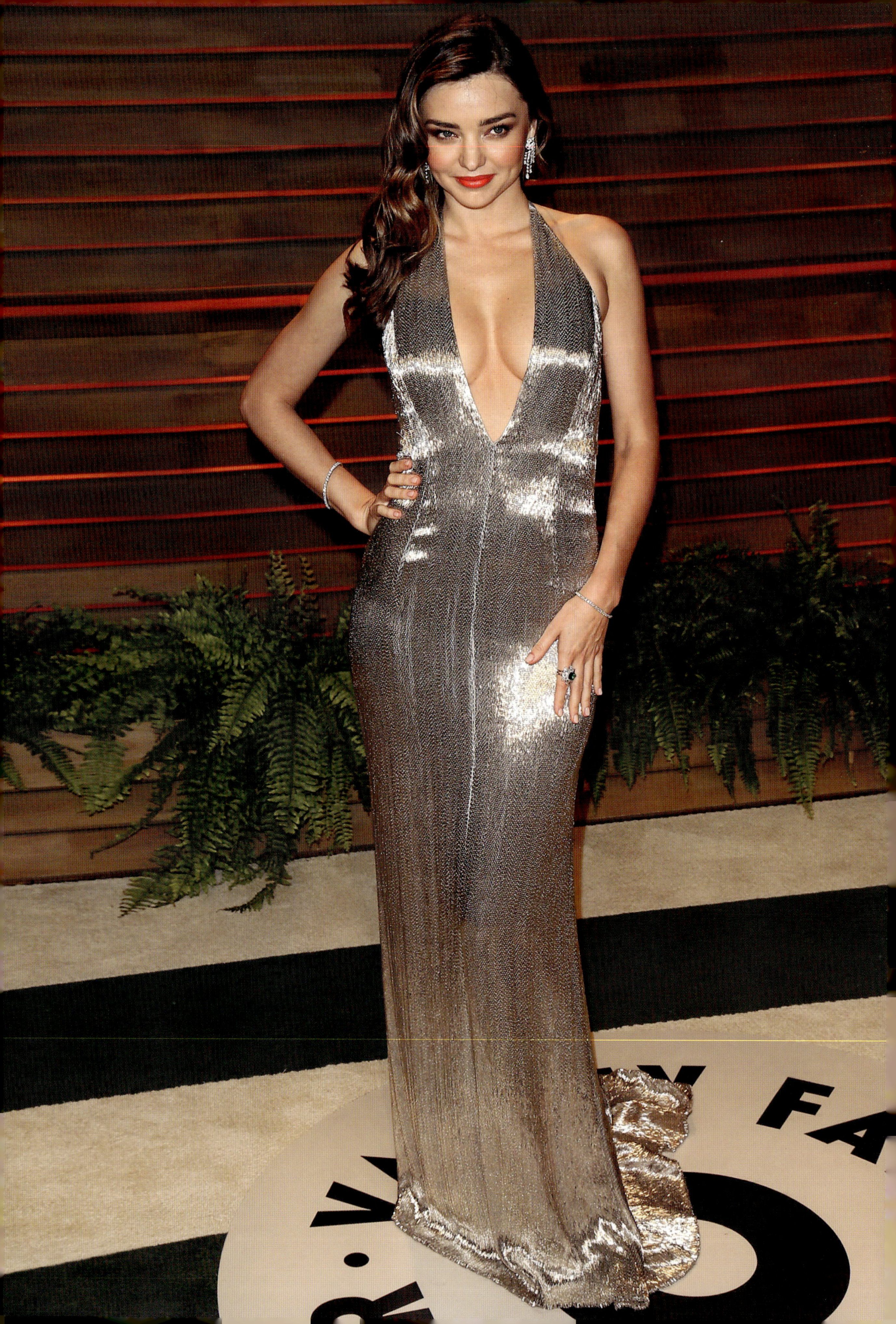

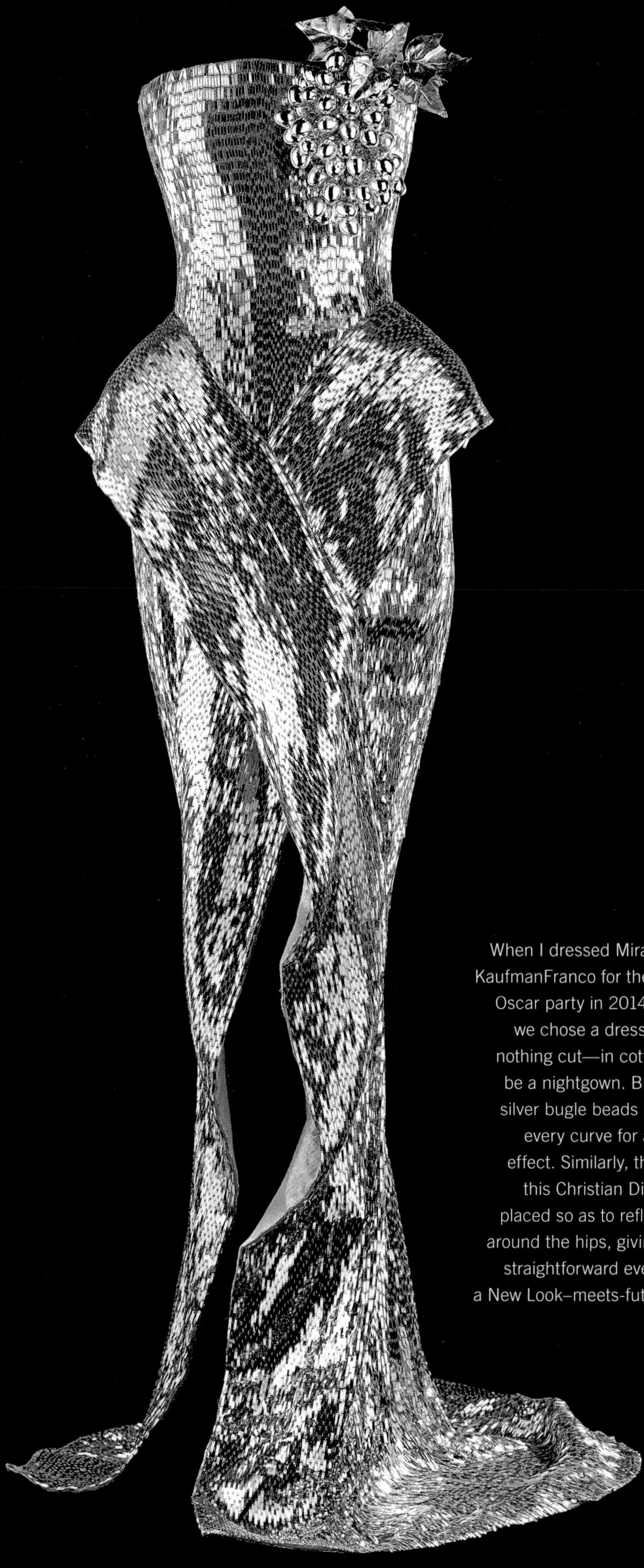

When I dressed Miranda Kerr in KaufmanFranco for the *Vanity Fair* Oscar party in 2014 (*opposite*), we chose a dress with a little nothing cut—in cotton, it could be a nightgown. But the liquid silver bugle beads shimmer on every curve for a supersexy effect. Similarly, the beads on this Christian Dior gown are placed so as to reflect the light around the hips, giving what is a straightforward evening shape a New Look–meets-futuristic vibe.

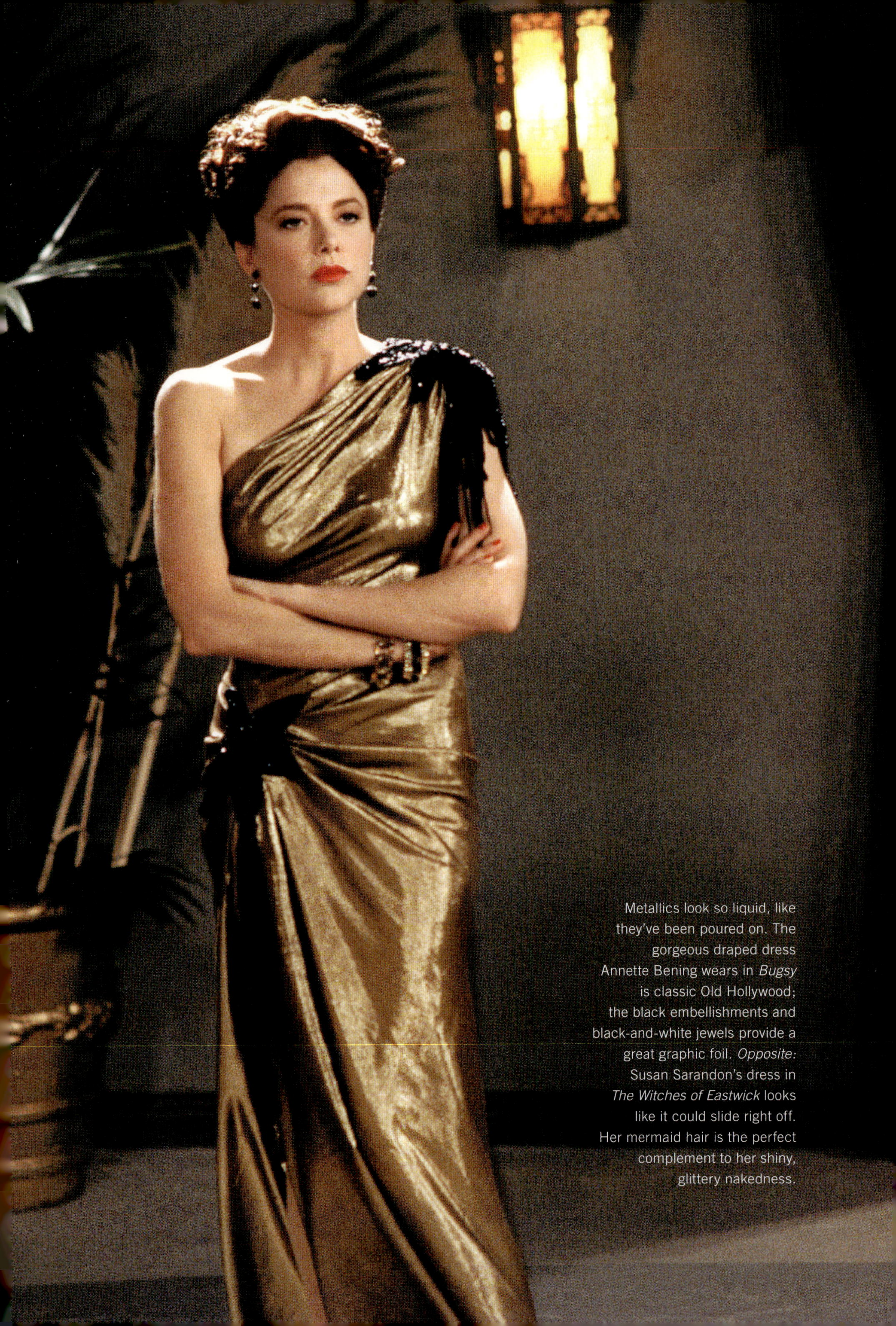

Metallics look so liquid, like they've been poured on. The gorgeous draped dress Annette Bening wears in *Bugsy* is classic Old Hollywood; the black embellishments and black-and-white jewels provide a great graphic foil. *Opposite:* Susan Sarandon's dress in *The Witches of Eastwick* looks like it could slide right off. Her mermaid hair is the perfect complement to her shiny, glittery nakedness.

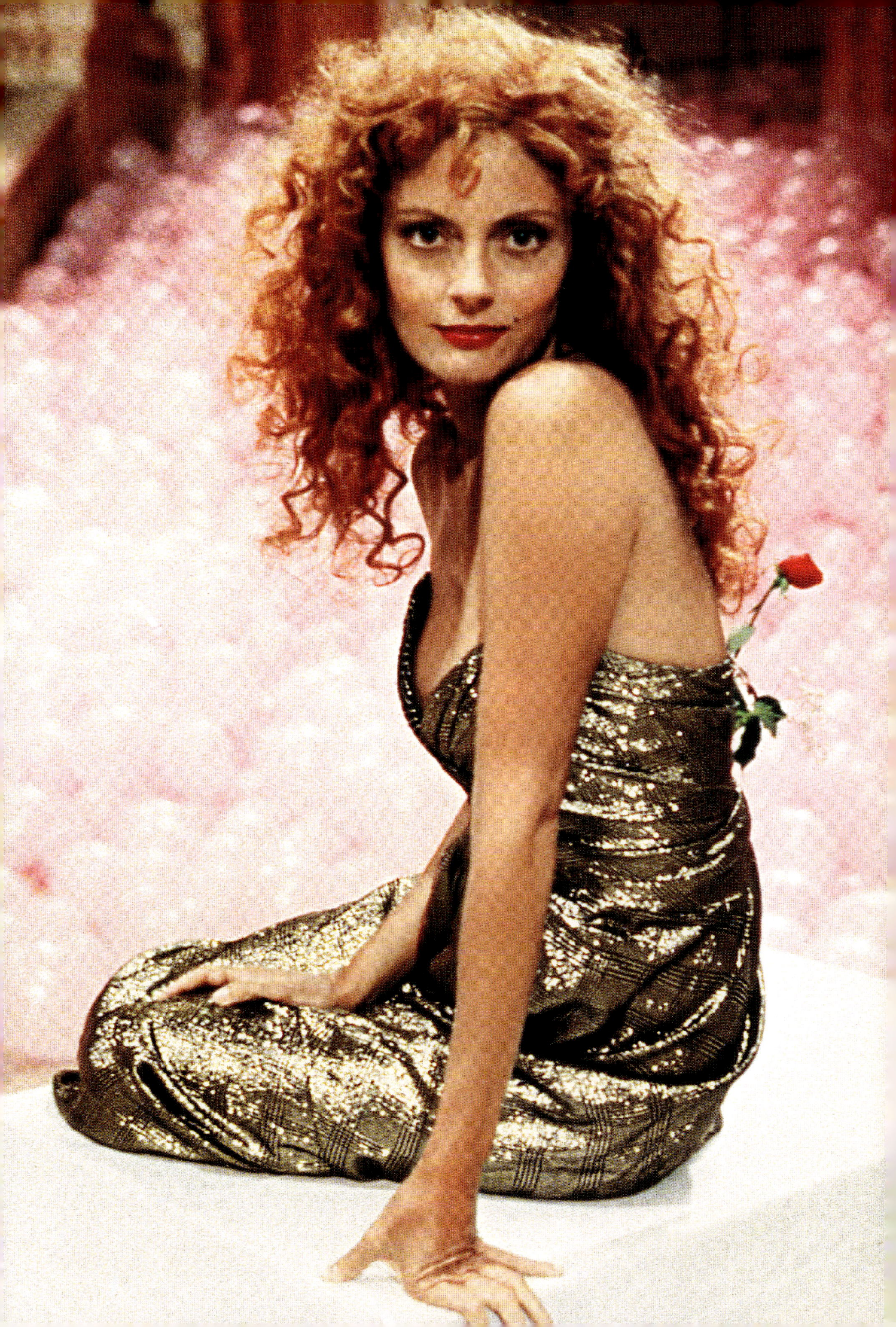

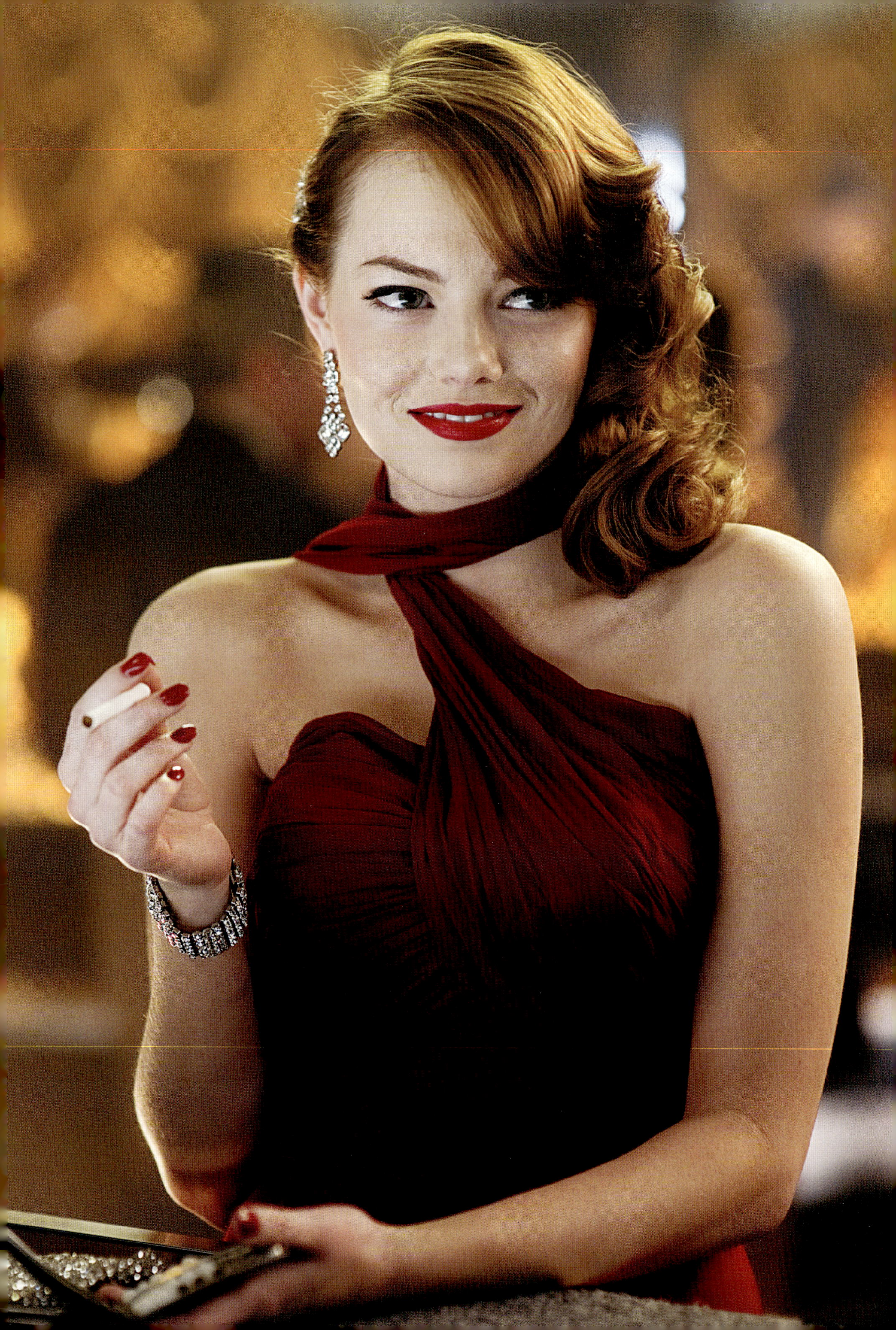

this instruction: Walk like there's a man behind you. I love that natural movement. People equate sexy dresses with breasts, but at least half the men in the world like the behind, so smashing it down is not necessarily the best idea. Instead, I love the Embracer Waist-cincher Thong by Victoria's Secret. We buy these by the case in my office. It goes up to your bra line so it keeps your waist really trim, and the bottom is a thong. If you wear it with a strapless bra, you look like you've got on an old Playboy bunny costume. You get the support, but you still have the jiggle. The only time I ask an actress to squeeze into Spanx is when it enhances the line of the dress. If you're wearing a bias cut, then they help the fabric glide over the body. Otherwise, shake your booty.

On the subject of what men like, keep your hair and makeup touchable. Guys love it when a woman looks as if she hasn't put any effort into looking amazing. A red lip can look too pristine to be kissable. Focus instead on a smoky bedroom eye and hair that looks like you could run your fingers through it. Another man-pleaser: looking a little undone. In *Suddenly,*

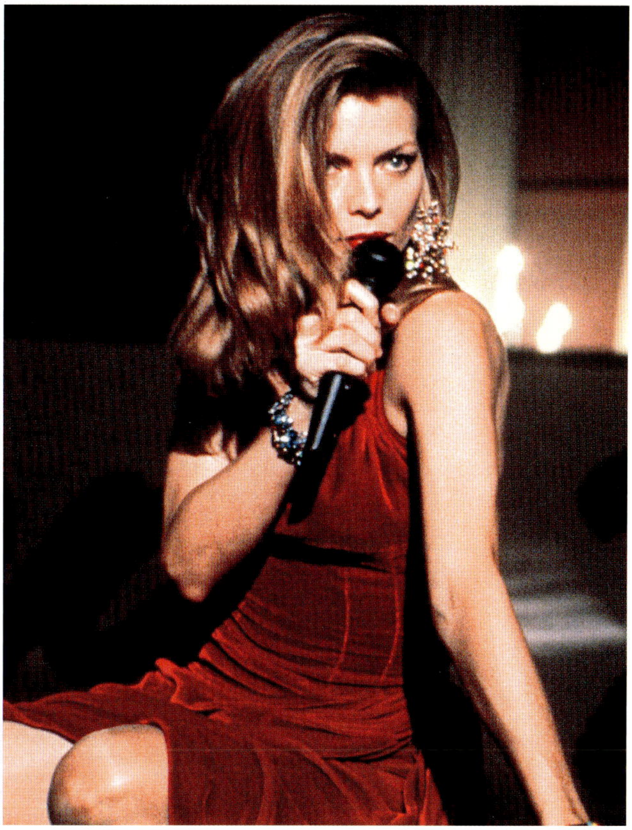

In *The Fabulous Baker Boys,* Michelle Pfeiffer wears a dress with a tight bodice and a twirly skirt, an old-school-sexy combination men love. The red velvet also makes you think of nineteenth-century bordellos, a great subliminal reference. *Opposite:* An element of the undone is always sexy. The halter of Emma Stone's dress in *Gangster Squad* looks as if you could unwind it, and her dress would tumble down.

> “My God, must I always wear a low-cut dress to be important?”
>
> Jean Harlow

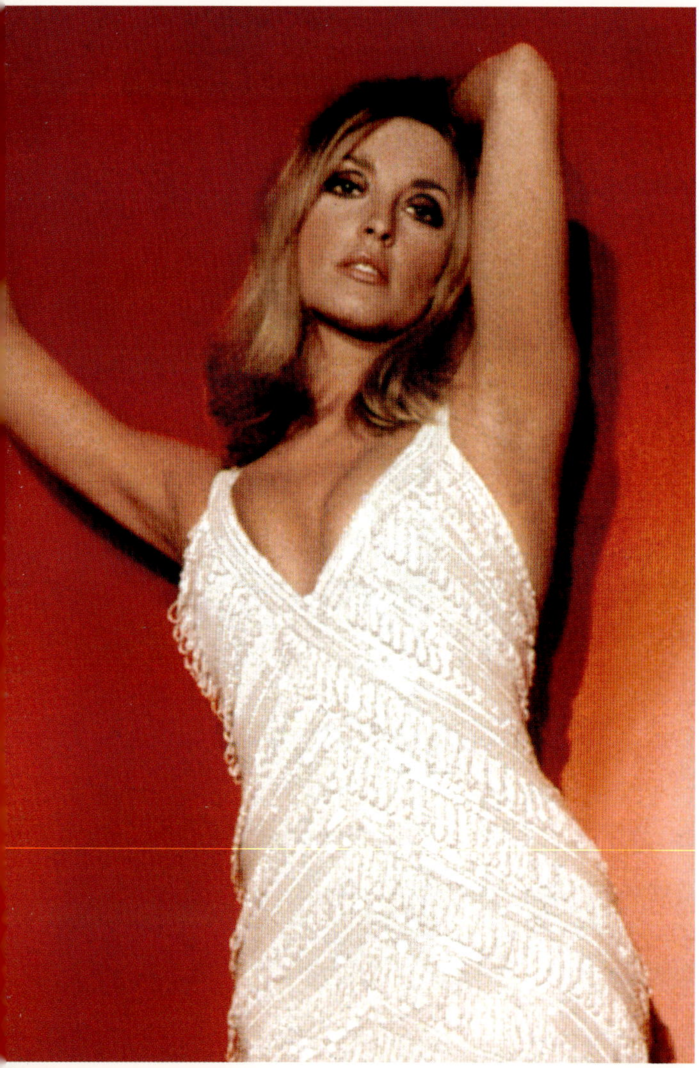

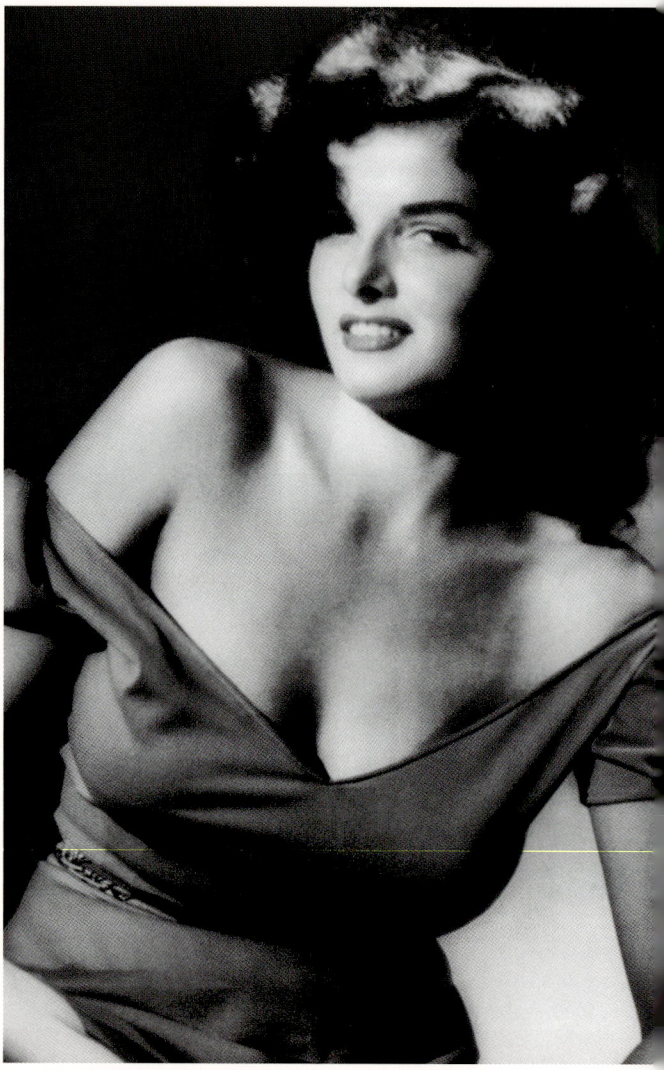

It's important to know what to show off and how. *From left:* Sharon Tate in *Valley of the Dolls* demonstrates how to do a more structured, formal kind of sexy in a form-fitting sheath dress that shows off her cleavage and shoulders. Jane Russell in *The Outlaw* and Halle Berry in *Introducing Dorothy Dandridge* wear dresses that present their shoulders and décolletage in a come-hither V-shape. And the delicate, criss-cross straps on Romy Schneider's dress in *Les innocents aux mains sales* draw attention to her back and shoulder blades.

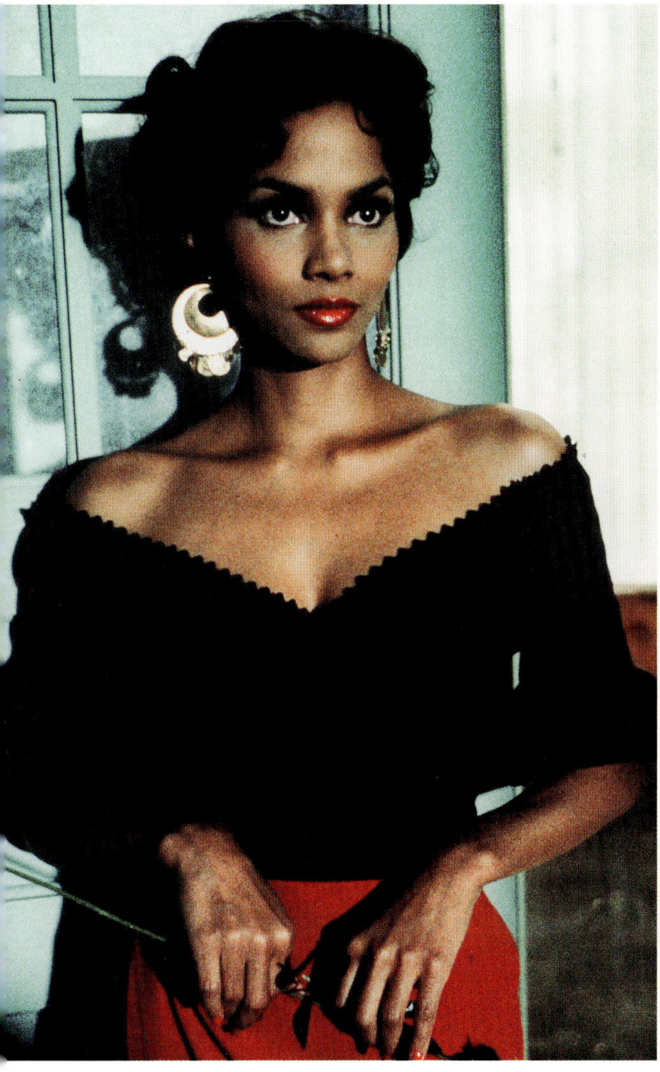

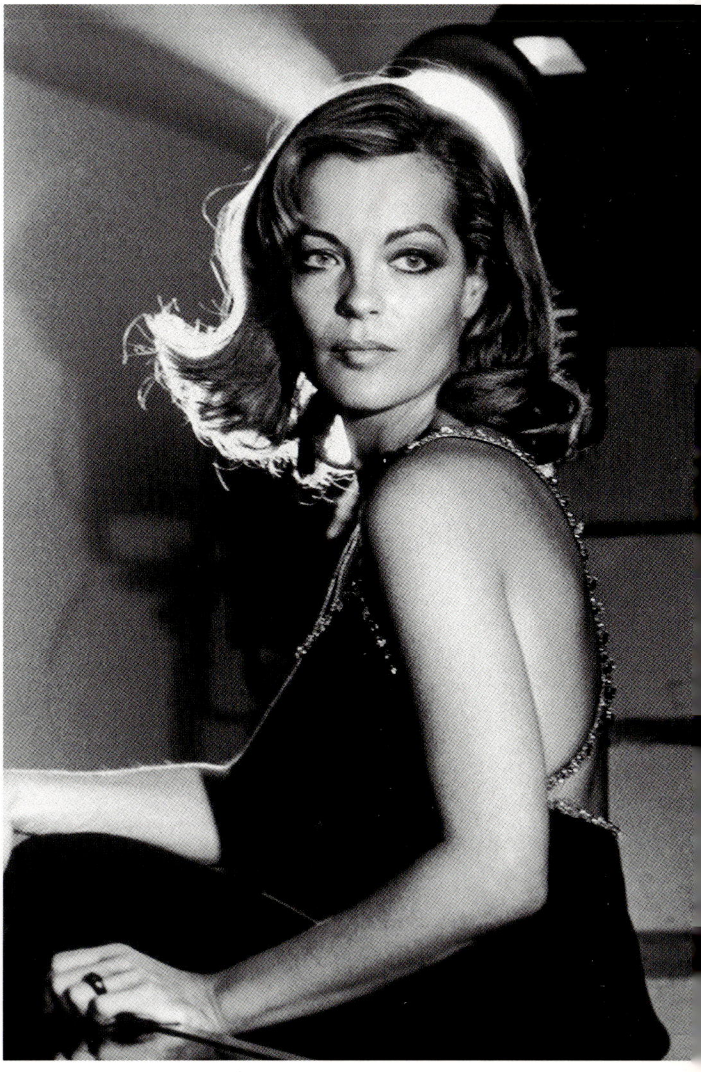

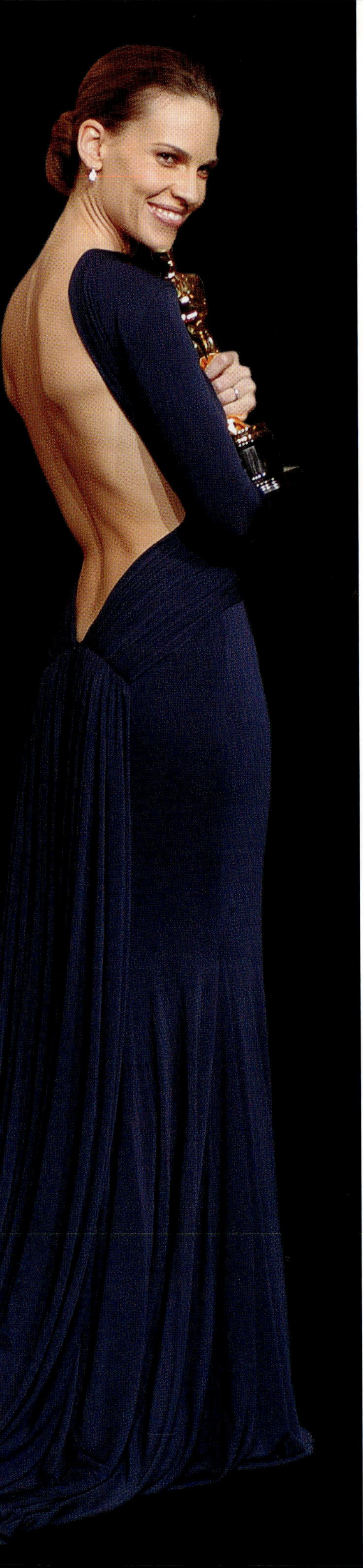

Last Summer, Elizabeth Taylor wears a rigidly fitted dress, but the rest of her is total sun goddess—you can practically smell the suntan oil on her skin and the saltwater in her hair as she lolls with her straps down.

In the end, finding the right sexy dress is like finding the right pair of jeans or the right bathing suit—there's no one-size-fits-all option. It's about how you feel in the dress and how it expresses your personality. The movie look that epitomizes this for me is Susan Sarandon's in *The Witches of Eastwick,* a film I've watched so many times I've lost count—that's how much I like it. In this shot, her character is in a scene where it's very clear that she's gone from repressed to oozing sensuality. Her dress isn't tight or revealing or falling off her. But you look at the gorgeous color and how incredible her shoulders and cleavage look, and you can tell it's not a romantic dress and she's not a wallflower. She's hot, and she knows it.

When I styled Hilary Swank for the Oscars in 2005, we knew immediately that this was The Dress. We didn't want to detract from the shockingly low back, so we kept the hair slicked away from her face and the makeup simple. The whole idea was to have her turn around and then—wow! *Opposite:* Sequins are part of the sexy-girl repertoire; if you wear them, prepare to be stared at. I like them best in a covered-up silhouette such as on this dress worn by Natalie Wood in *Gypsy.* It's the ideal combination of siren and serious.

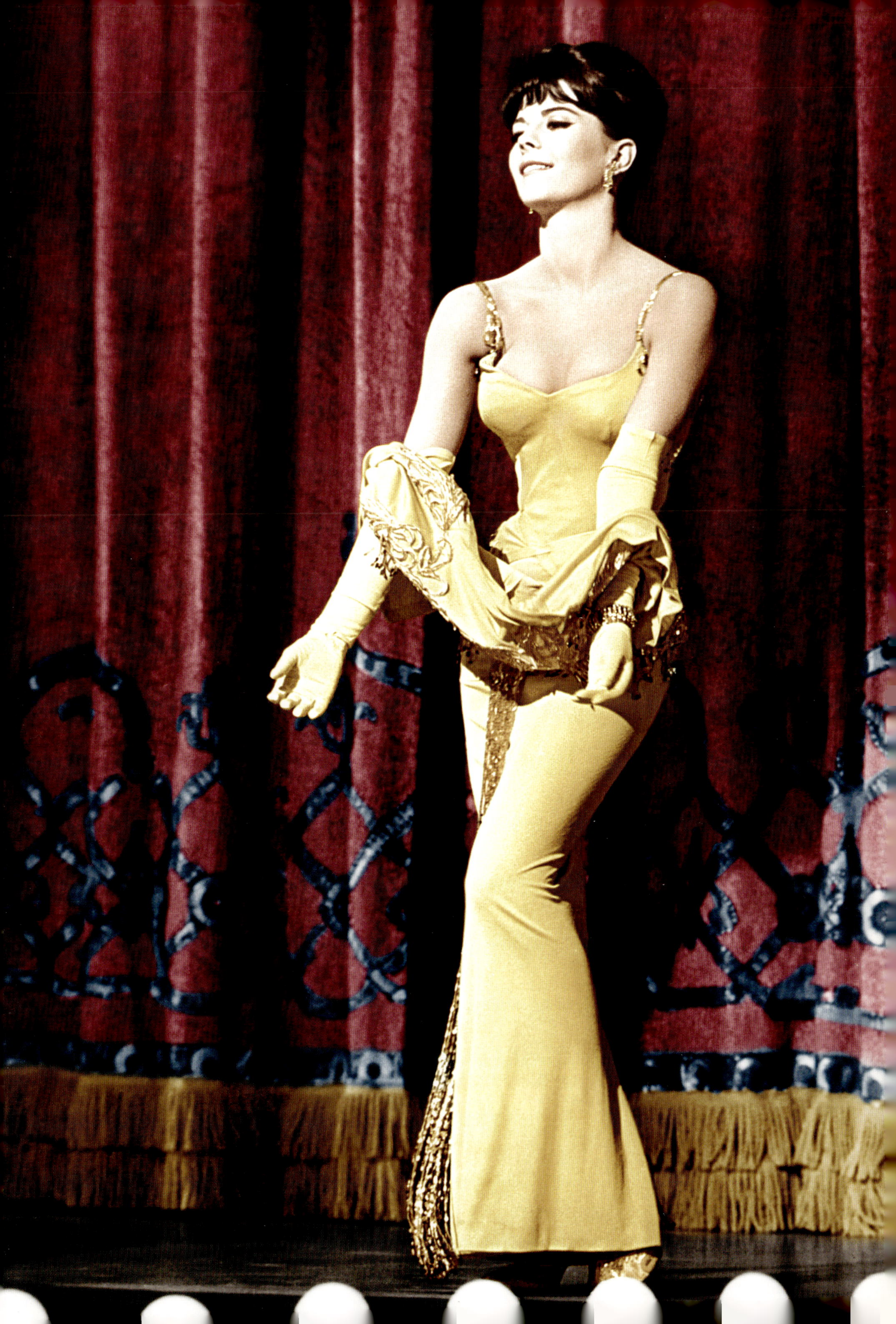

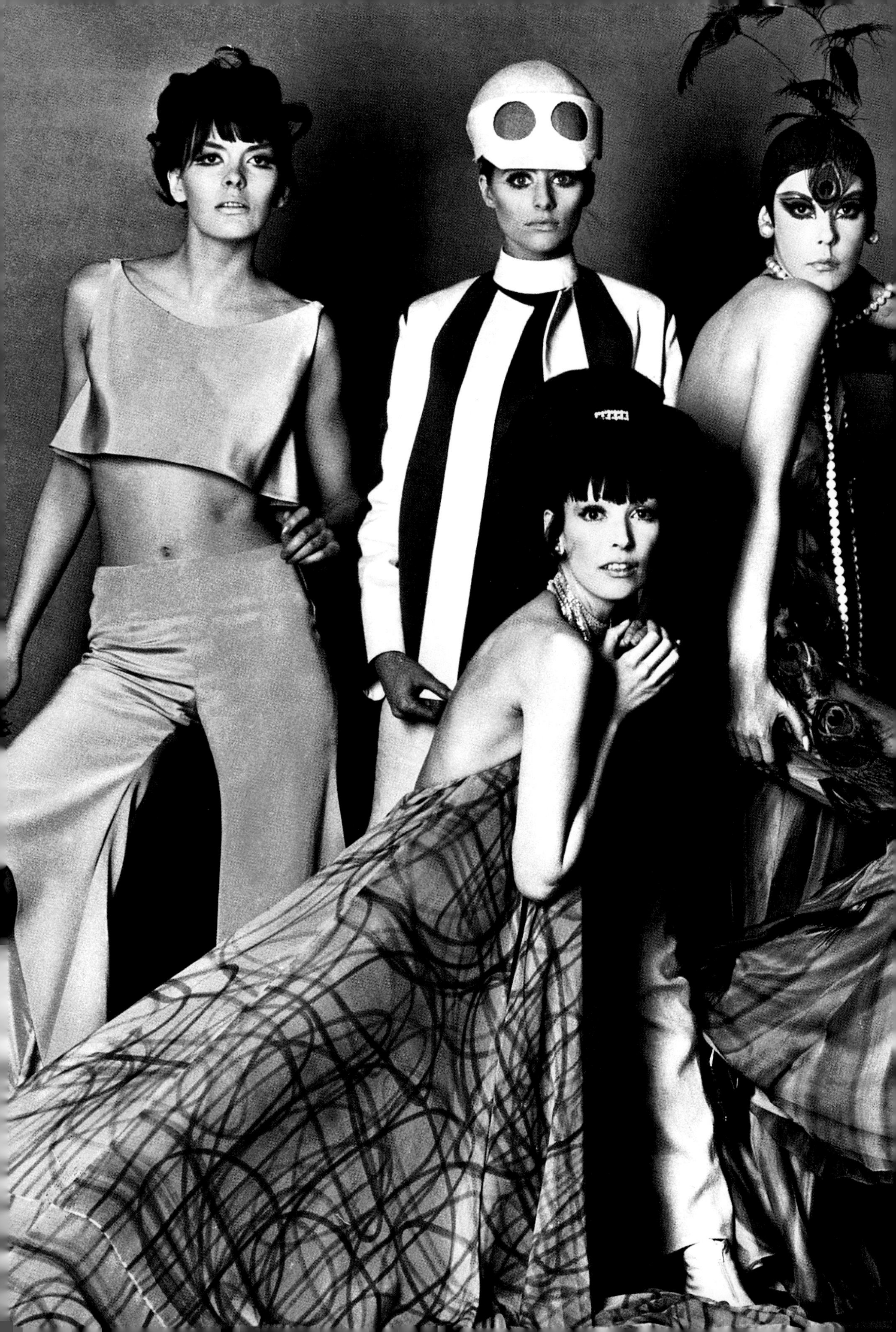

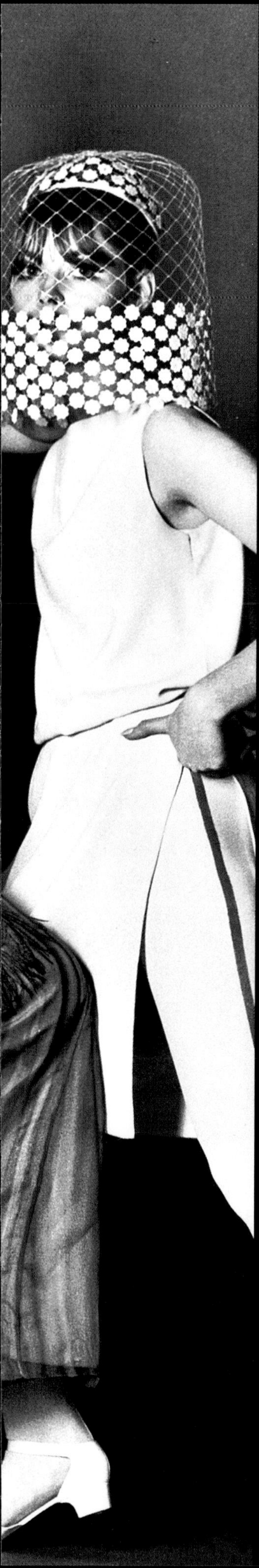

Fashion Forward: The Statement Dress

Most dresses are about something other than the dress. A sexy dress is really about your body; a black dress is really about you. But a fashion dress isn't about anything but Fashion-with-a-capital-F. When you choose one—and the only time you're likely to is for a white-tie affair, which is an occasion for something out of the ordinary—you're very deliberately deciding to make your dress the most important thing about your look, something that's trickier than it sounds. I'm going to come right out and say it: A fashion dress may not be the most flattering thing you can wear. People who aren't head-over-heels with fashion are probably not going to appreciate it. One actress I work with wore a conceptual gown we chose, and when she stepped out onto the red carpet, she texted me to ask if she looked like Björk. I texted back, "Yes. But do it anyway." Because sometimes, provided it brings you joy, I think it's okay to be made fun of. It means you're taking chances, and part of the fun of fashion is stepping outside of your comfort zone, even if it's going to raise eyebrows.

Many of the looks in this chapter seemed shocking at first. When I put Michelle Williams in a 1930s-inspired egg-yolk-yellow

Avant-garde clothes likes these worn in *Blow-Up* can be shocking; it takes the eye a while to adjust to new ideas. But that's part of the fun of wearing them.

“Why change? Everyone has his own style. When you have found it, you should stick to it.”

Audrey Hepburn

chiffon Vera Wang gown for the Oscars in 2006 (see page 59), the reviews ranged from hyperbolic to puzzled. But that's the way it is with this kind of dress. You need to have the courage of your convictions to wear something dramatic. Michelle and I adored it because it was a gorgeous color, had beautiful details, and, most important, it made a strong statement, which is exactly what a fashion dress is all about. It's not about being pretty or sexy; it's about being amazing. Fashion dresses exist purely for the delight of them, inspired by draping, beading, feathers, embroidery, and all the rest of the couture arts. You look at a dress like this and instantly feel the romance of fashion—the violins start playing. It may not be the dress you meet a man in, but it is the one that will bring you bliss. That's the reward for taking the risk of wearing it.

I should also say that there's nothing utilitarian about a fashion dress. It will very likely be worn only once, which makes it incredibly extravagant. It almost always has some sort of detail that defies logic, like the feather collar on Delphine Seyrig's dress in *Last Year at Marienbad* (a film that launched a thousand fashion shoots) or the oversize pinwheel-shaped organdy sleeves on Katharine Hepburn's white frock in *A Bill of Divorcement* (see pages 60–61). Some people look at those details and wonder, “What's the point? Why wear something so impractical?” I look at them and think, “God, I love fashion, and isn't it amazing that you can wear feathers around your face

This gorgeous dress that Nicole Kidman wears in *Moulin Rouge* looks like it would be heaven to touch. The strong color, the tiny waist, the spiny origami details of the bustle all make me think of some exotic creature. It's an incredibly fancy, very serious dress.

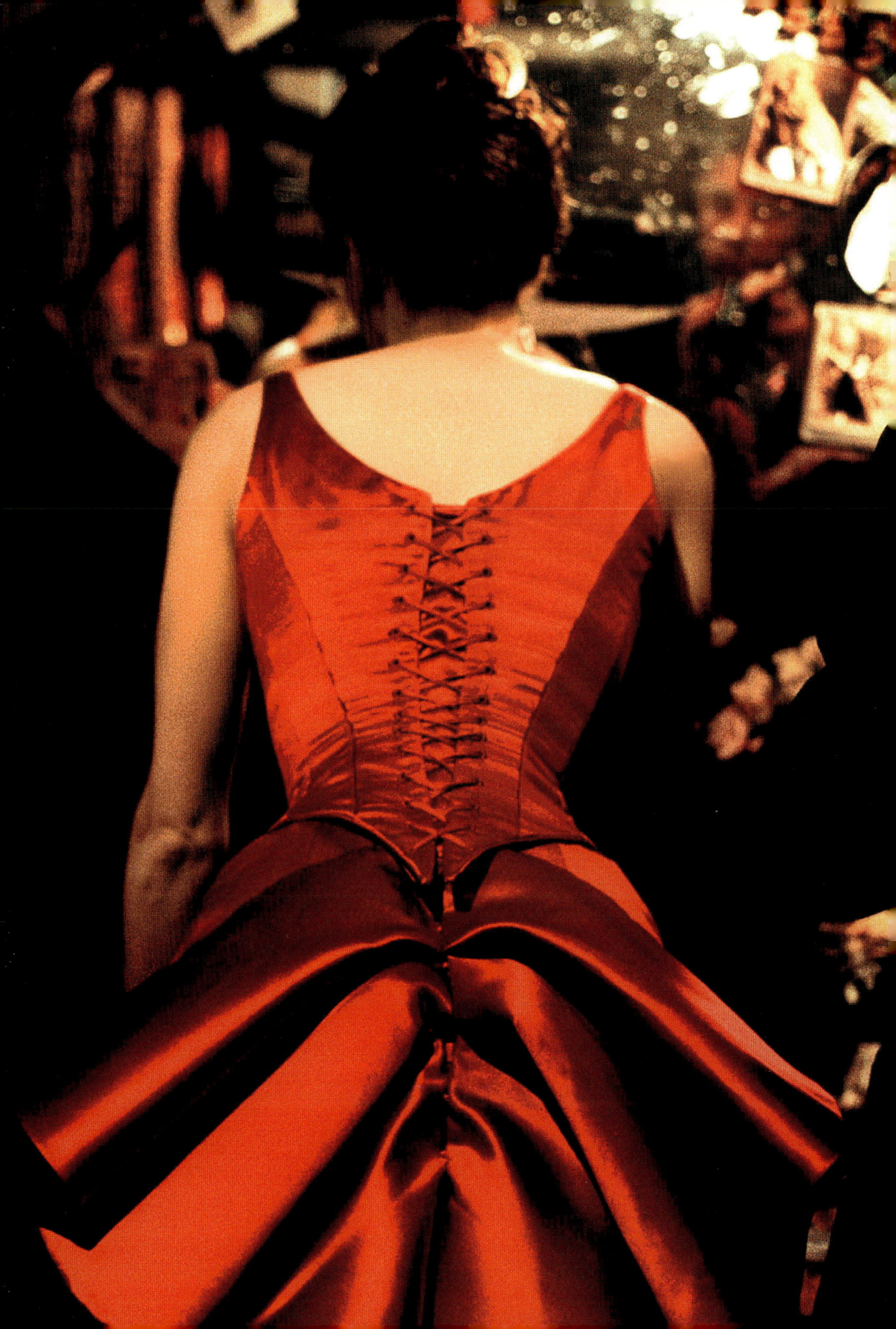

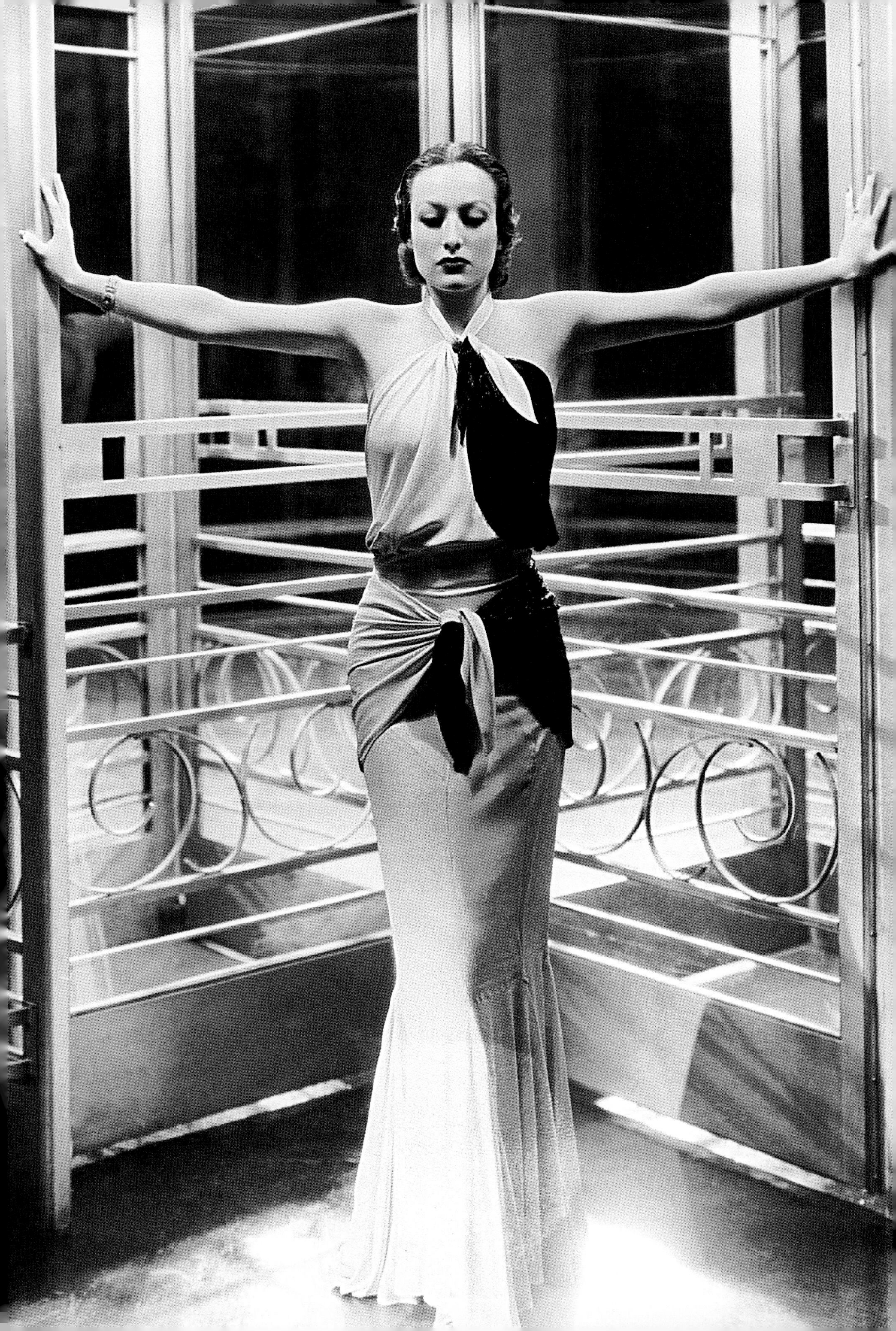

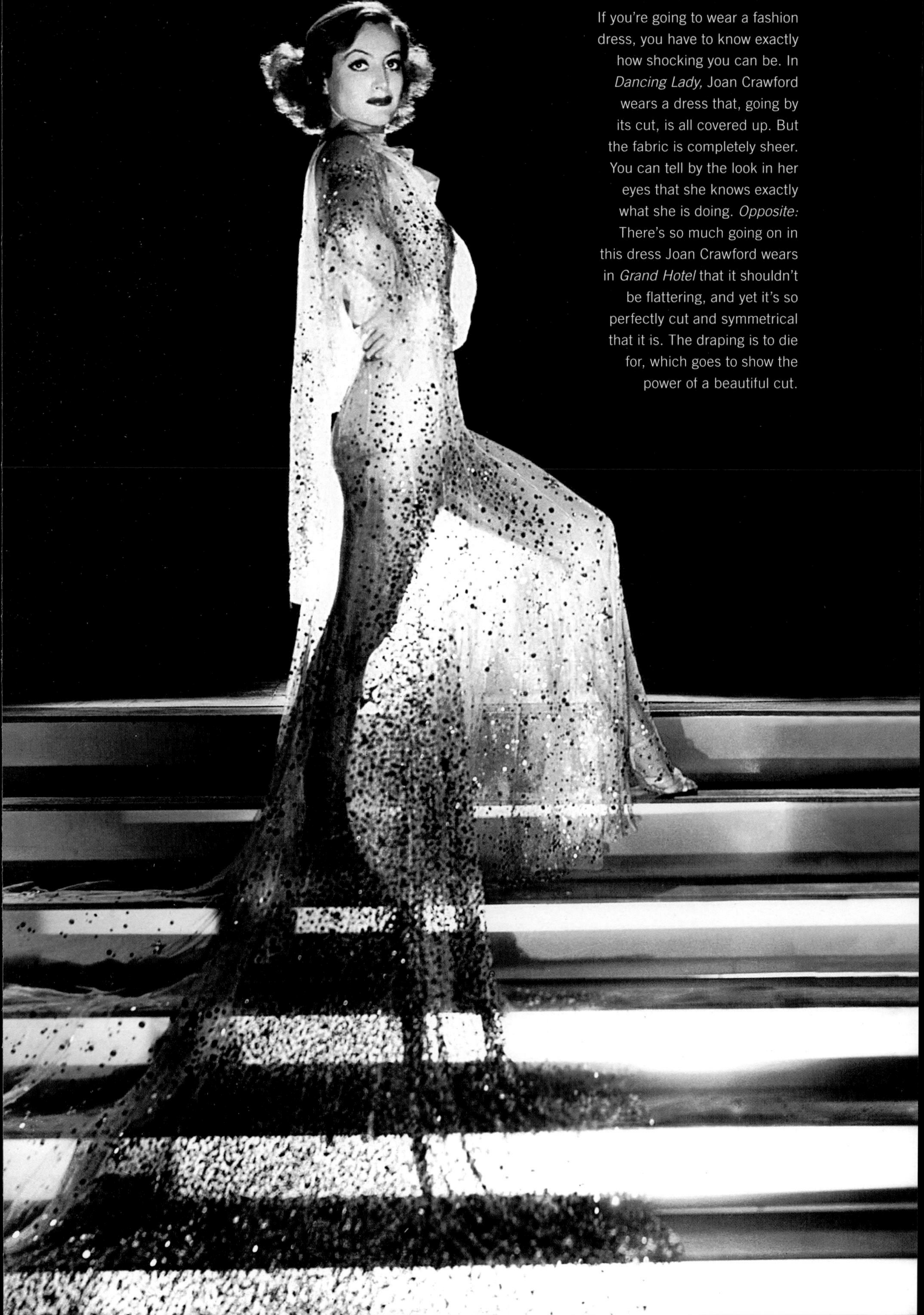

If you're going to wear a fashion dress, you have to know exactly how shocking you can be. In *Dancing Lady,* Joan Crawford wears a dress that, going by its cut, is all covered up. But the fabric is completely sheer. You can tell by the look in her eyes that she knows exactly what she is doing. *Opposite:* There's so much going on in this dress Joan Crawford wears in *Grand Hotel* that it shouldn't be flattering, and yet it's so perfectly cut and symmetrical that it is. The draping is to die for, which goes to show the power of a beautiful cut.

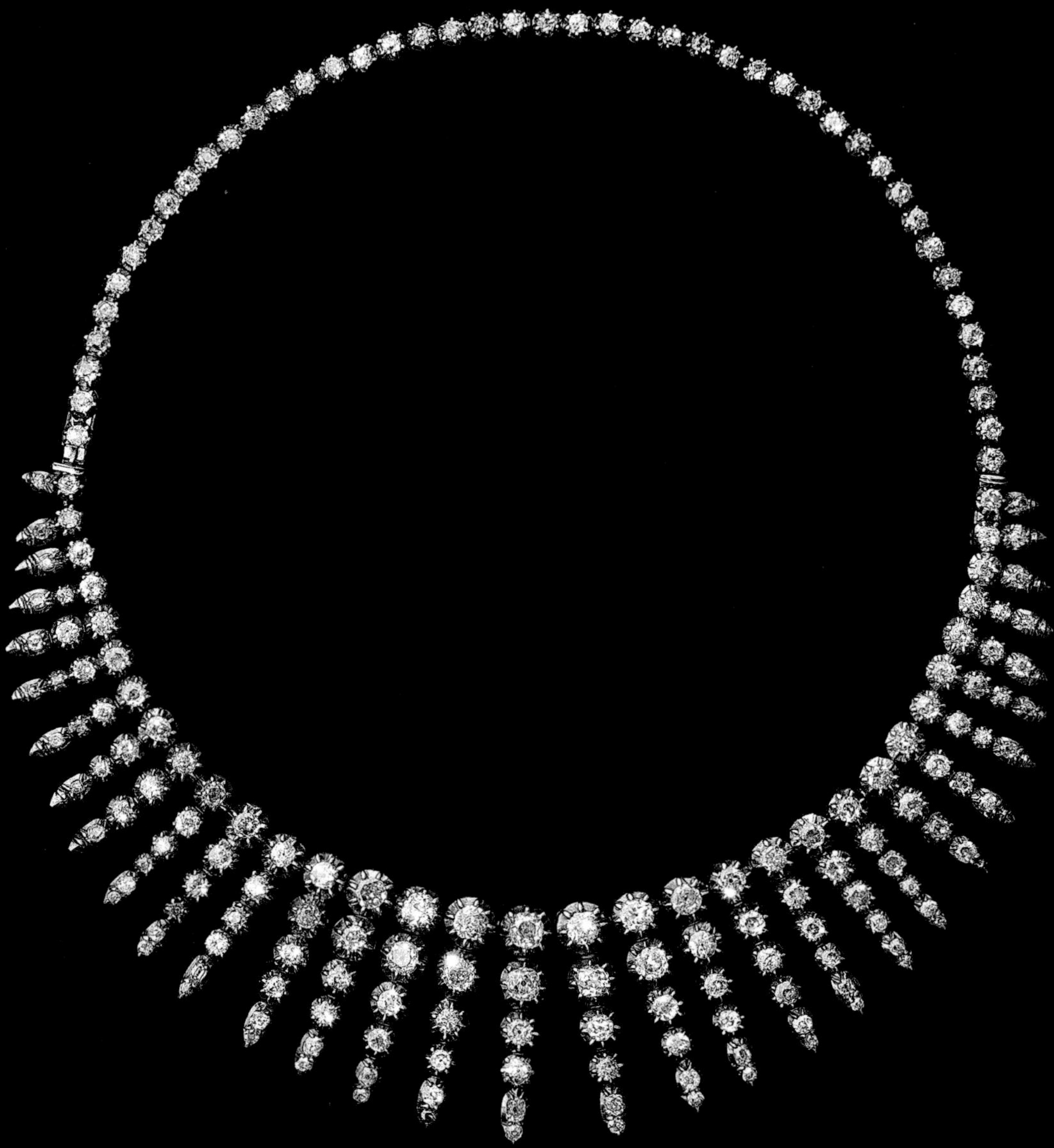

“Pour yourself a drink,
put on some lipstick,
and pull yourself together.”

Elizabeth Taylor

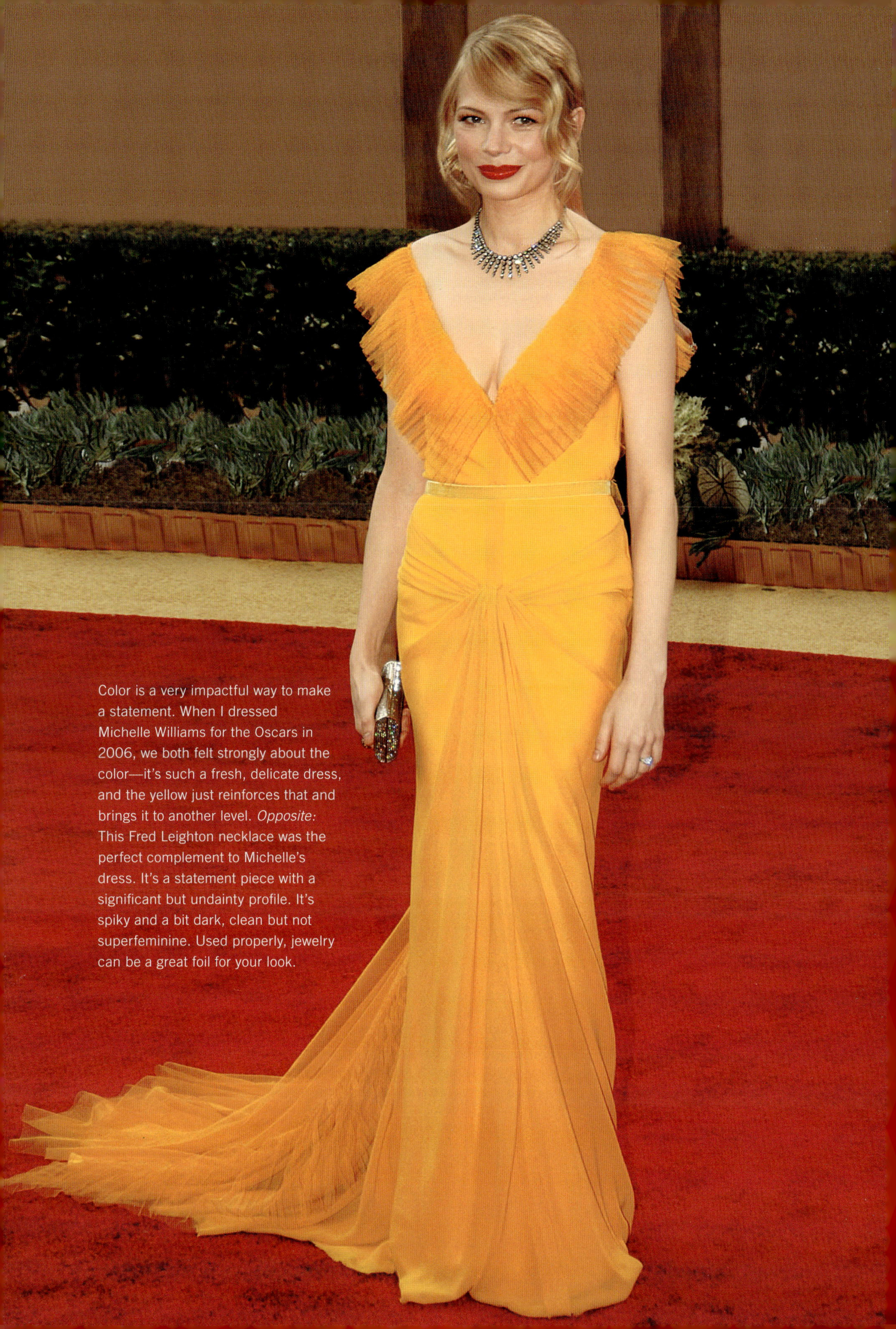

Color is a very impactful way to make a statement. When I dressed Michelle Williams for the Oscars in 2006, we both felt strongly about the color—it's such a fresh, delicate dress, and the yellow just reinforces that and brings it to another level. *Opposite:* This Fred Leighton necklace was the perfect complement to Michelle's dress. It's a statement piece with a significant but undainty profile. It's spiky and a bit dark, clean but not superfeminine. Used properly, jewelry can be a great foil for your look.

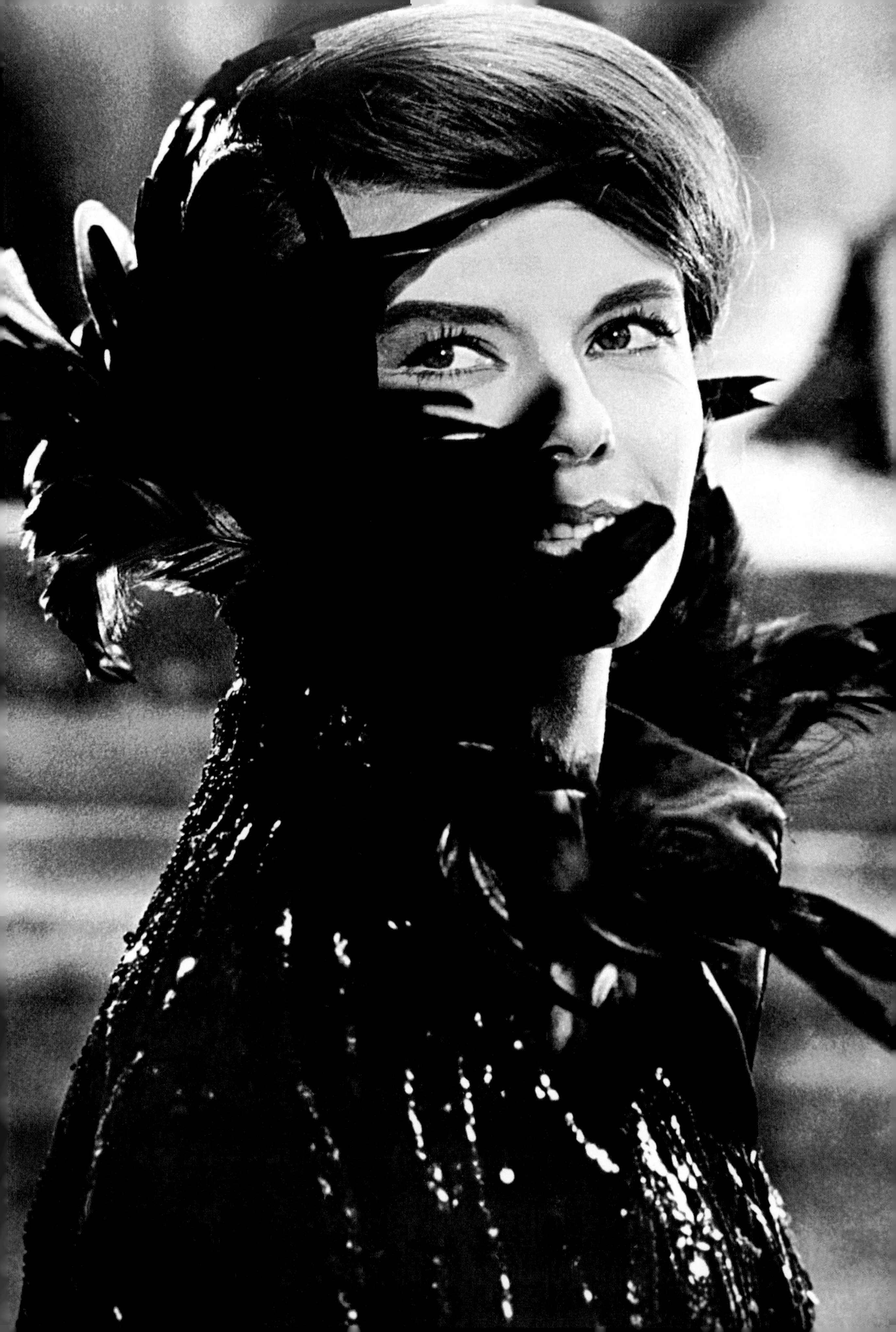

and organdy wings?" It makes me so happy that someone stitched those feathers in place and that someone else knew how to make those organdy wings. These artisans are the people who make fashion beautiful.

When an actress and I determine that we're going with a fashion dress, my advice to her is to pretend she's playing a part, whether that's a 1930s screen goddess or a Victorian matron with a naughty secret; whatever scenario is appropriate for the dress. Posture, hair, and makeup all play a part in the role. When you look at

Katharine Hepburn wore this in her first film, *A Bill of Divorcement.* It's a super-romantic gown—but at the same time it's really bold. The one outrageous detail of the giant organza wings on an otherwise pretty dress makes it impossible to forget. *Opposite:* In *Last Year at Marienbad,* Delphine Seyrig plays a mysterious character. That's reflected in this dress, which has a great dramatic effect while partly concealing her features. There's nothing quite like feathers—if you dare to wear them, they're great at framing the face. *Following pages:* In *Atonement,* Keira Knightley's character is in a state of high emotion, and the brilliant emerald green dress she chooses to wear reflects that. Just remember that you can't hide in a dress like this—you must wear it with confidence.

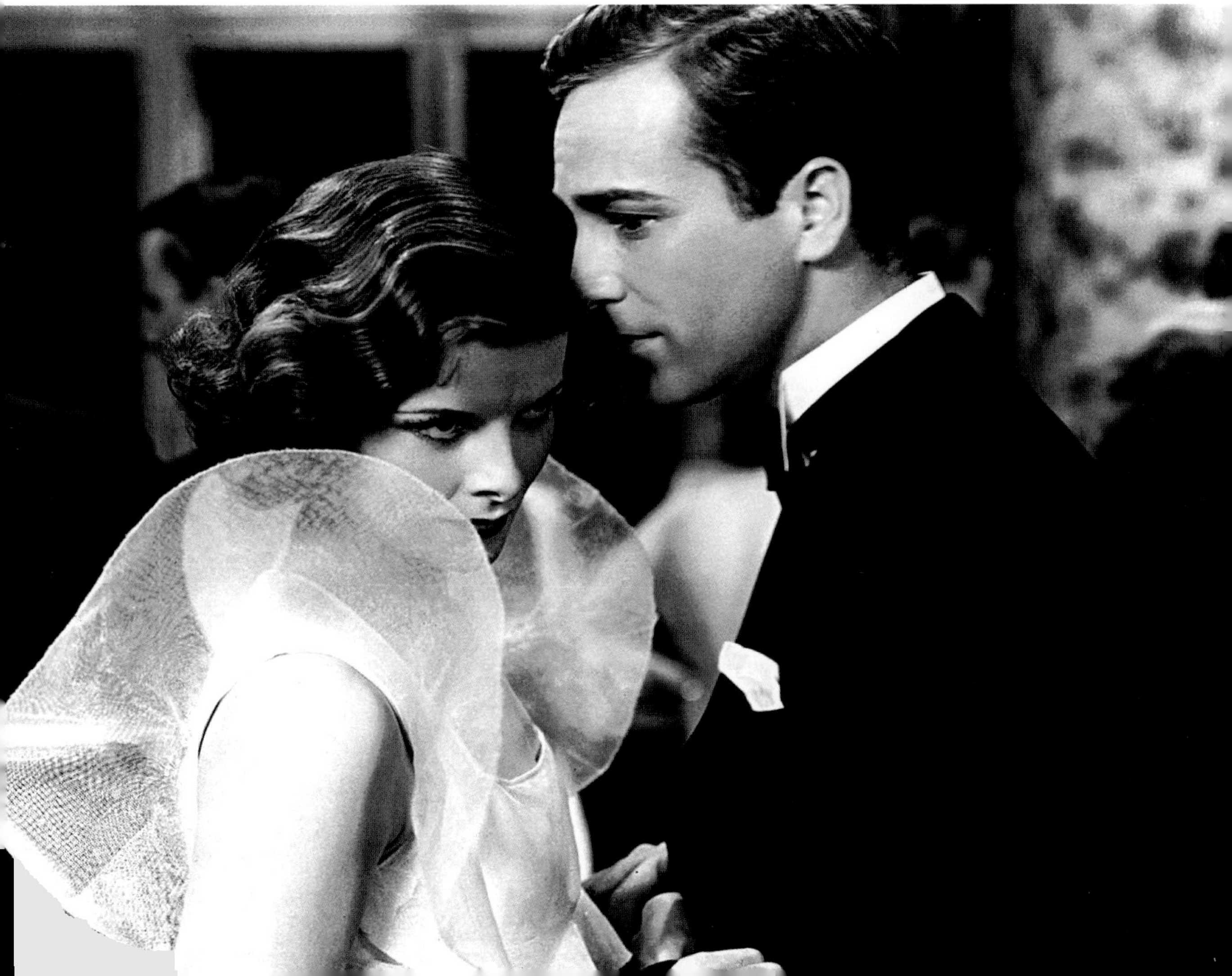

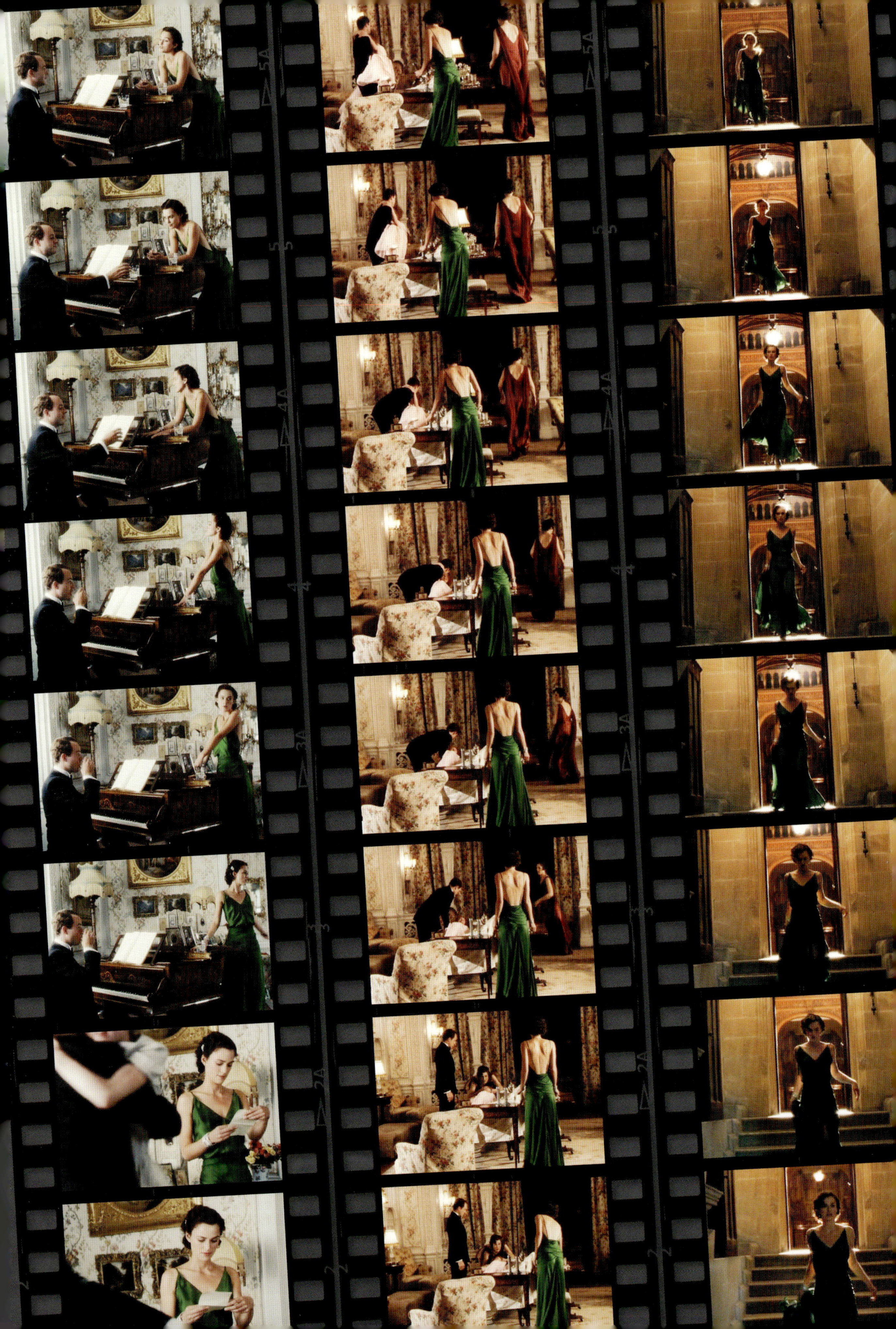

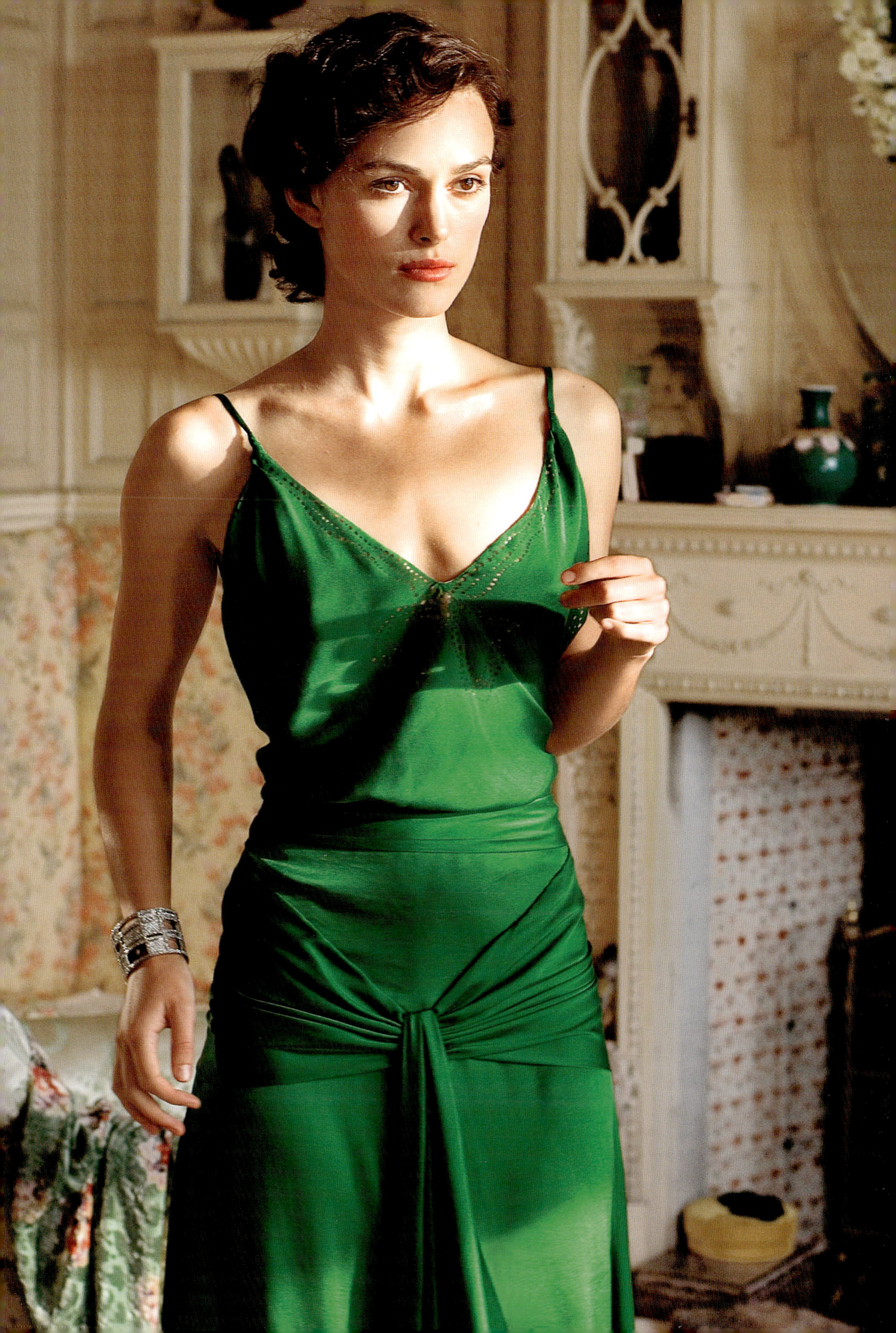

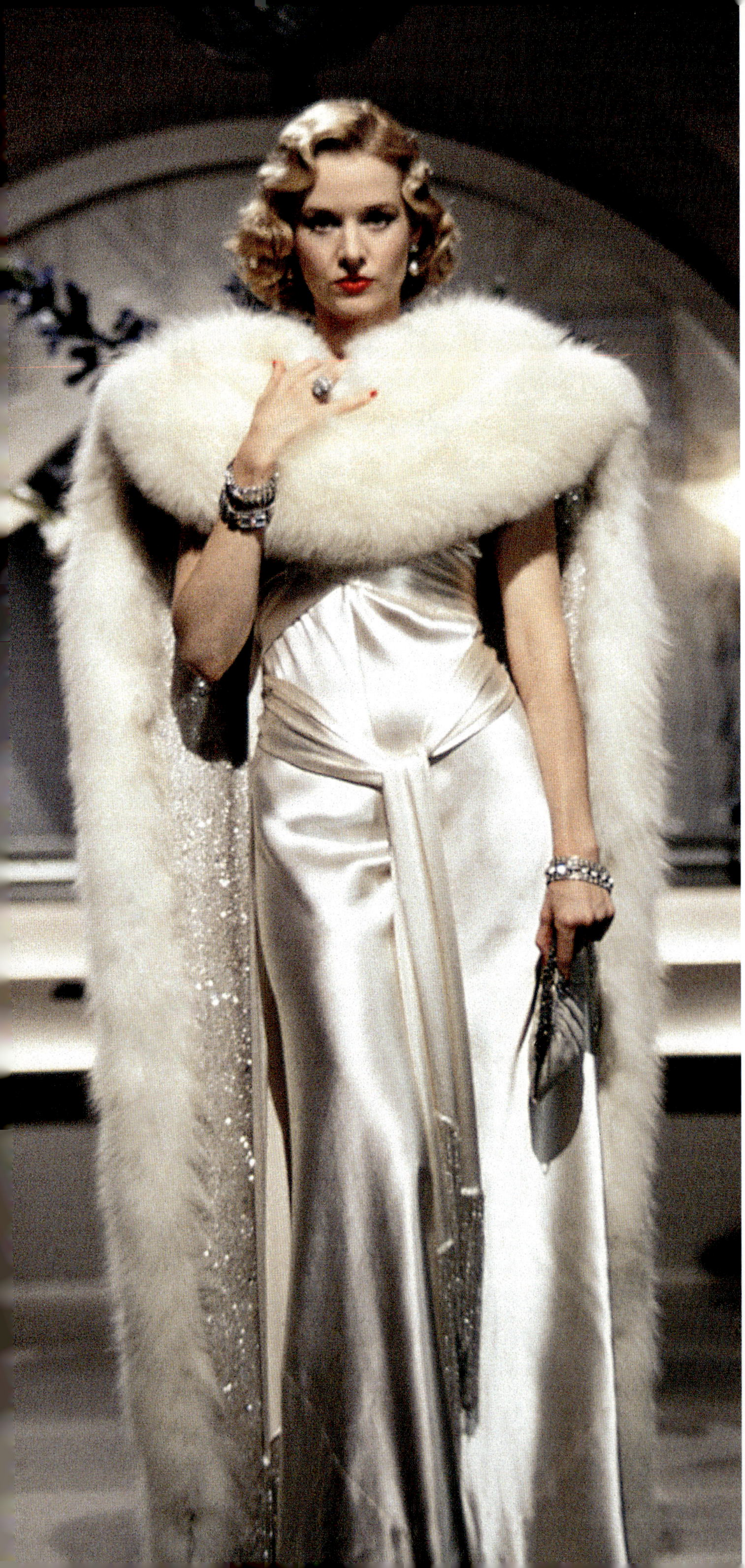
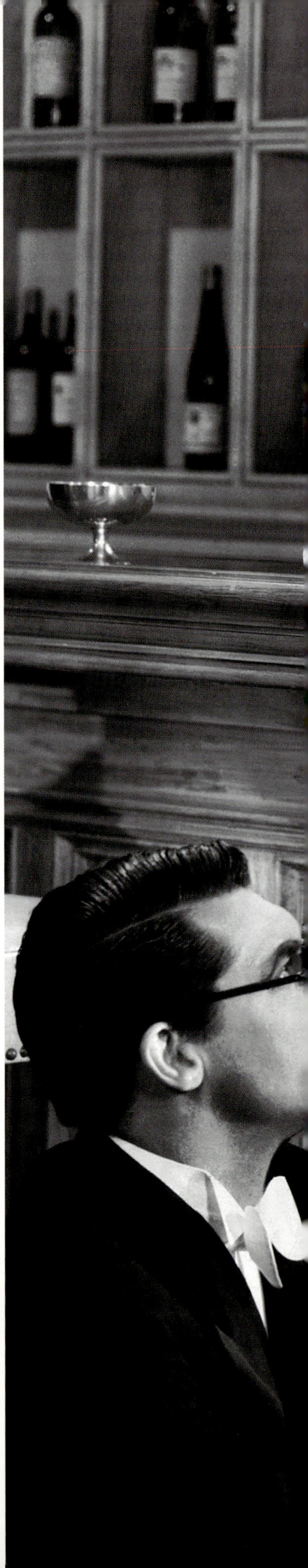

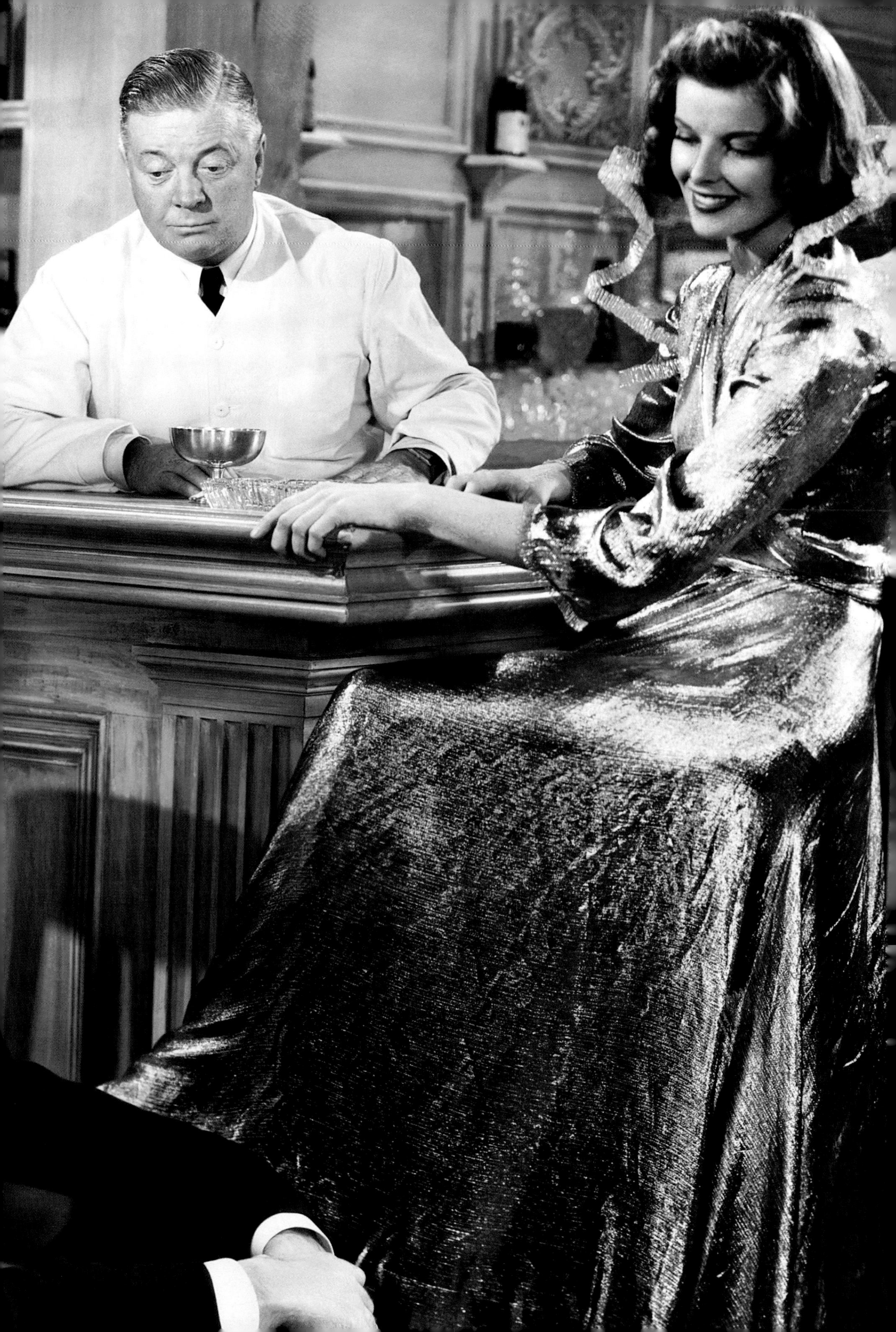

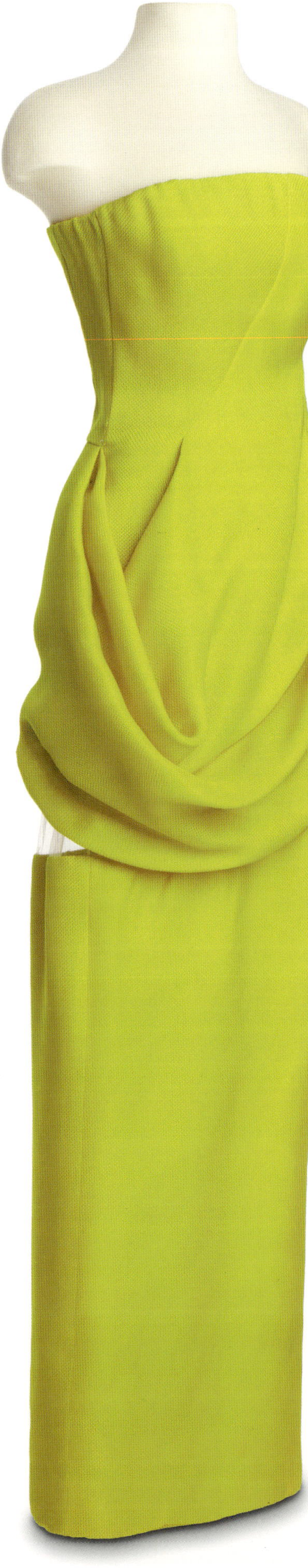

There's an interesting play between classicism and modernism in this Dior dress. The draping is pure old-school, while the see-through panel is a little surreal. Plus, it's acid yellow. *Opposite:* In *Prizzi's Honor,* Anjelica Huston shows how striking it is to be completely coordinated. Her dress, her makeup, her hair, her accessories—everything comes together into one outstanding whole. There's so much fashion in this image that it's almost overwhelming, but the purity of the look makes it work. *Previous pages, left:* Can one outfit contain so much drama? Penelope Ann Miller in *The Shadow* is wearing bias-cut satin with serious draping and a giant, glittery fur stole. What keeps it gorgeous is that it's tonal; everything's in harmony. *Right:* In this scene from *Bringing Up Baby,* Katharine Hepburn is wearing a metallic dress with a crazily dramatic neckline—yet she's still approachable and real. Why? Because while her outfit might be a bit wacky, it's basically a shirtdress. Balance is key!

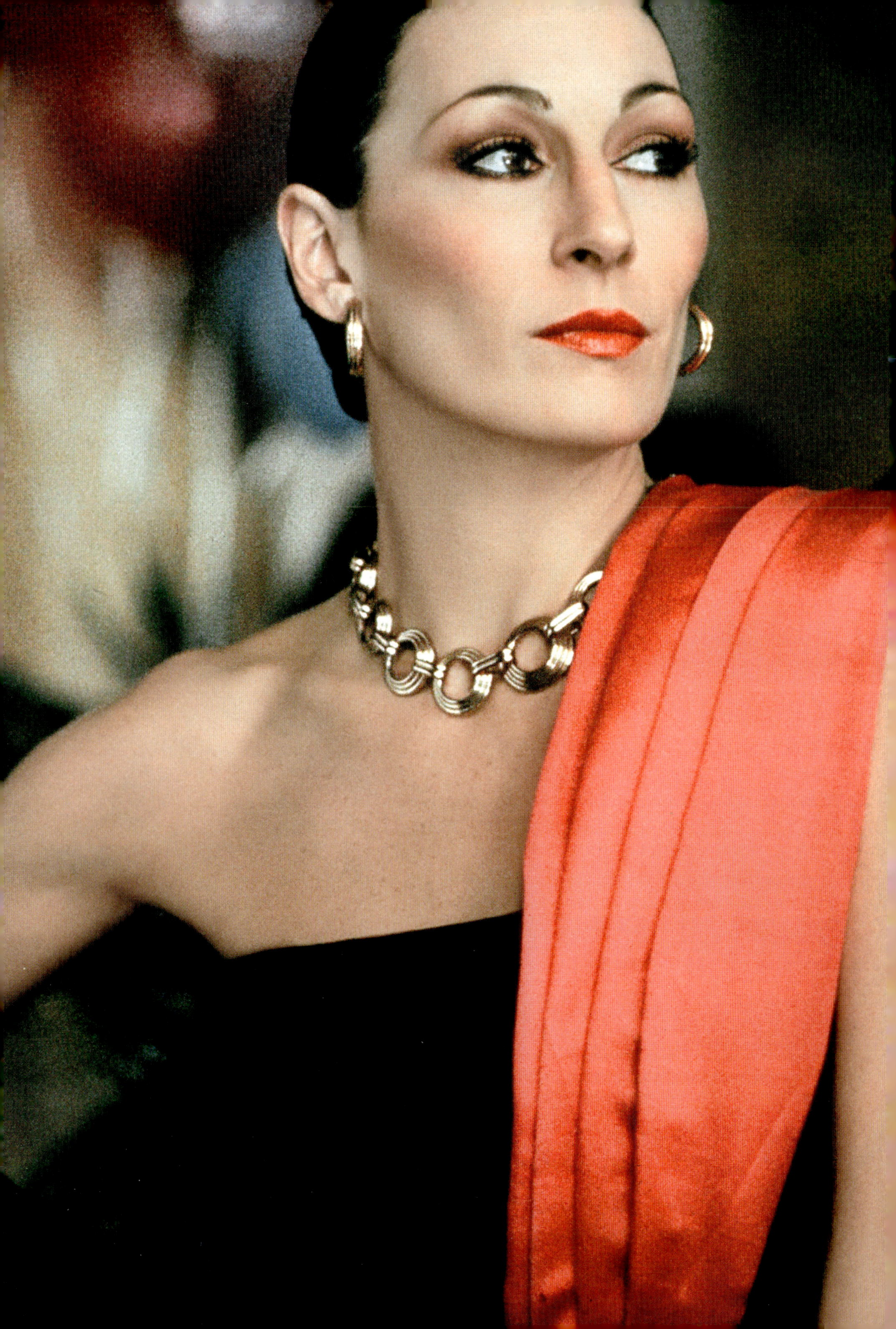

> “It takes too much time to be a well-dressed woman. I have watched others. Bags, shoes, hats. They must think of them all the time.”

Marlene Dietrich

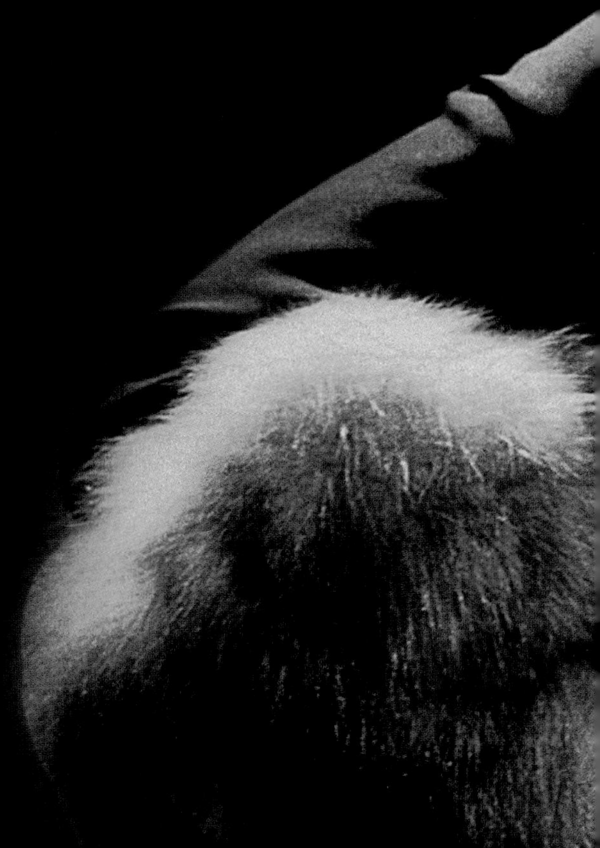

If there’s one woman who lived the concept of this chapter, it was Marlene Dietrich, seen here in *Blonde Venus.* “I dress for the image,” she said. “Not for myself, not for the public, not for fashion, not for men.”

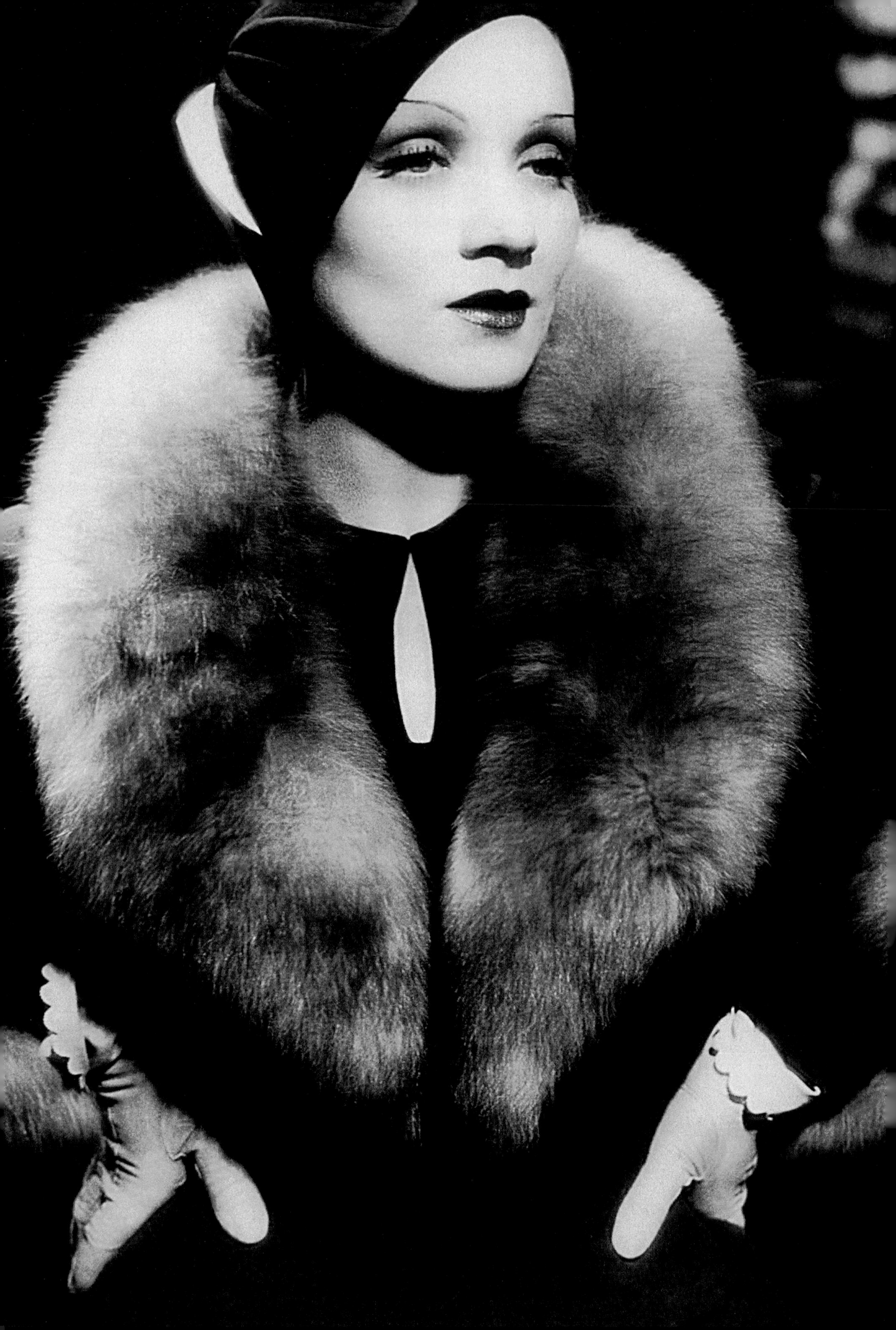

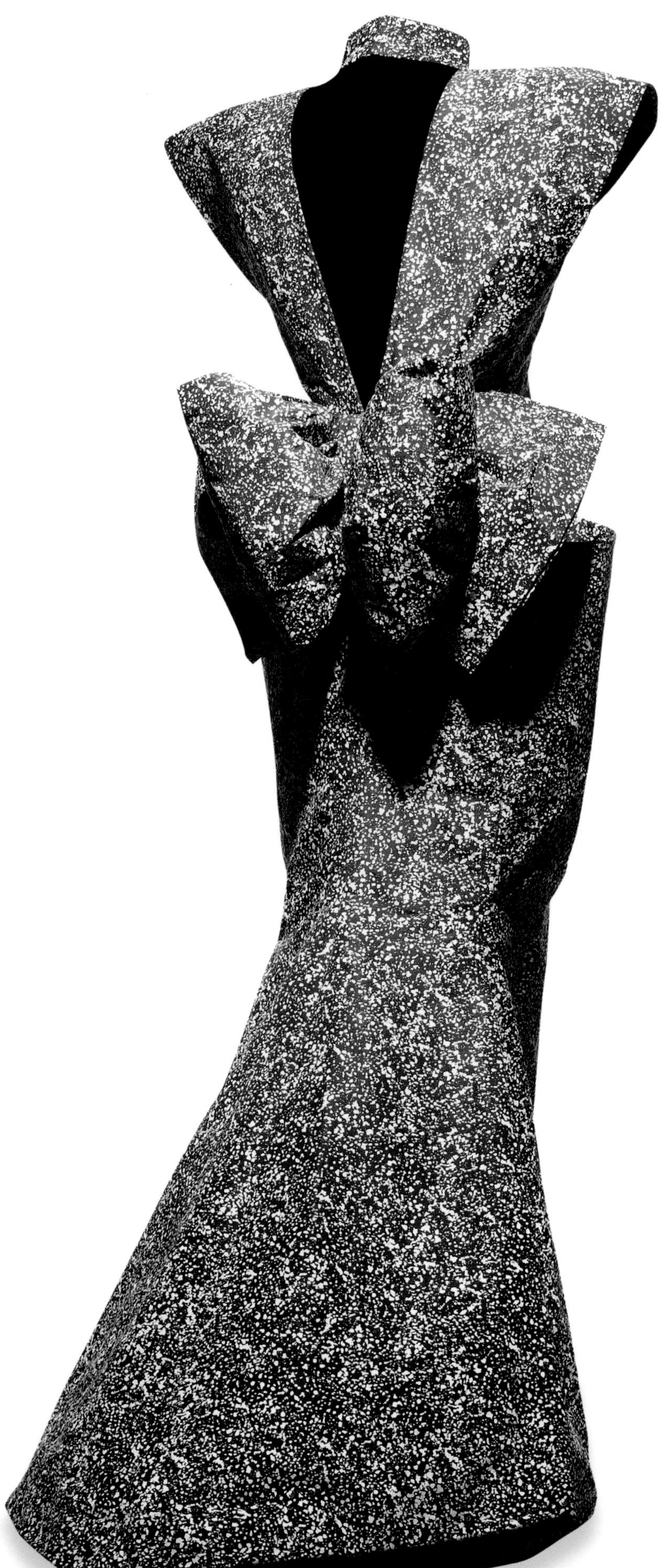

"I'm not ashamed to admit it: fashion is superficial, but I love it."

Chloë Sevigny

Anjelica Huston in *Prizzi's Honor,* she became one with her outfit. The dress is so strict and Japanese in its purity. The sculptural accessories underscore this, as do her hair and makeup, which are so stylized they're practically Kabuki. I don't think this dress would have been successful on a blonde. The fact that her hair is the same color as her dress is part of the package. She's working it, which is what fashion dresses require. They're not the sort of thing you throw on and forget about—they're physically demanding and tend to require hypervigilance on the part of the wearer to ensure that she's living up to her outfit. Do you think that after Nicole Kidman was laced into that nineteenth-century-style red satin ball gown in *Moulin Rouge,* she threw herself down on the couch and put her feet up? Not a chance. She would have been aware of every movement she made and would have avoided sitting so as not to crush that gorgeous bustle. And it was worth it, because she looked incredible. But if a dress feels like too much effort, find another one.

Some of the women who are known for their unique fashion choices—Marlene Dietrich, Cher—have strong personalities. However, that's not always the case. Keira Knightley, for example, frequently wears fashion dresses. You can be a vamp in a fashion dress or fall in love with the poetry of it or the concept it conveys. But for a fashion dress to do its job, it really has to mesh with your personality as well as your body. Selecting one is a process. Often you fall in love with it on the rack and hope that it looks as good on you as it does on the hanger. Before you commit, though, make sure it's the dress for

The shape of this Dior dress is designed to make a woman's body look amazing. The shoulders are structured; the waist is tiny; the bow plays up the curve of the hips; the skirt veers in to make the knees look tiny, then widens again. It's a classic that gets extra oomph because of the stiff, shiny material, which makes it look like it's crafted from metal.

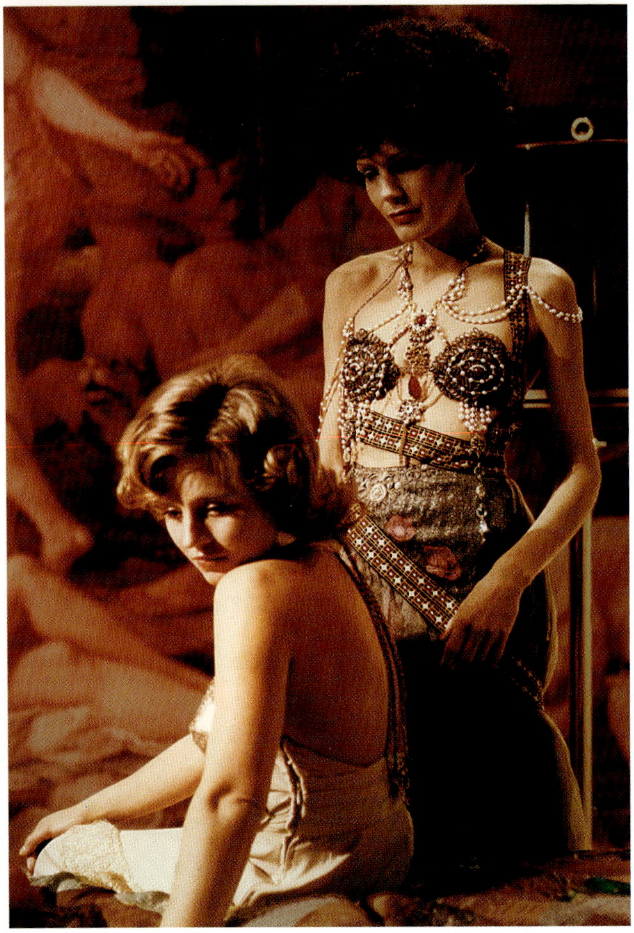

you. They tend to come in strong colors, so it should be one that's flattering for you as opposed to one that's on trend. I love jewel tones on brunettes, pink on blondes, and redheads really sing in green. Women with dark skin can wear very strong, unusual colors and look phenomenal. Everyone looks glamorous in some shade of red. But these are guidelines; always take a long look in the mirror before you buy. If the dress has volume, make sure it's in a place that flatters your body. If it's tight, it should only be because that was the designer's intention—and even then, you shouldn't be struggling to breathe.

I've said it before, and I'll say it again: Undergarments are crucial. A fashion dress will have a definite structure, and you need the correct underpinnings to support it. Your hair and makeup shouldn't be in a tussle for dominance over your dress. To wear a fashion dress successfully, you have to love it, and you have to let it be the star. Everything else, including you, is support.

I don't know if the above is a gown or jewelry or a bathing suit or art, but I love it. For me, this dress from *The Bitter Tears of Petra von Kant* represents how inspiring creative insanity can be. Even if you aren't going to wear something like this yourself, you can riff on some part of it. Designers from Tom Ford to Miuccia Prada have referenced this dress, and I'm sure the costume designer for *Blow,* who created the dress Penelope Cruz is wearing (*opposite*), did too. Her character has status and power and can consequently make bold fashion choices.

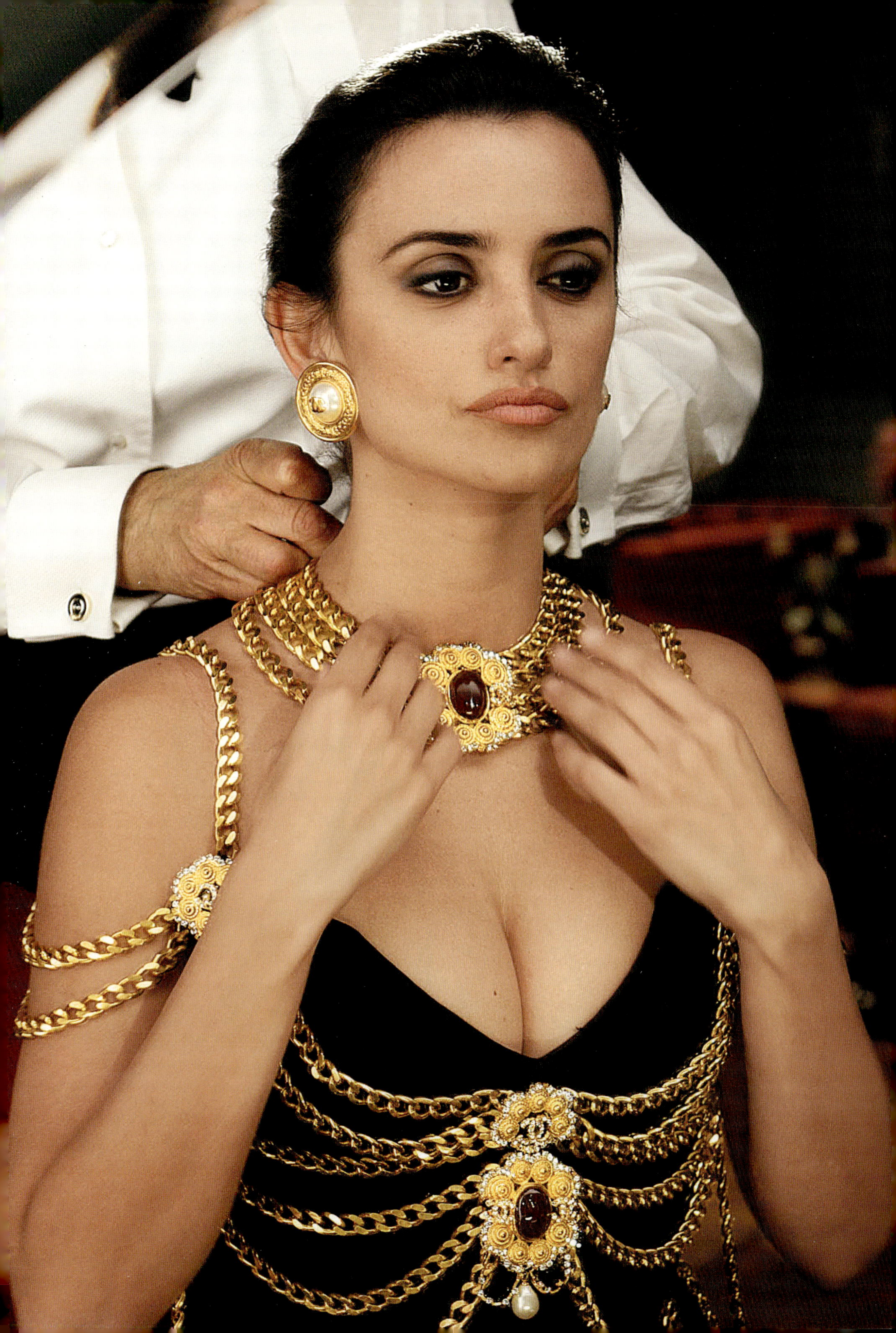

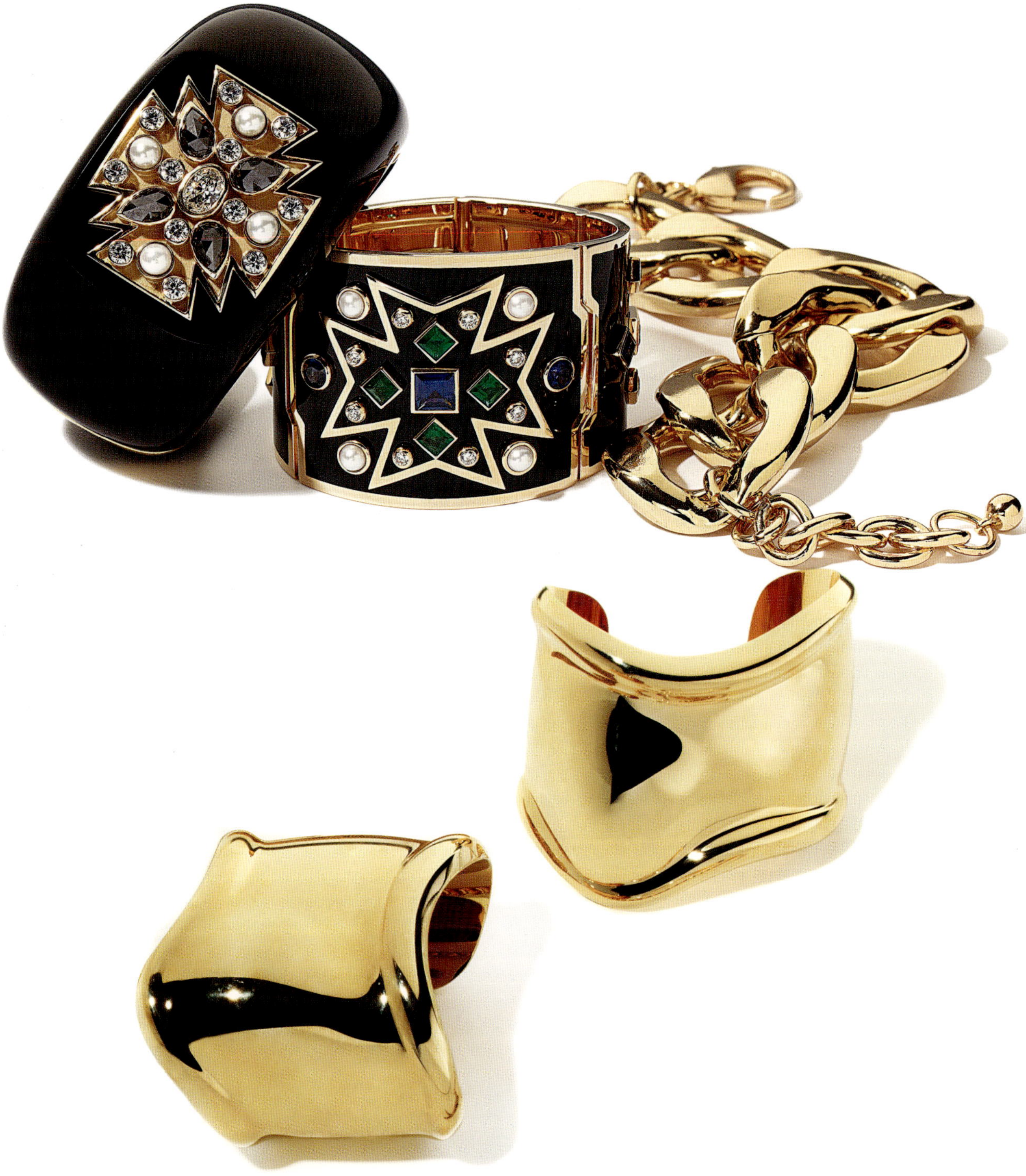

Bracelets highlight one of the prettiest areas of a woman's body—the wrists. I love a strong bracelet, because it's a way to wear jewelry that isn't prim or princess-y. My favorites are by Fulco di Verdura and Elsa Peretti. Verdura, who designed the three bracelets in the top row, was the go-to jeweler for leading ladies during Hollywood's golden years. Peretti, who designed the biomorphic cuffs (you can buy them to fit your right or left wrist), worked closely with Halston in the 1970s. *Opposite:* What this image of Marlene Dietrich from *Blonde Venus* says to me is to have fun. Don't be afraid to wear something ridiculous if it brings you joy. There's something incredibly freeing in knowing that's okay.

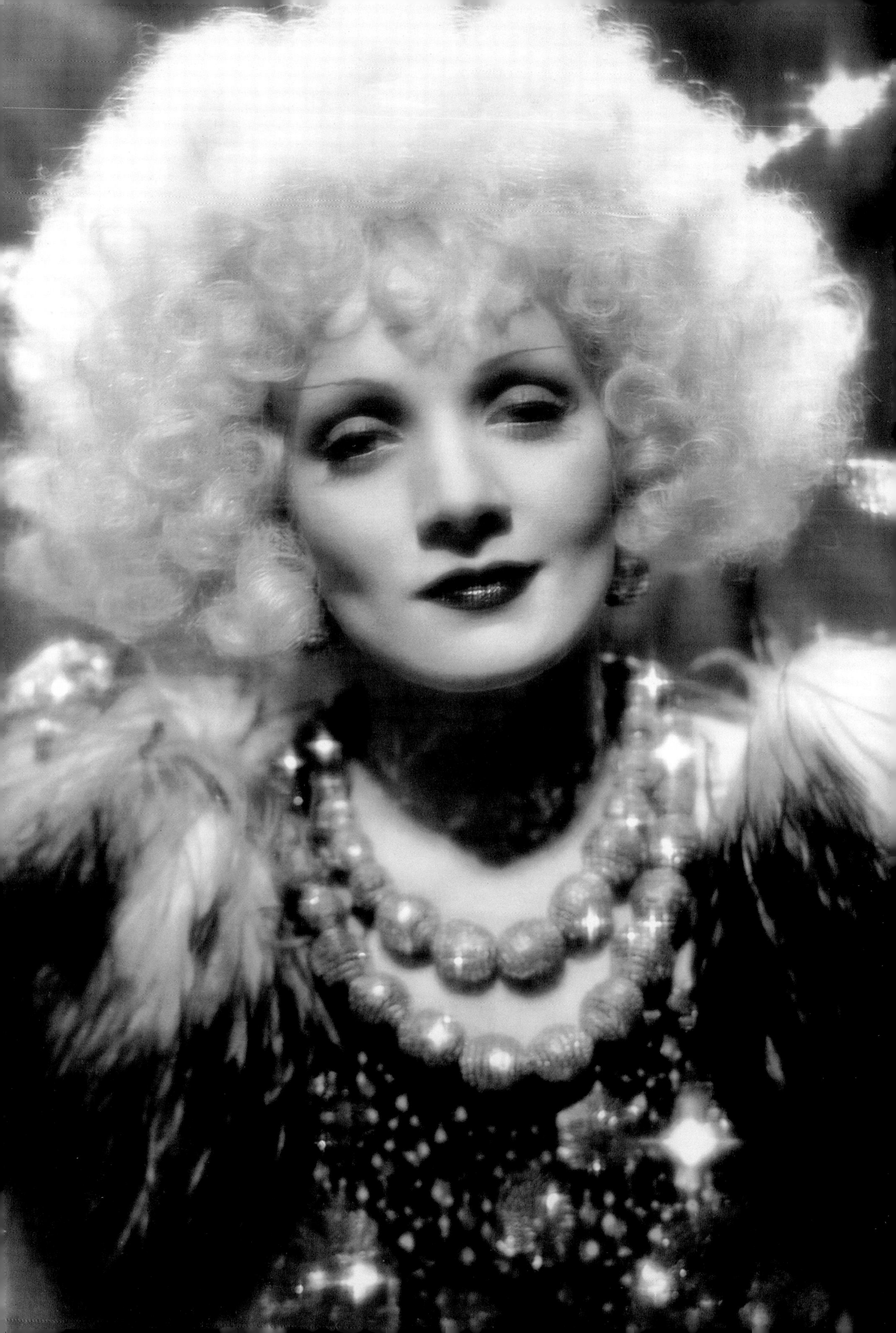

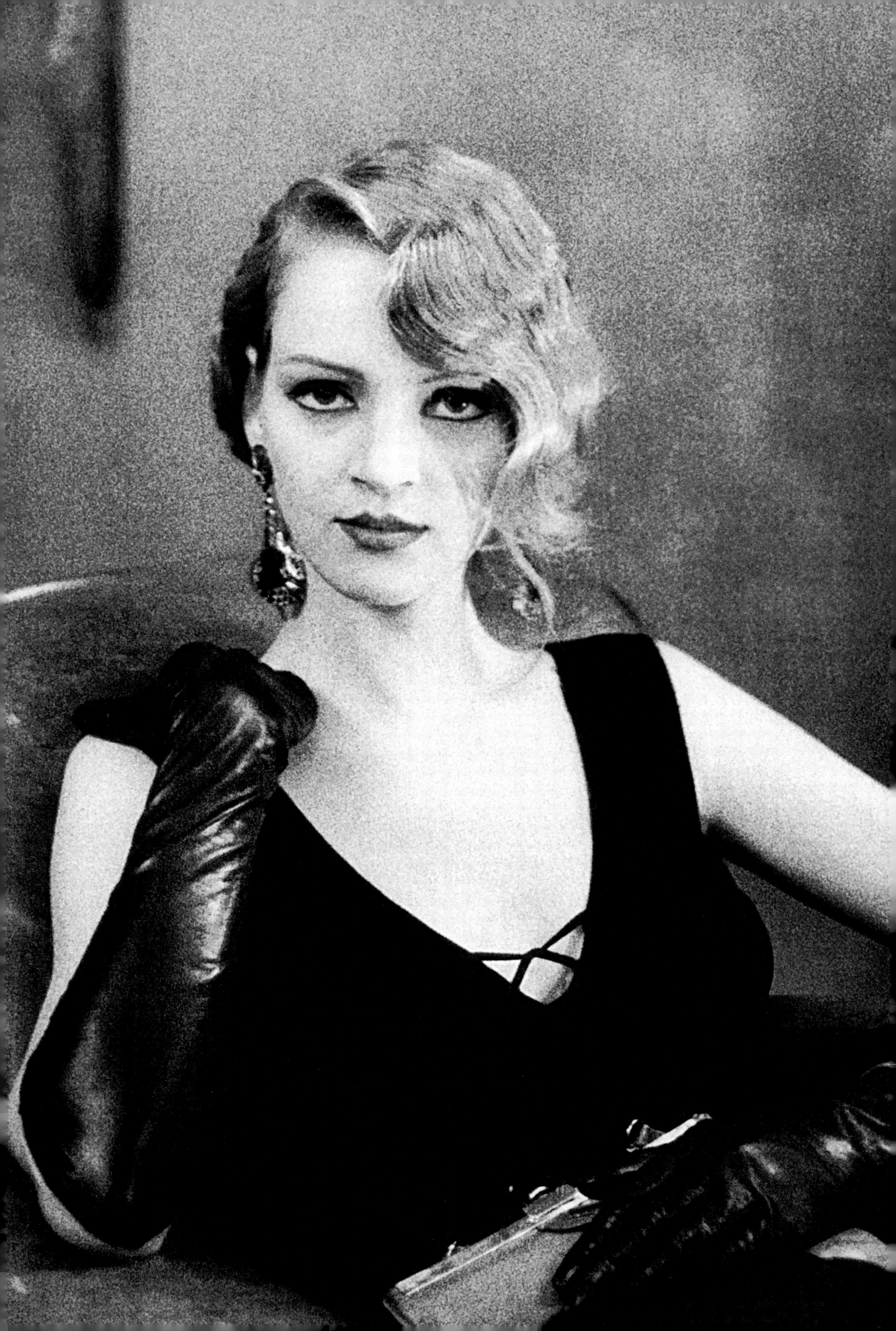

Film Noir: The Black Dress

Every few seasons, fashion magazines will announce that black is over. There will be headlines declaring that green is the new black or pink is the new black or cornflakes are the new black or whatever. The implication is that if you persist in wearing black, you're hopelessly out of it, darling. Resist being taken in by all of this. Fashion thrives on change, and these sorts of dictates are always going to be issued. But dismissing black as passé is like saying that sugar is over or asking if you're sick of air. Of course not! Just look at Anouk Aimée in *La Dolce Vita,* wearing a dress that is just as relevant today as it was in 1960 (see page 78). It has a body-enhancing shape, an interesting play of textures, and an eye-catching neckline, and is proof that a good black dress endures.

There are very real reasons why black is perennially popular. It's flattering—if you're feeling fat, it will make you look thinner. It's practical—you can wear a black dress with tights in the winter and sandals in the summer. It's expensive looking—you can buy a cheap black dress and have it look like a million bucks, something that will never work,

With a black dress, the details are key. It's the tiny lingerie detail at the bust of this dress, which Uma Thurman wears in *Henry & June* that makes it for me. It draws attention to the sexiest part of the dress without making a big fuss about it. She's paired the simple dress with heavy, vampy makeup, which makes the look smolder.

for example, with a red dress, because the dyes are too unpredictable. It's versatile—with just a change of accessories, a black dress can go from conservative to sexy. Christian Dior said it best: "You can wear black at any time. You can wear it at any age. You can wear it for almost any occasion. A little black frock is essential to a woman's wardrobe."

From my point of view, what black really has going for it is its innate correctness. Who doesn't want to look like they have great taste without having to try too hard? Take Angelina Jolie. She's one sexy lady (see pages 128–129 for proof...if you need any). With her va-va-voom hair and face and body, she could easily veer into the cartoonish. But when she puts on a black dress, as she often does, she gains gravitas and elegance. The only downside to black is that it can be a bit subtle for the red carpet, which is why I don't tend to put my clients in it very often. (The other time I stay away from

Black is the most classic, never-fail color: You could confidently wear Anouk Aimée's dress from *La Dolce Vita* (*below, left*), which was made more than 50 years ago, today. There's nothing like black for creating contrast. In *Dick Tracy* (*below, right*), Madonna's deep V-neck matte black dress makes her skin look like magnolia petals. Black can also save the day when you're pressed for time and feel like a wreck. In *Quantum of Solace* (*opposite*), Olga Kurylenko appears to be walking away from a plane crash but still looks pulled together in her black dress.

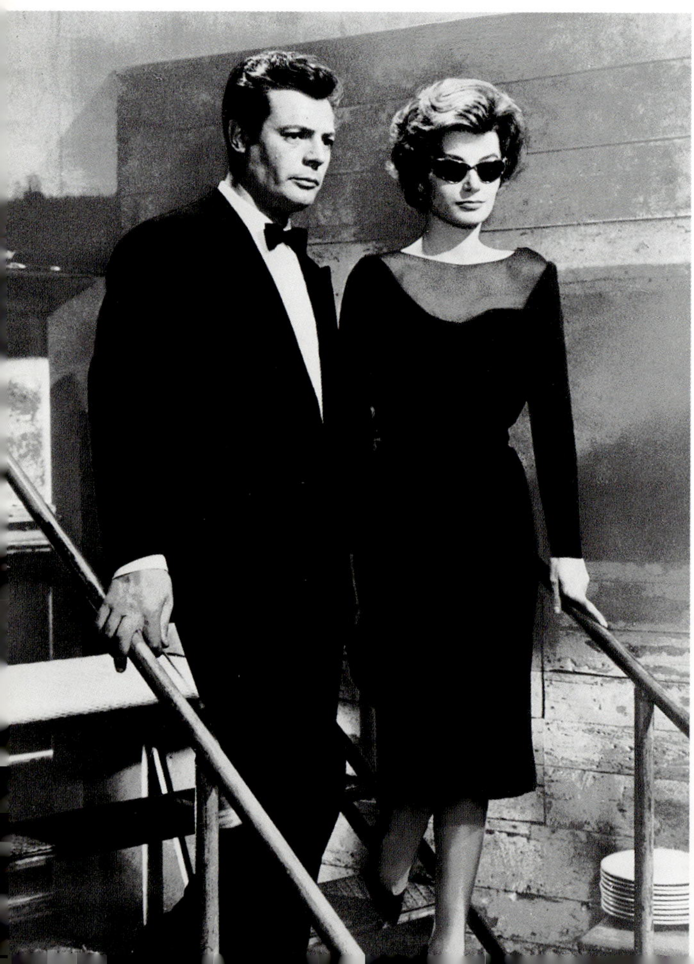

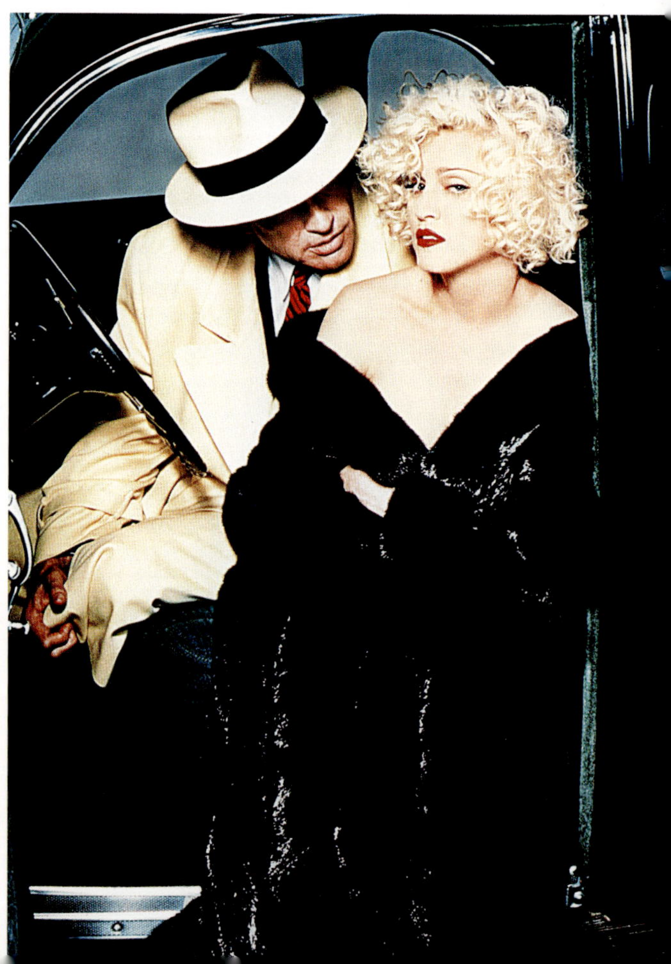

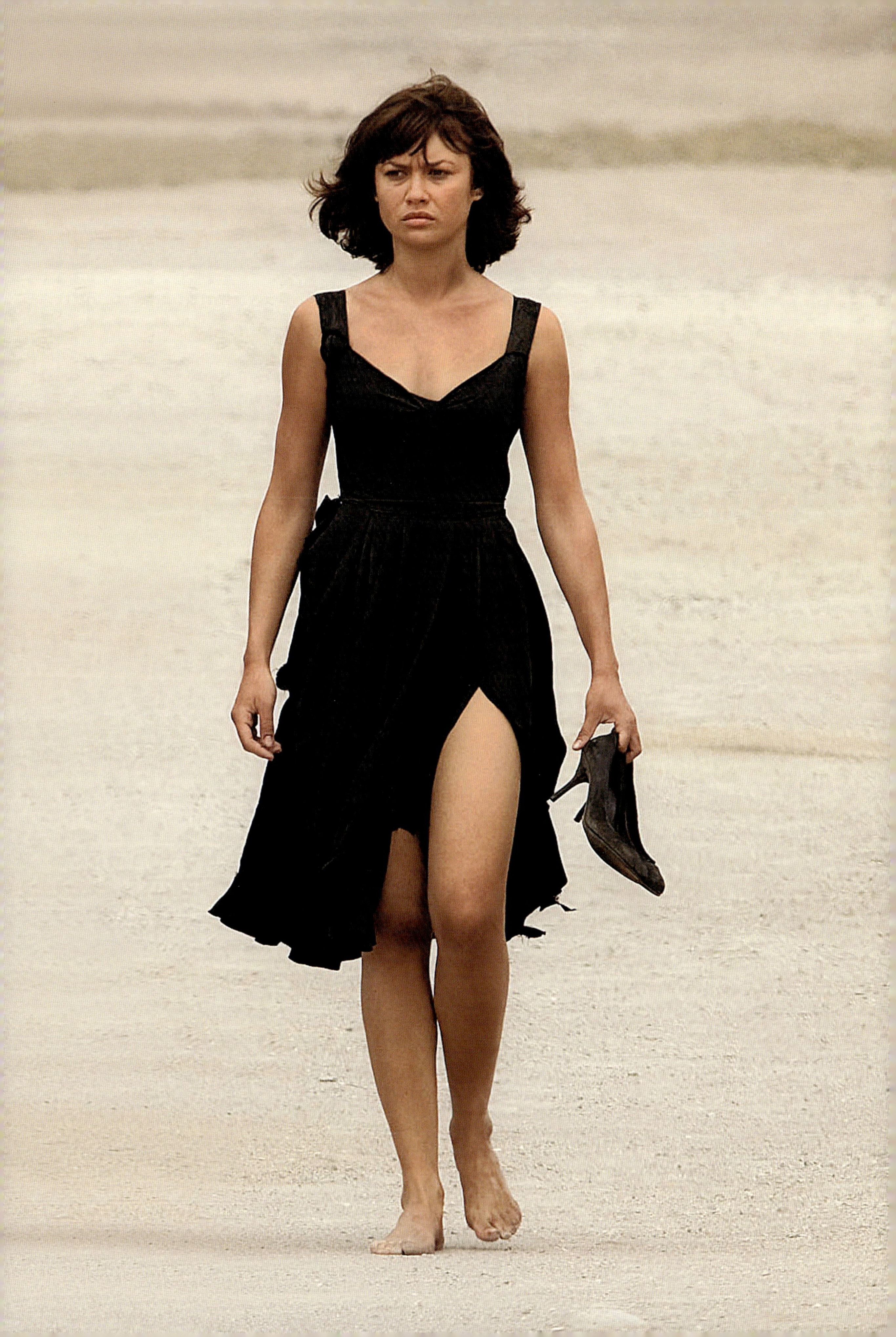

The perfect black pumps, cocktail ring, and clutch will carry you far. These pumps, by Charlotte Olympia, show just the perfect amount of toe cleavage. The diamond and onyx cocktail ring, by Fred Leighton, is both futuristic and classic. And the metal clutch by Lee Savage is like a portable piece of sculpture. *Opposite:* Gwyneth Paltrow in *The Talented Mr. Ripley* is all about the correctness and formality of black. It feels respectful and fancy and beautiful, especially styled with an updo and quiet jewelry. It's an old-fashioned sort of formality that's still always modern.

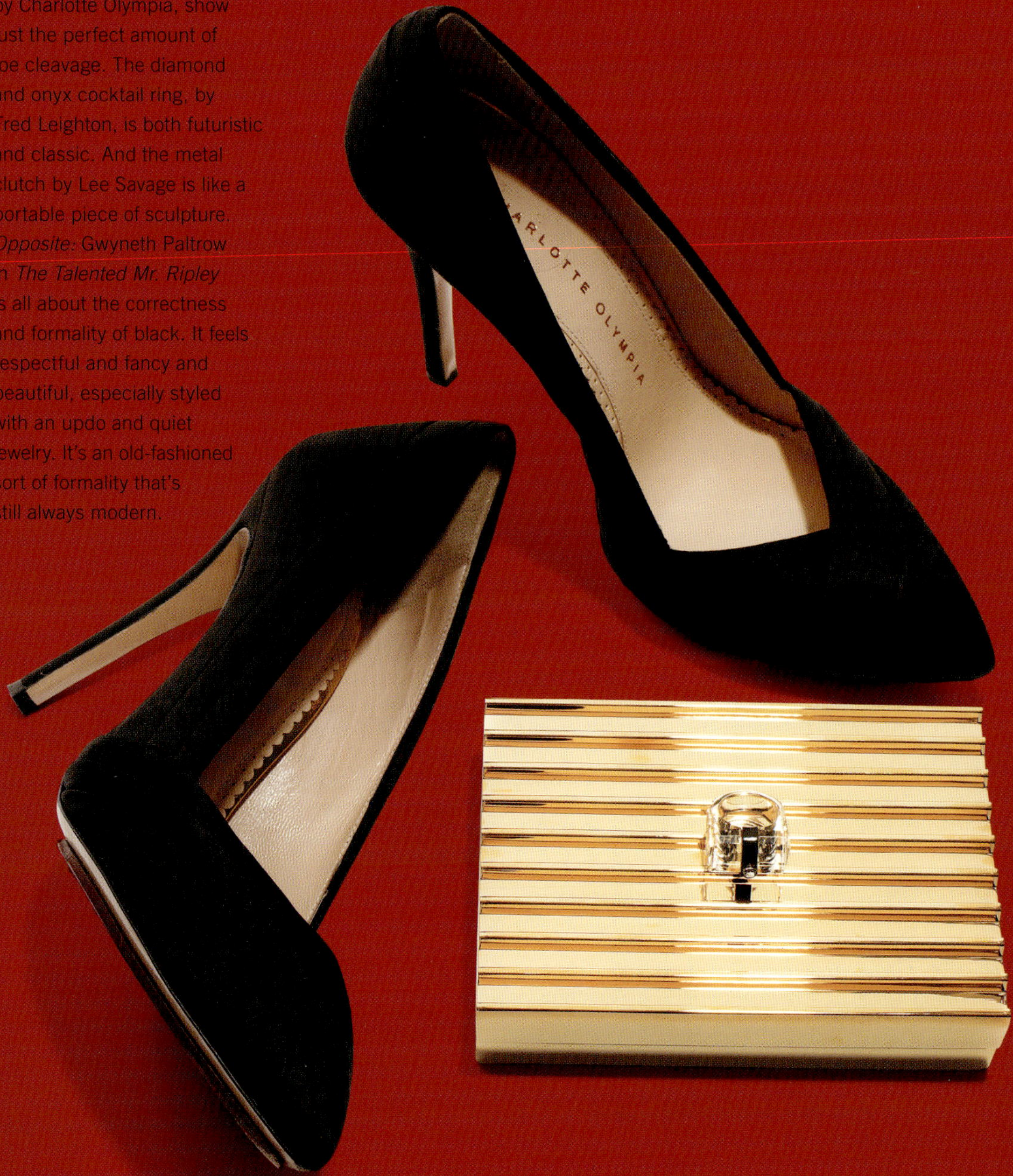

"Beauty and femininity are ageless and can't be contrived, and glamour cannot be manufactured. Not real glamour; it's based on femininity."

Marilyn Monroe

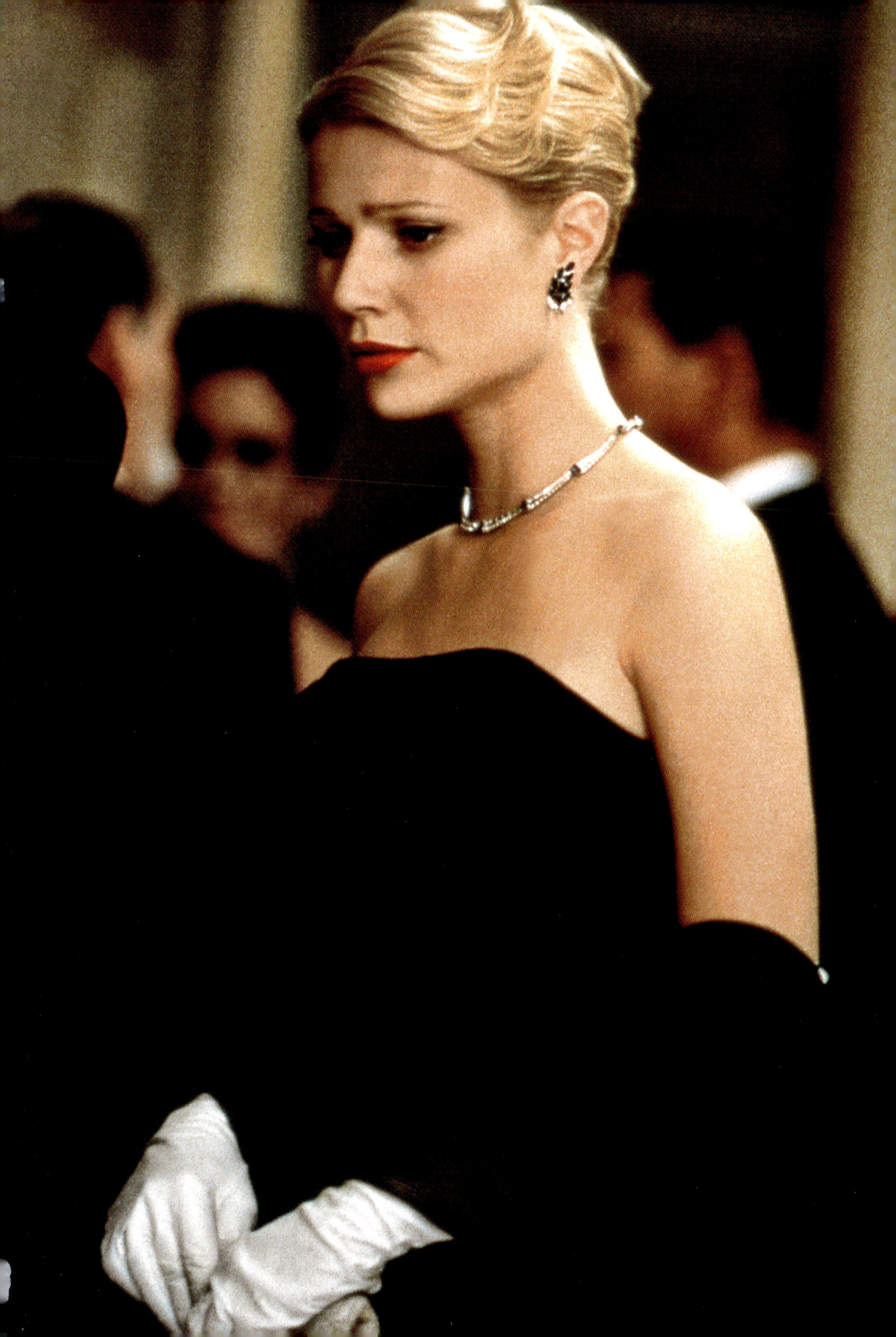

“Beautiful? It's all a question of luck. I was born with good legs. As for the rest...beautiful, no. Amusing, yes.”

Josephine Baker

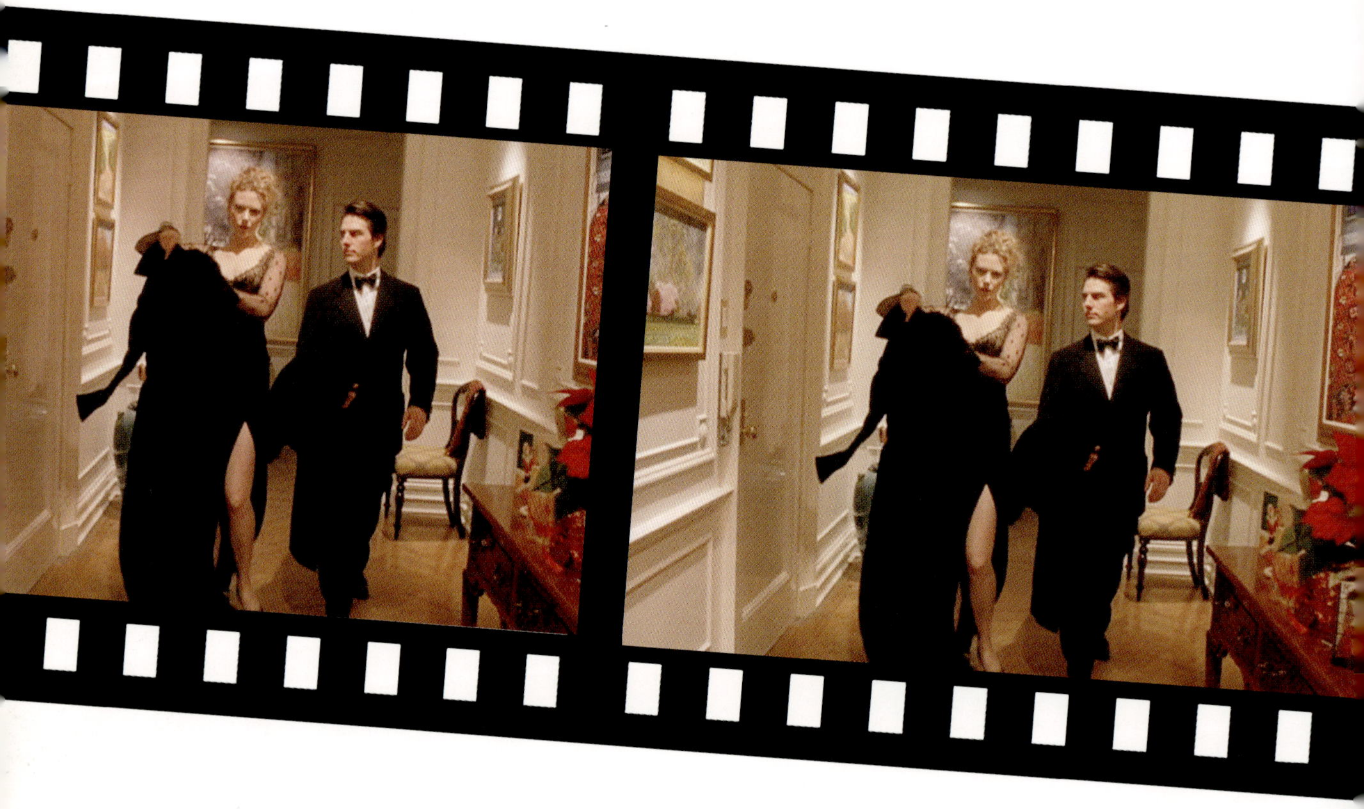

The ideal black dress is really a showcase for you—it's the epitome of Coco Chanel's observation: “Dress shabbily and they remember the dress; dress impeccably and they remember the woman.” In *Eyes Wide Shut,* you don't even see Nicole Kidman's black dress. Instead, you see her décolletage, her hands, and her leg—all areas the dress calls attention to.

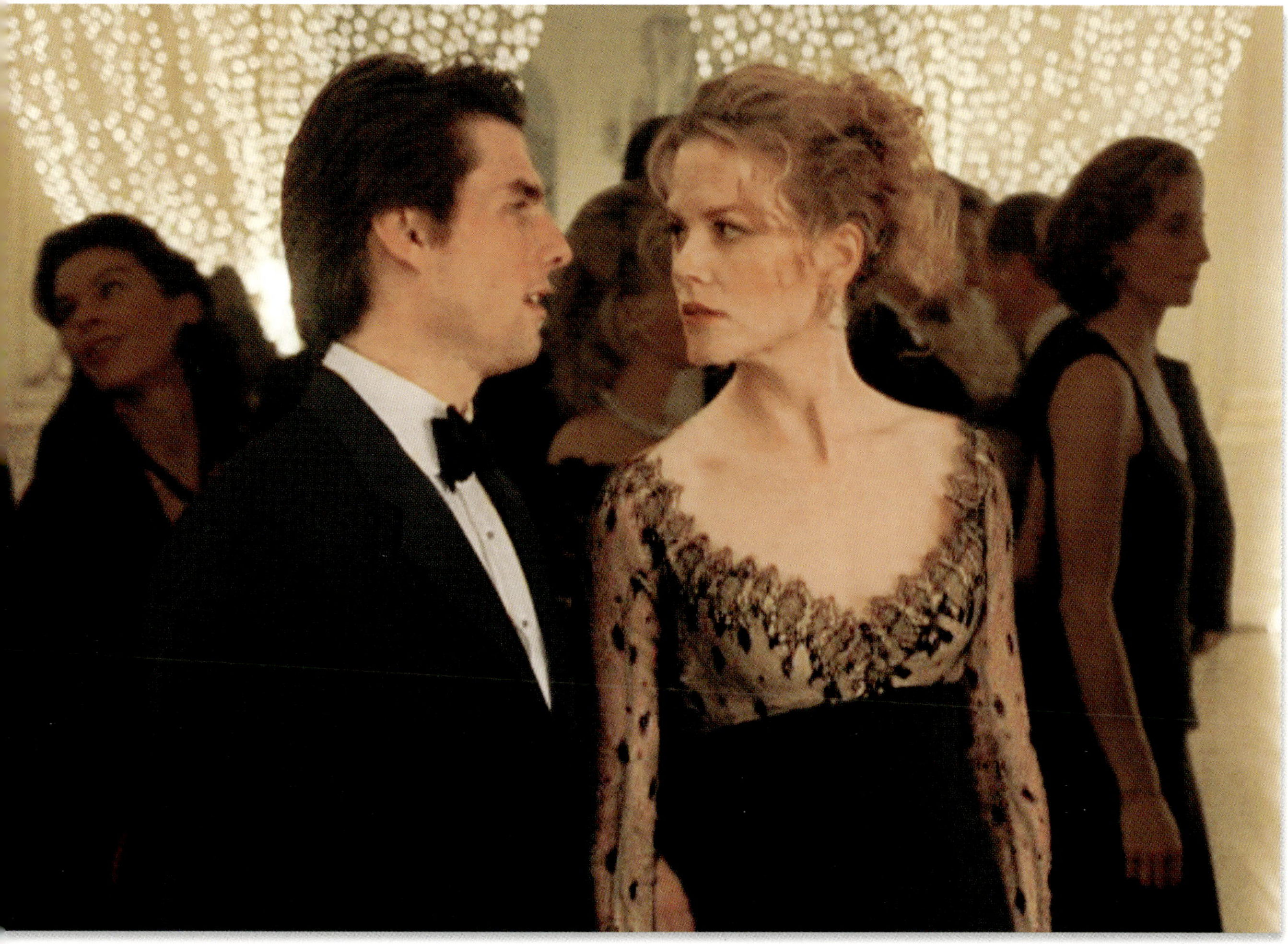

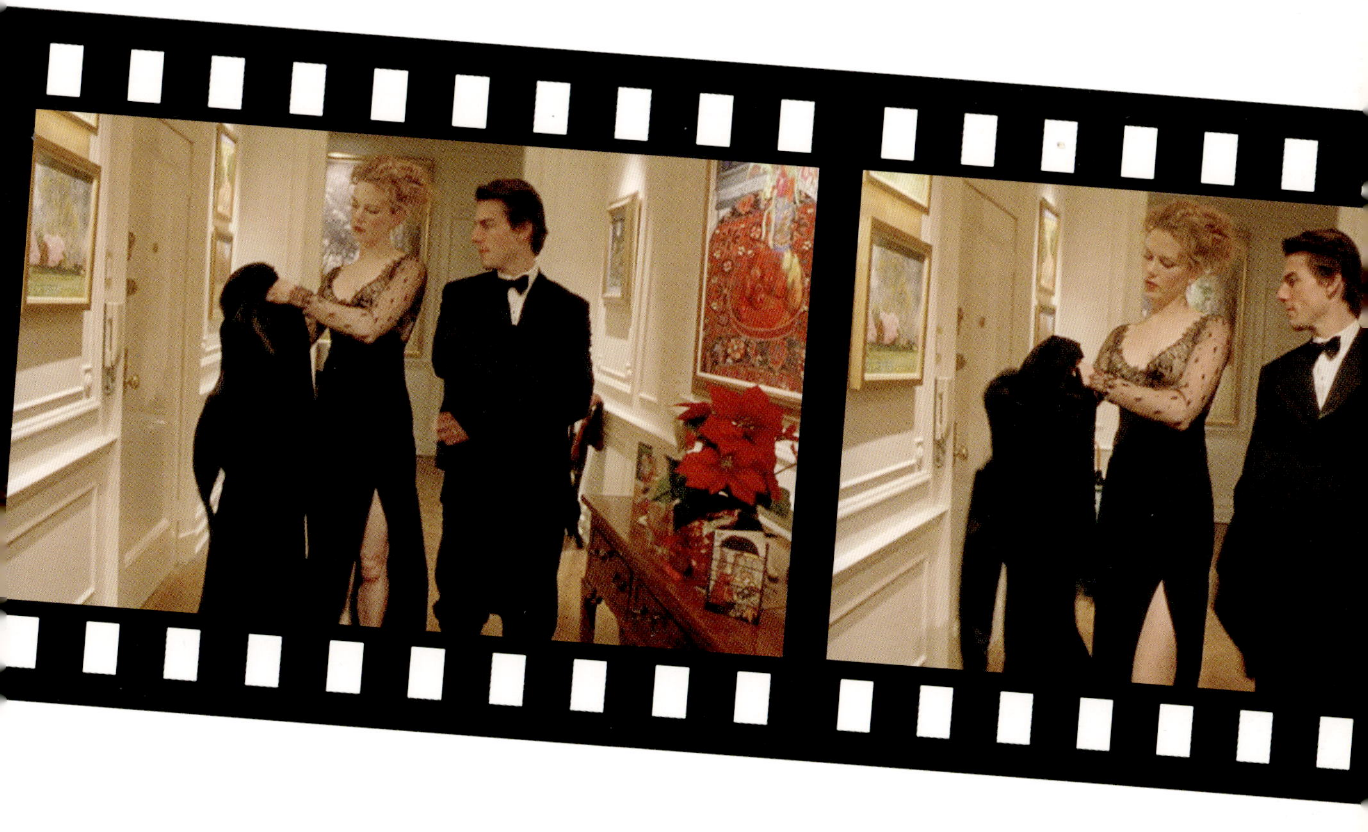

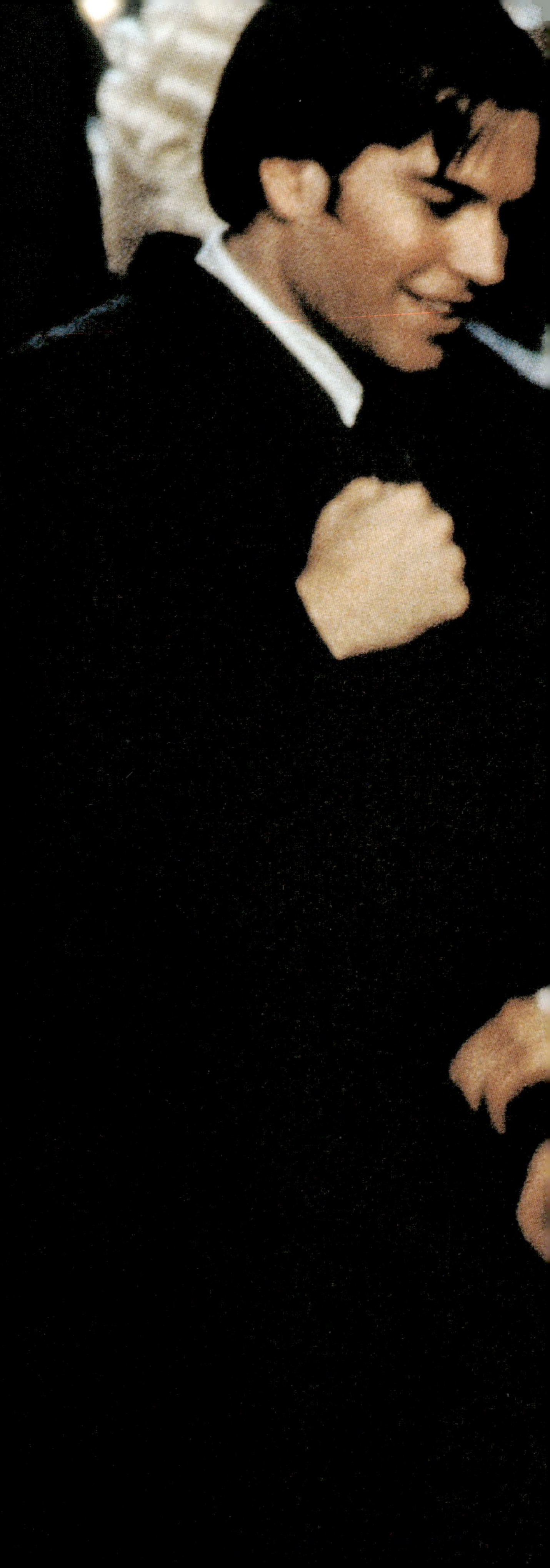

Black can make even flashy embellishments, like the sequins on Chloë Sevigny's dress in *The Last Days of Disco,* seem subtle. In a bright color, sequins can easily look overdressed; in black, they're versatile enough for a black-tie event or regular old party.

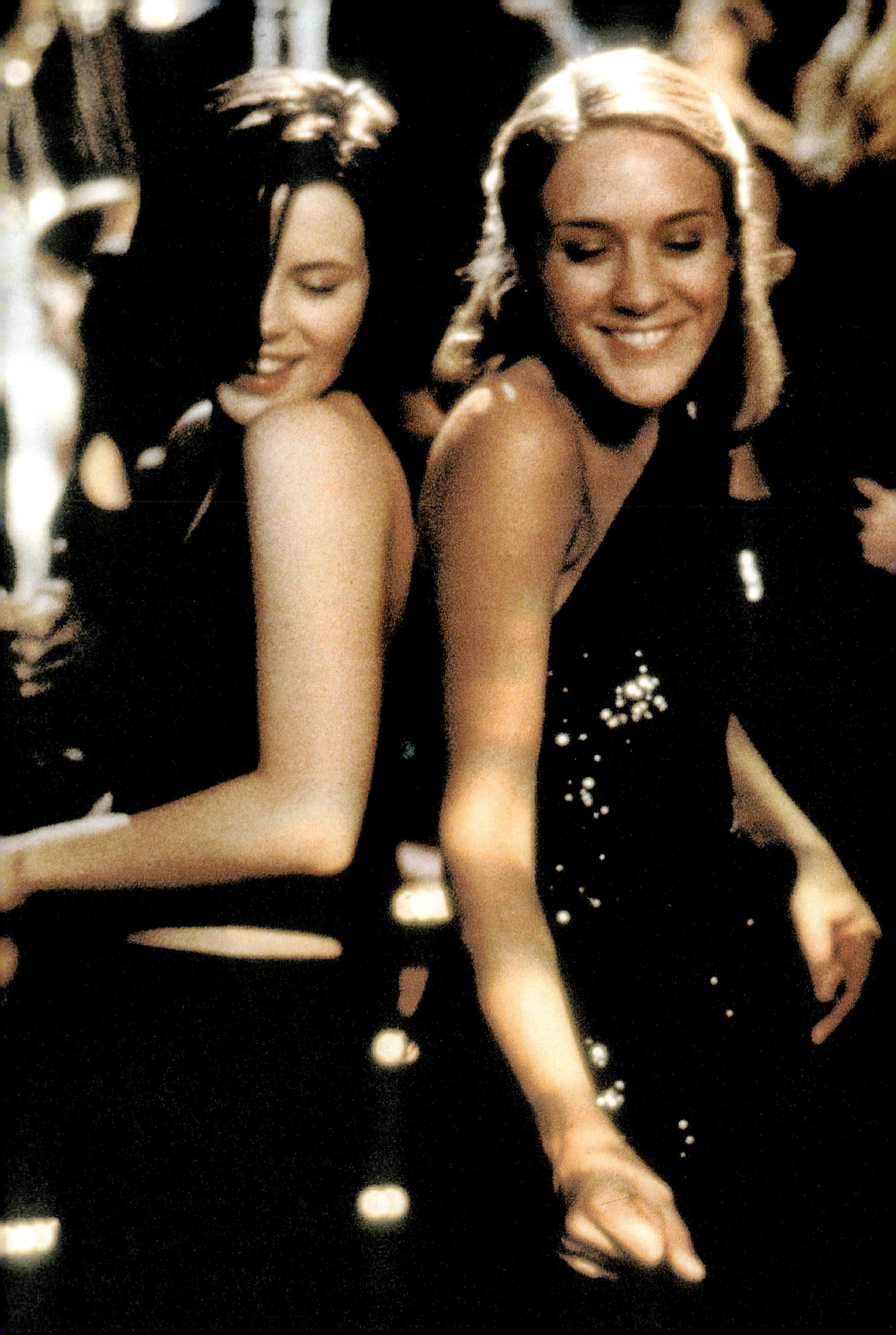

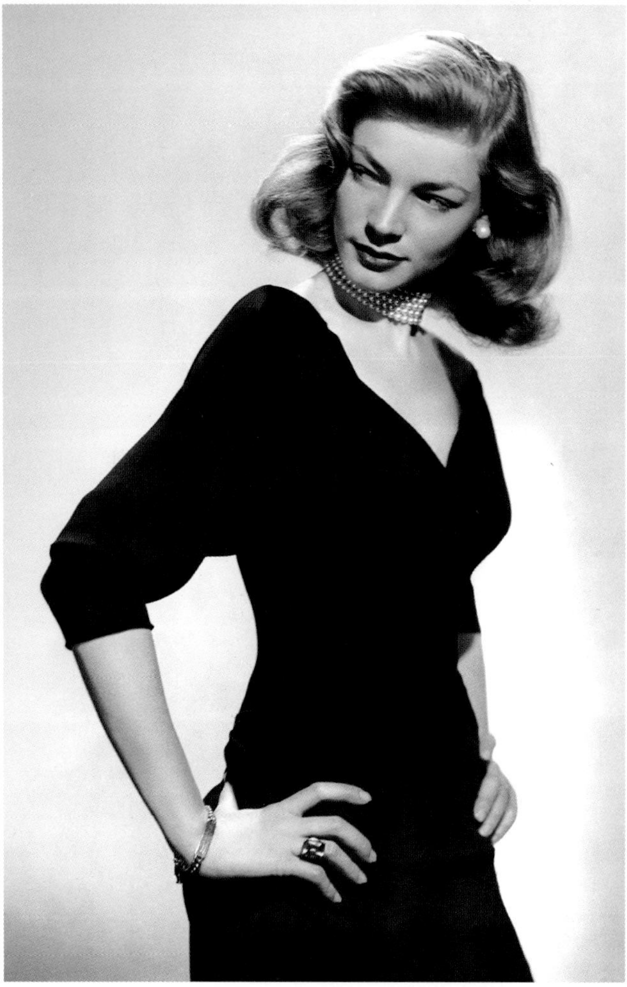

> “There was a reason for the cost of those perfectly plain black dresses.”
>
> Dorothy Parker

black is for summer weddings, where I think it can look a bit heavy.) On the other hand, the black dress is frequently the most beautiful dress, and sometimes that's all that matters. The vintage Chanel couture black lace dress Natalie Portman wore to the Golden Globes in 2006 (see page 90) is a prime example. The combination of the fragile-looking lace and the classic silhouette were a perfect match for her short hair. She looked feminine but fresh, which is another thing I love about black: It cuts the sweetness of a romantic look.

It's no coincidence that this dress Natalie wore is from the House of Chanel: It was the streamlining, forward-facing Coco Chanel who made the little black dress a staple of women's wardrobes in the 1920s. But the power of black to be both seductive and subversive was appreciated well before that. In *Anna Karenina,* written in the 1870s, Tolstoy has Anna wear “a black, low-cut velvet gown, showing her full throat and shoulders” to the ball at which she embarks on her disastrous love affair with Count Vronsky. It gives a sartorial clue to Anna's essential sensuality, which costume designer

Whether it's demure, as in Lauren Bacall's 1945 look (*above*), or ultrasexy, as in Sophia Loren's 1957 strapless number (*opposite*), black is the ultimate foil for a woman's personality. You get a window into the personalities of these actresses by the way they wear black.

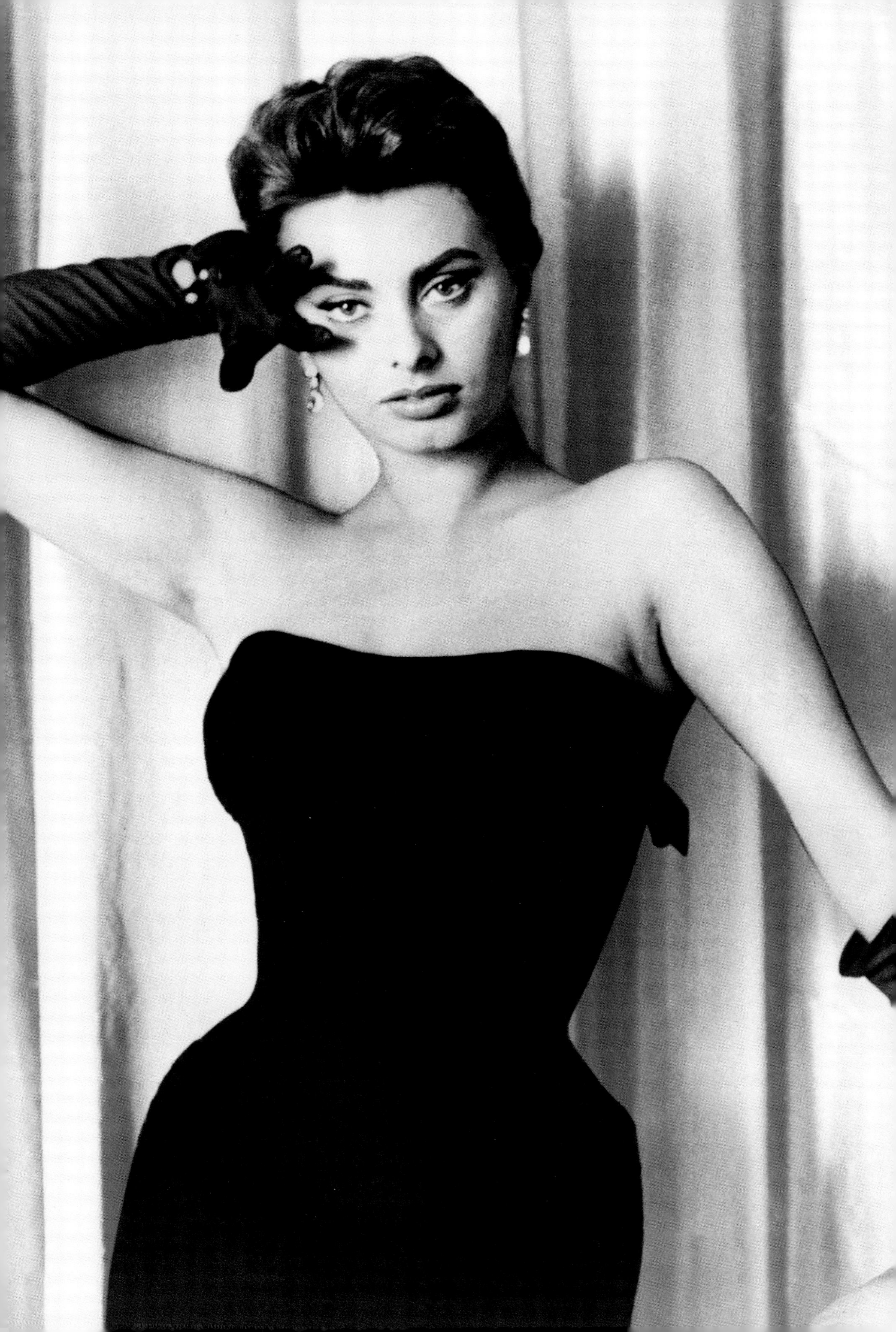

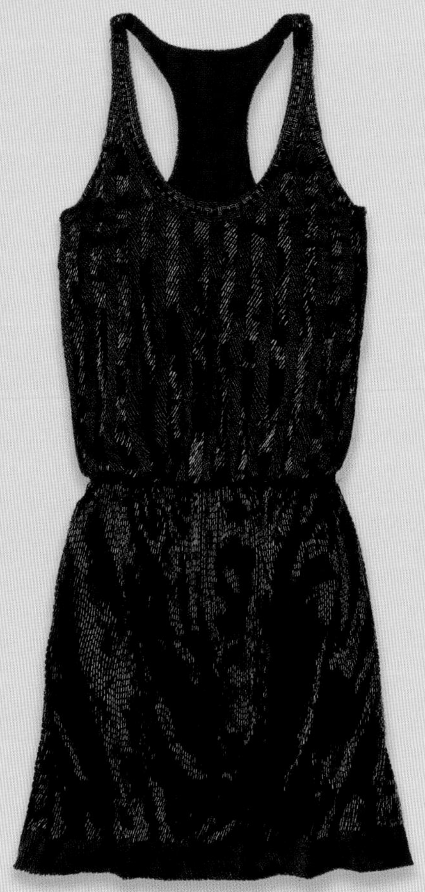

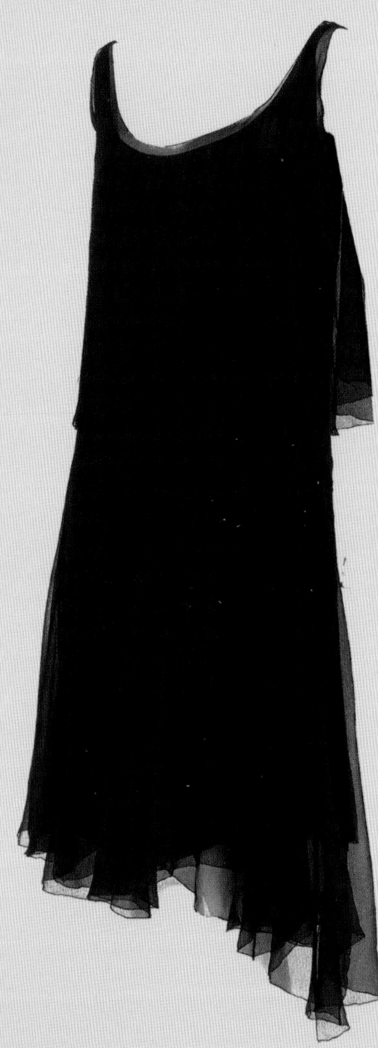

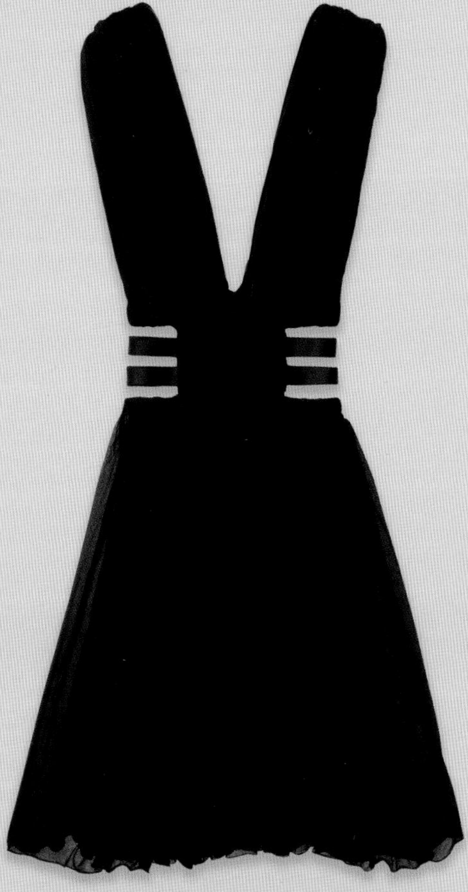

> Five out of five men are said to look twice at any girl in a black dress.
>
> Elizabeth Hawes

A quartet of little black dresses, each with a different feel. *Clockwise from top left:* I love that this Balenciaga dress mingles a sporty, pull-on shape with dressy bugle beads. The chiffon Chanel is transparent and flowing—breathtaking in motion. And the Alaïa is a modern goddess gown with cutouts for interest. *Opposite:* This Saint Laurent dress is one of my favorite design conceits: a strapless dress with a transparent top and sleeves (in this case, faux demure dotted Swiss). The combination is formal without leaving you feeling exposed.

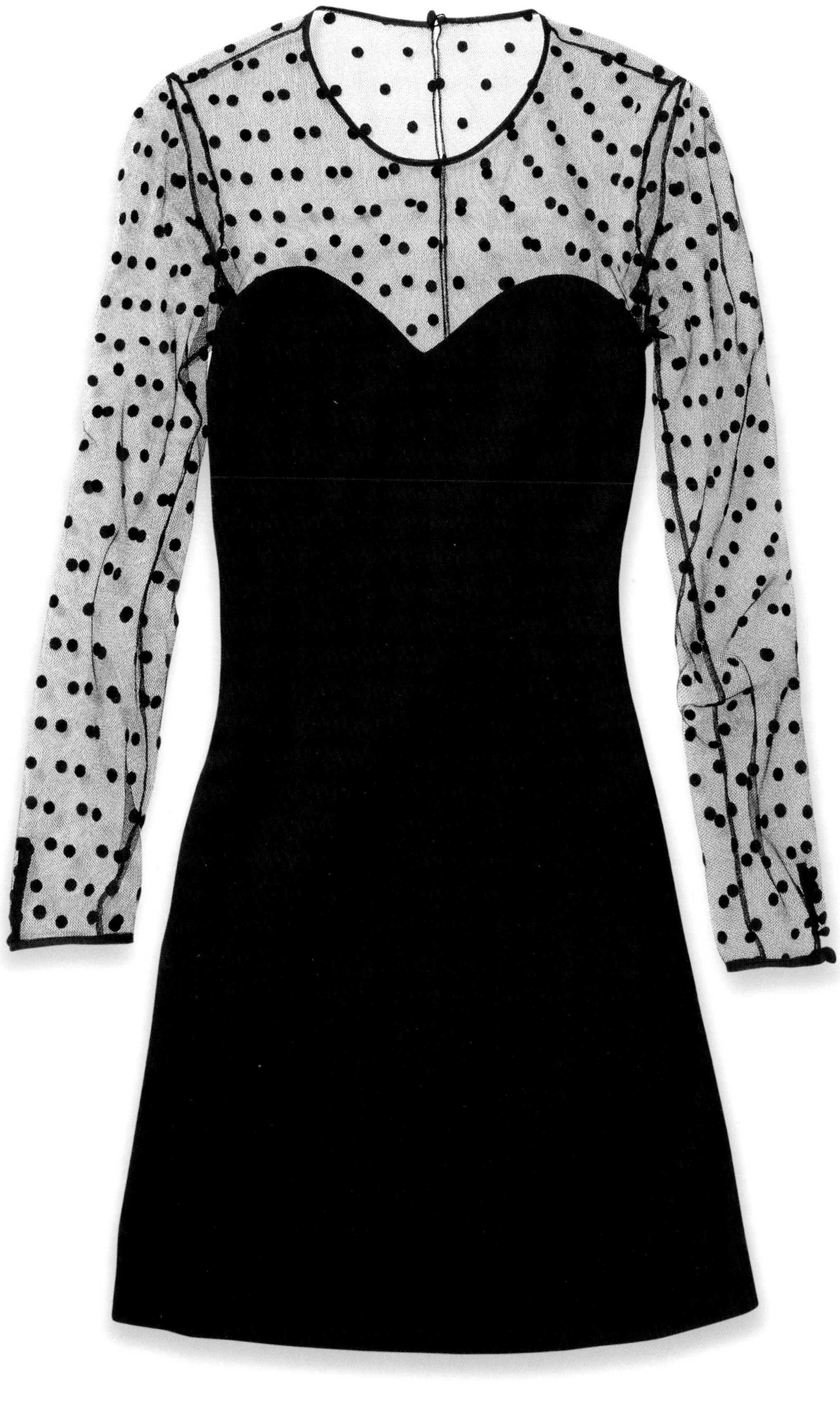

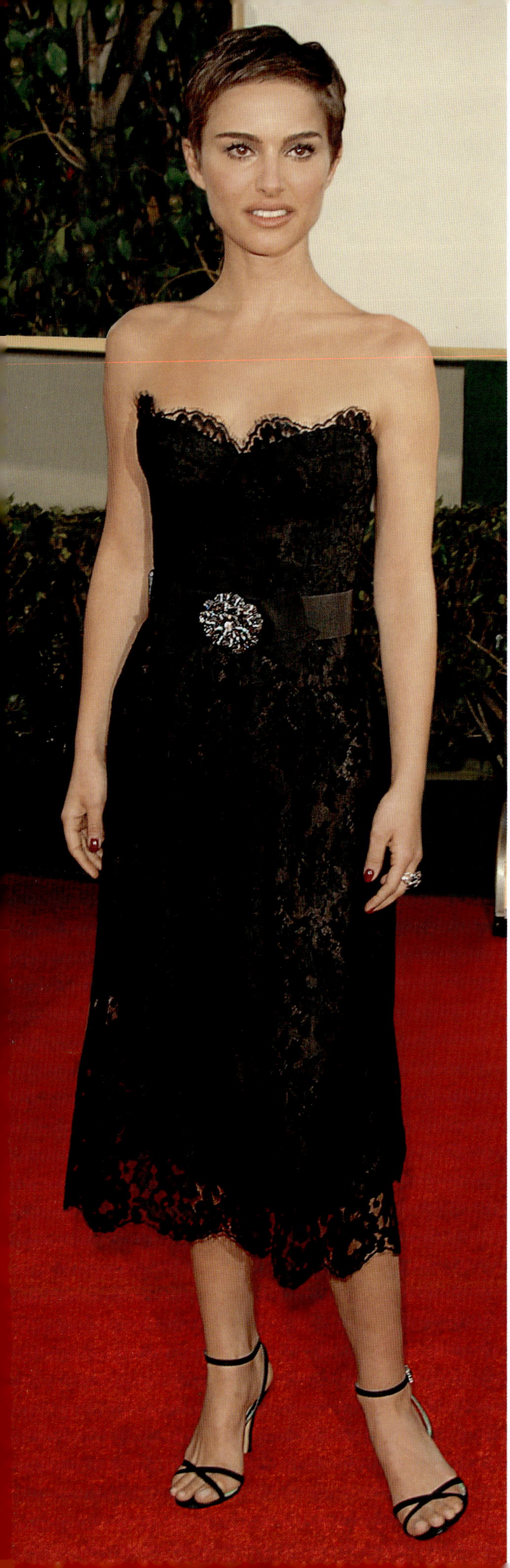

Jacqueline Durran followed through on for the 2012 film version, starring Keira Knightley (see page 95). For the ball scene, Keira wears a sublime black gown that's a masterpiece of sculptural pleating. In another color, it would be a pageant dress, and the dress would be memorable instead of the woman wearing it. But in black, the volume is controlled. A black dress like this one is a frame. Instead of overwhelming Keira, it's a lovely pedestal for her beautiful neck and shoulders, and the perfect setting for her necklace. (If there's a piece of jewelry you want to show off, black is the way to go.) She looks womanly, sophisticated, and ever so faintly unmanageable.

Black can also be flat-out racy, as with Anita Ekberg frolicking in the Trevi Fountain in *La Dolce Vita,* which is one of the most erotically charged dresses ever designed (see page 99). It's

Black is an excellent way to do a superfeminine shape while keeping a sophisticated edge. I don't often choose black for actresses on the red carpet, but for the Golden Globes in 2006, this black lace vintage Chanel couture dress looked perfect on Natalie Portman. The dress is opaque but the edges are transparent—the kind of small touch that black shows off so perfectly. *Opposite:* The dress Audrey Hepburn wears in *Funny Face* is a serious one, but because it's paired with girlish accessories like kitten heels and little white gloves, it comes off as light. For a modern take on little white gloves, try a clutch shaped like a domino or some other slightly off, nonmatchy accessory.

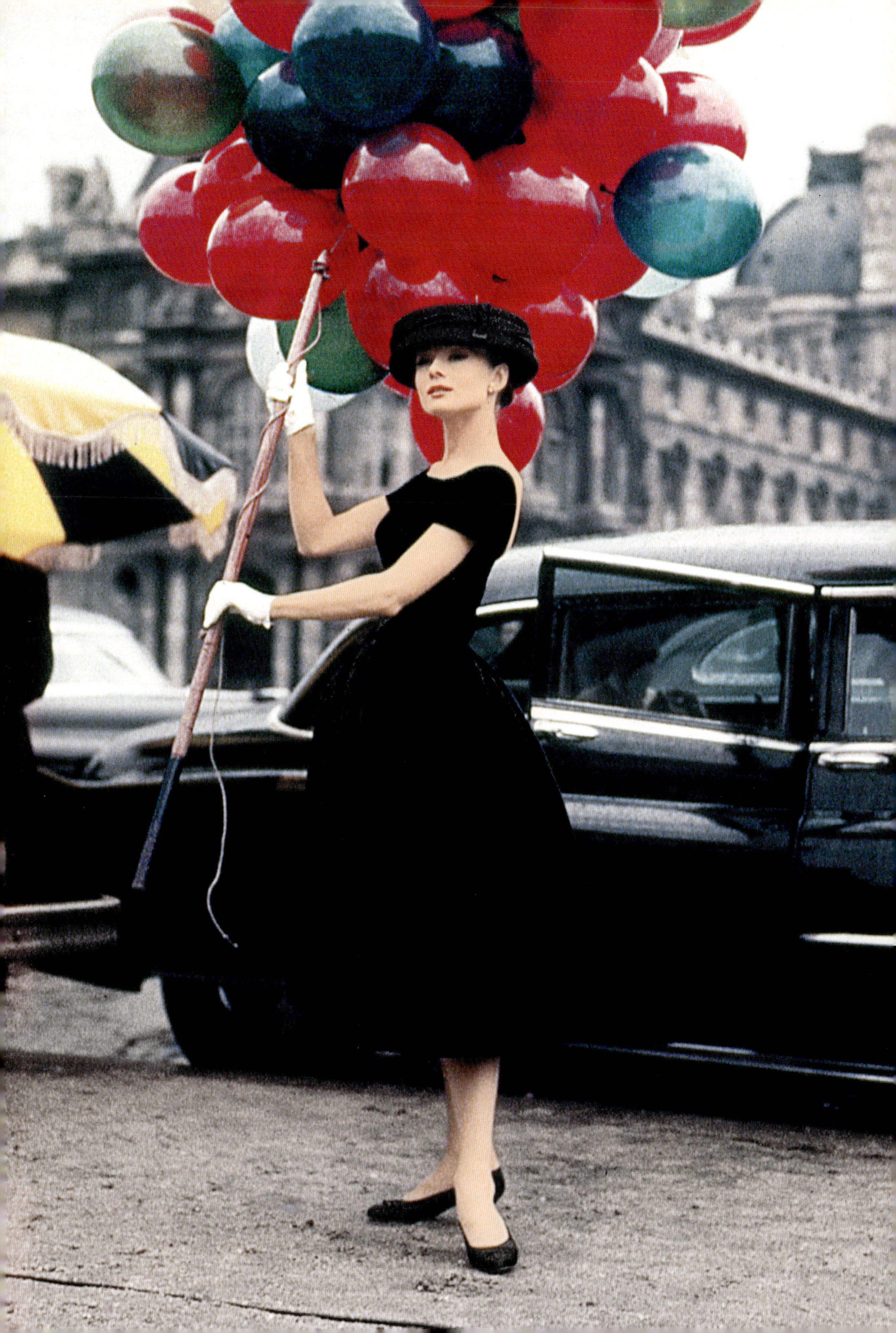

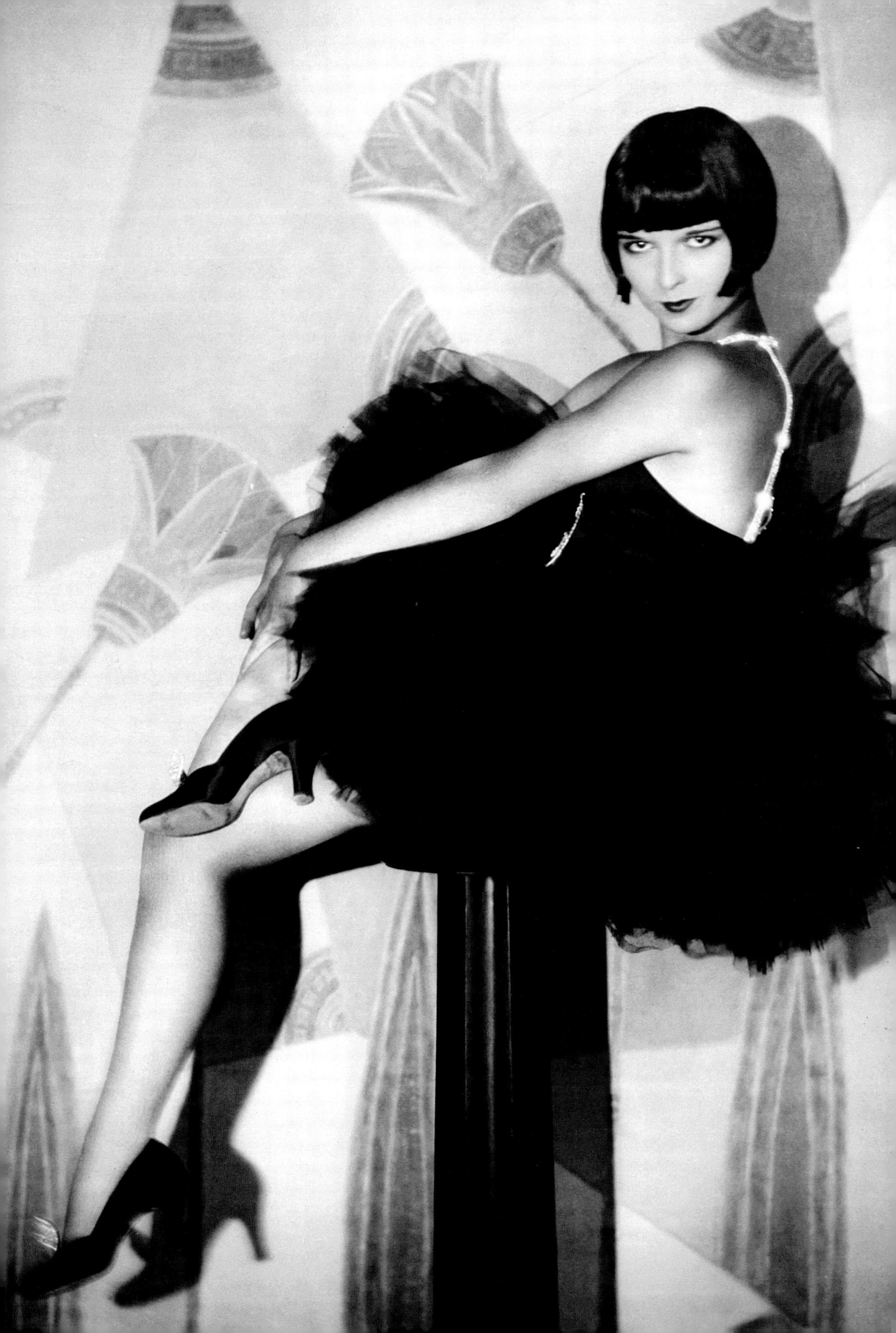

> "I love photo shoots where I can be like a pinup, not myself. Where I can be feminine, glamorous, dark...not like in real life."

Eva Green

The dress Veruschka wears in *Blow-Up* demonstrates that black can be just as interesting as brighter colors. Between the textured surface and the string sides, there's a lot going on. But because it's all in black, it still feels streamlined rather than overdone. *Opposite:* The one and only Louise Brooks is wearing what is basically a baby's dress in black, which is precisely what makes it so sexy and vampy. In black, even an innocent-looking tutu can be devastating.

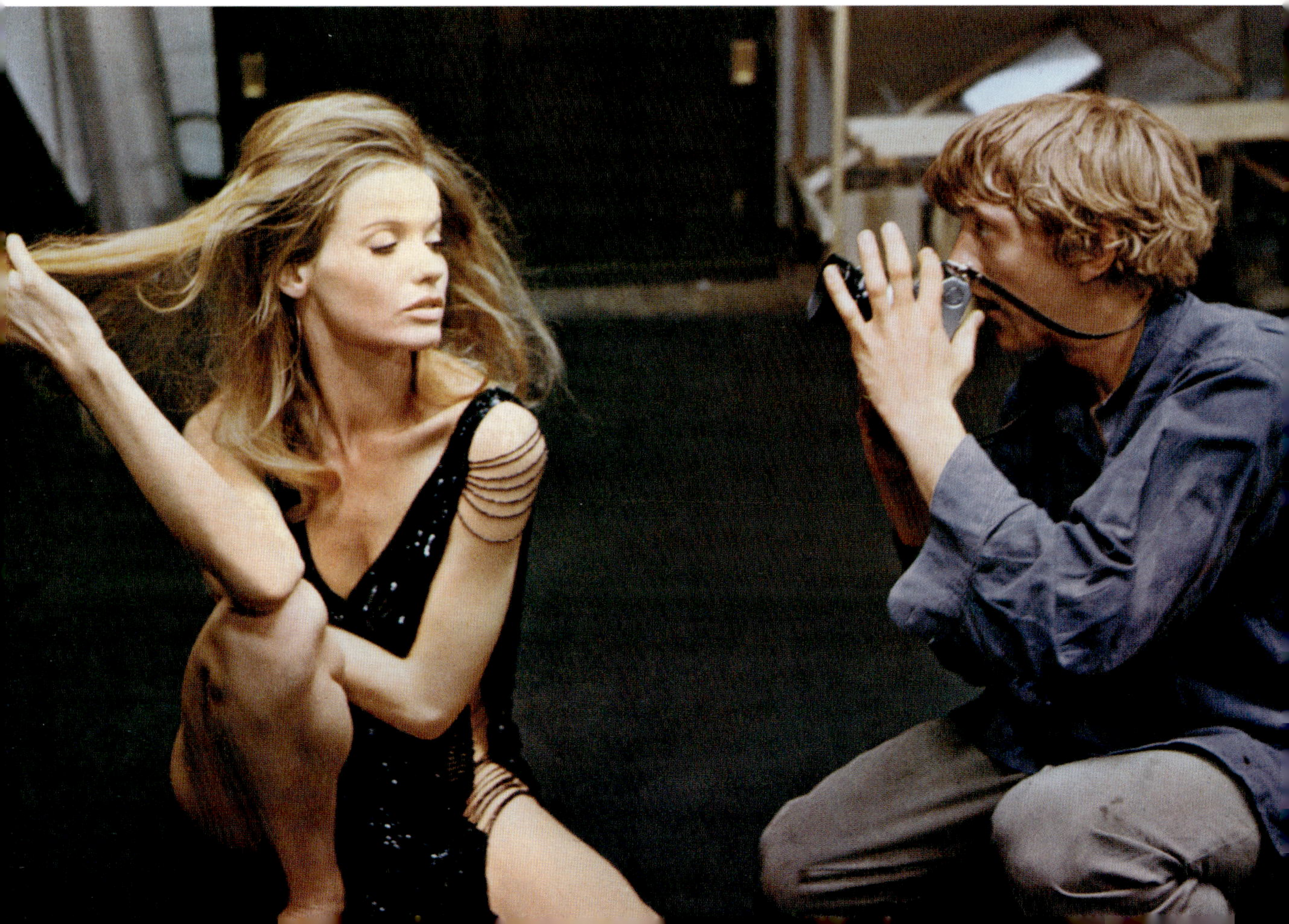

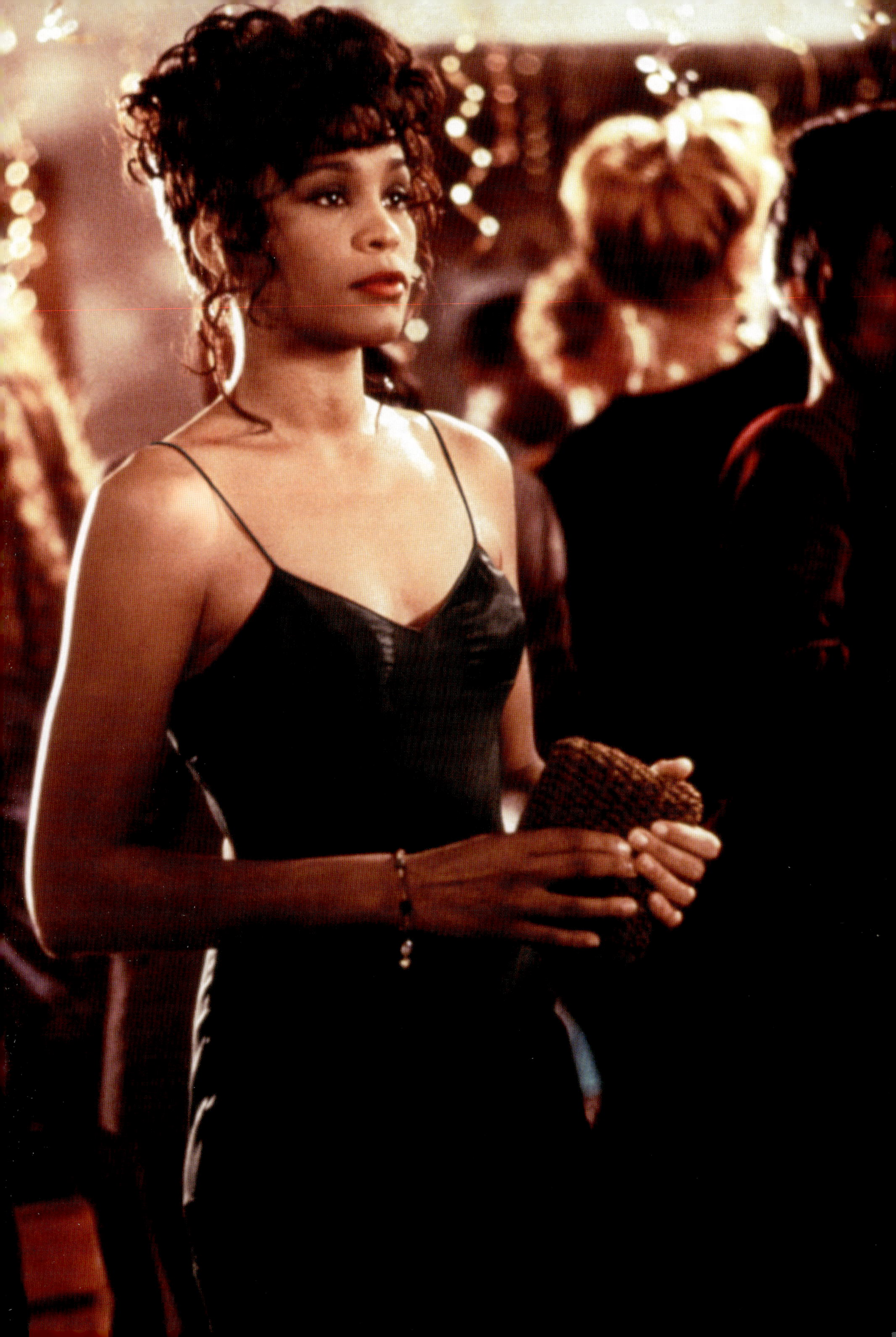

actually more of an idea of a dress, or maybe, given how low it's cut in the front and how deeply it dips behind, a feat of engineering. What this dress really epitomizes is how much of an archetype a black dress is. If you had a picture of yourself naked and colored in a dress with a black marker, it would look like this. It's so simple and yet so powerful. It's almost not there, which is the beauty of a first-rate black dress. It disappears enough to let you take center stage.

Given the emphasis it puts on the wearer, it's very important to choose the right black dress. Evening gowns tend to be unforgiving on the figure—you're almost as exposed in an evening gown as you are in a bathing suit—but you have a little more leeway with black. You can wear a stretchy bandage dress in black, and it won't look like you're trying to get a man's attention, which is why I like a black dress in a scuba fabric. I'm also a fan of black crepe, which always looks smart and elegant. And I love how expensive and couture black lace is. As for silhouettes, if you have an hourglass figure, then a fit-and-flare shape will look great. If you have amazing shoulders, a halter style

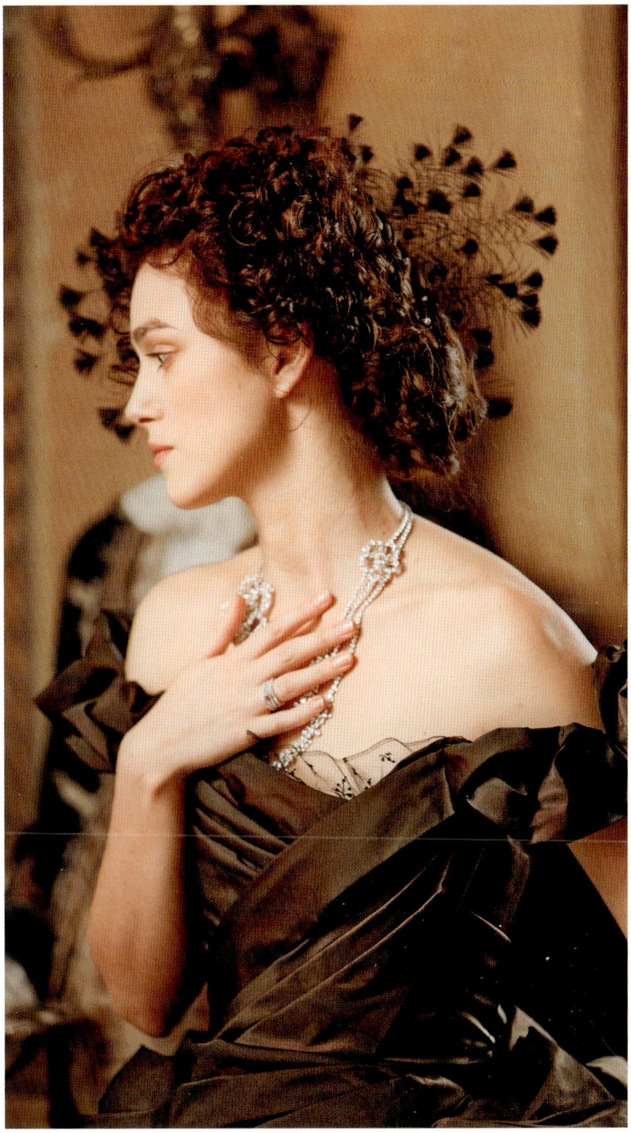

If you're going to wear something really dramatic, like this elaborately draped and pleated gown seen on Keira Knightley in *Anna Karenina,* make it black. Black will keep the emphasis on the line and the silhouette, ensuring the dress doesn't overwhelm you. *Opposite:* This lingerie-inspired look on Whitney Houston in *Waiting to Exhale* is ultrasexy. It looks like she's in her slip and should have another dress on over it; the piled-up hair is also very I'm-about-to-have-a-bath-and-slip-into-bed. *Following pages:* If you have the body for a black slip dress, it's your best friend. The simplicity of the one sported by Rene Russo in *The Thomas Crown Affair,* with nothing but a sheen of beads as embellishment, needs just a change of accessories to go anywhere. I love the idea of throwing a trench or a man's suit jacket over it.

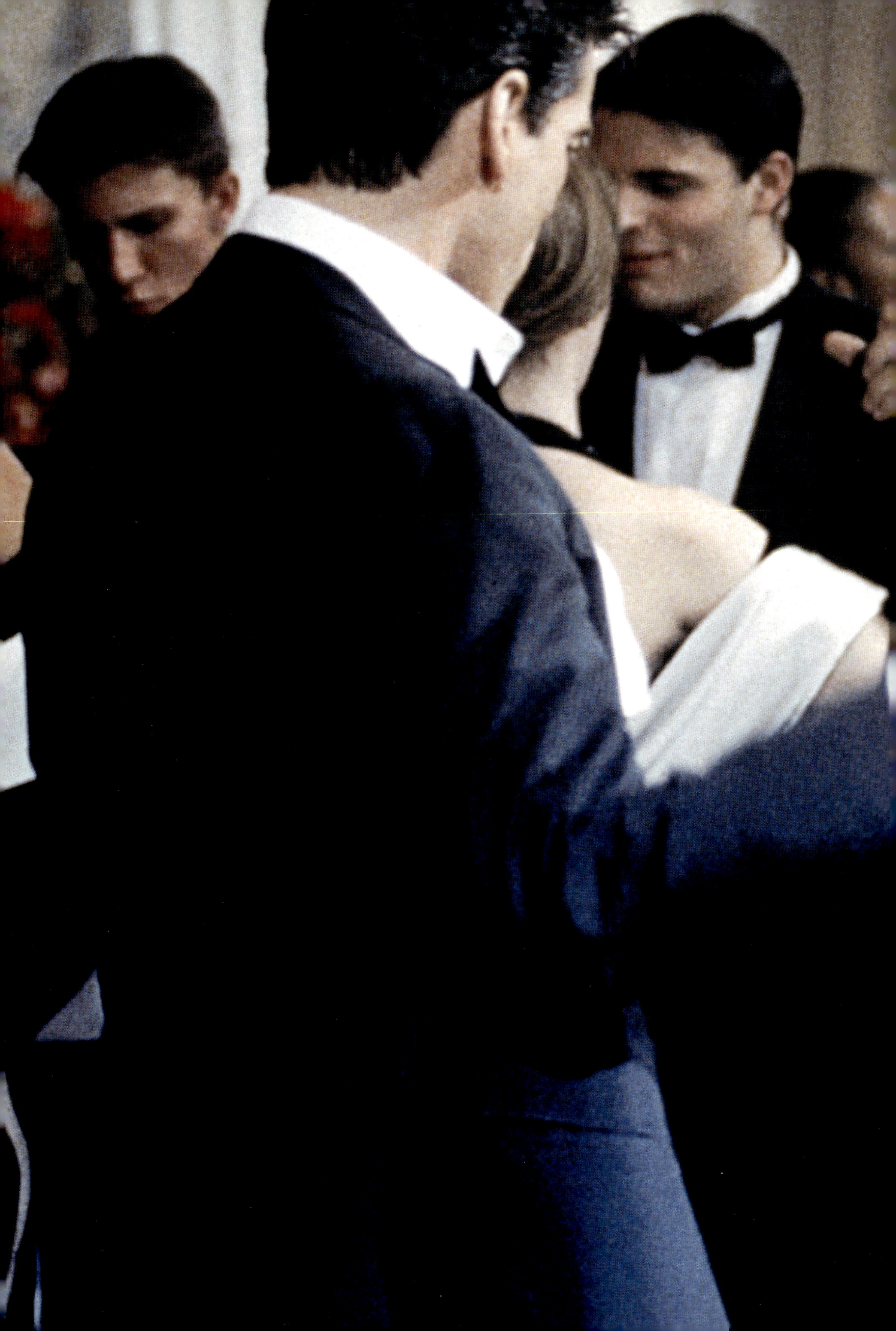

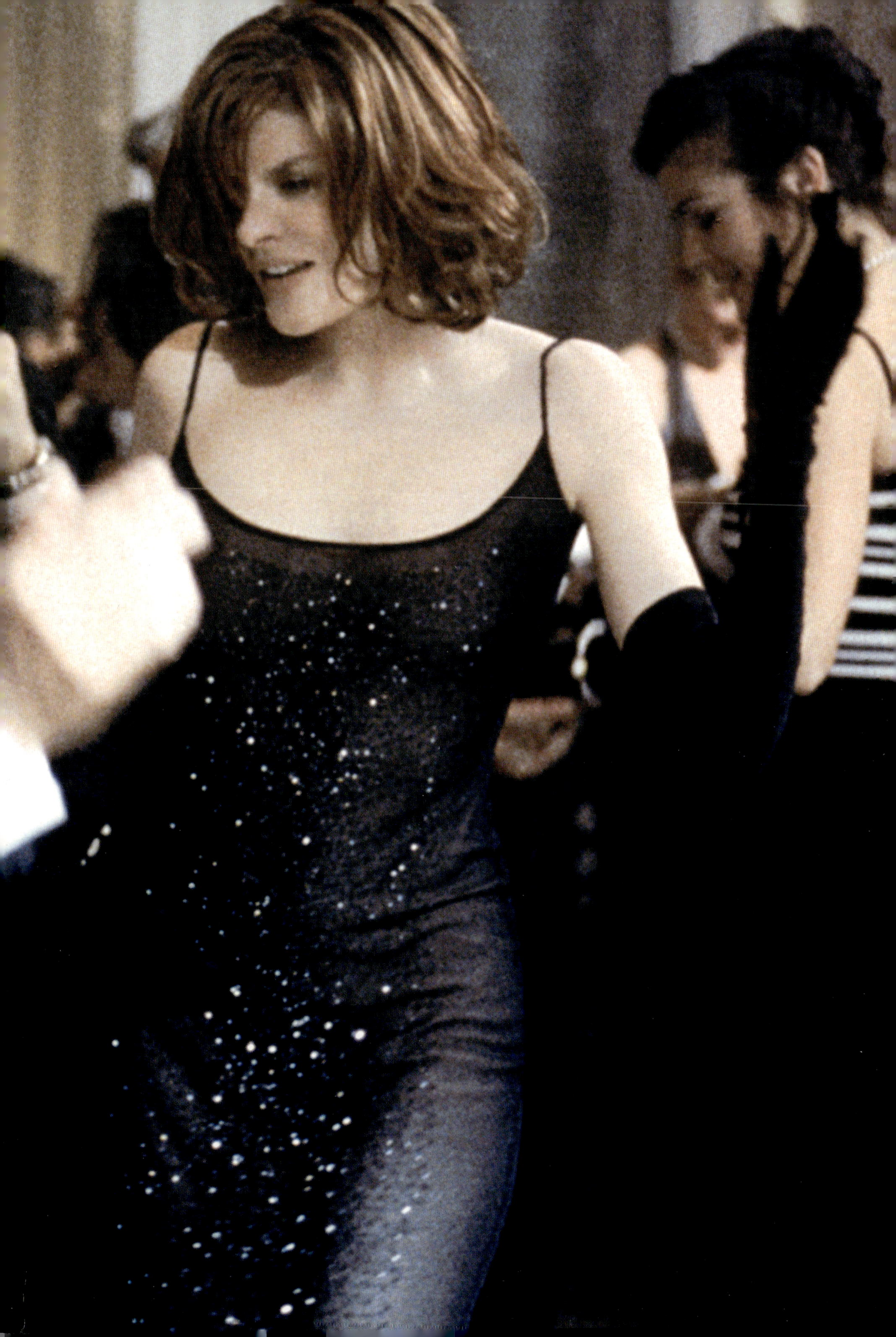

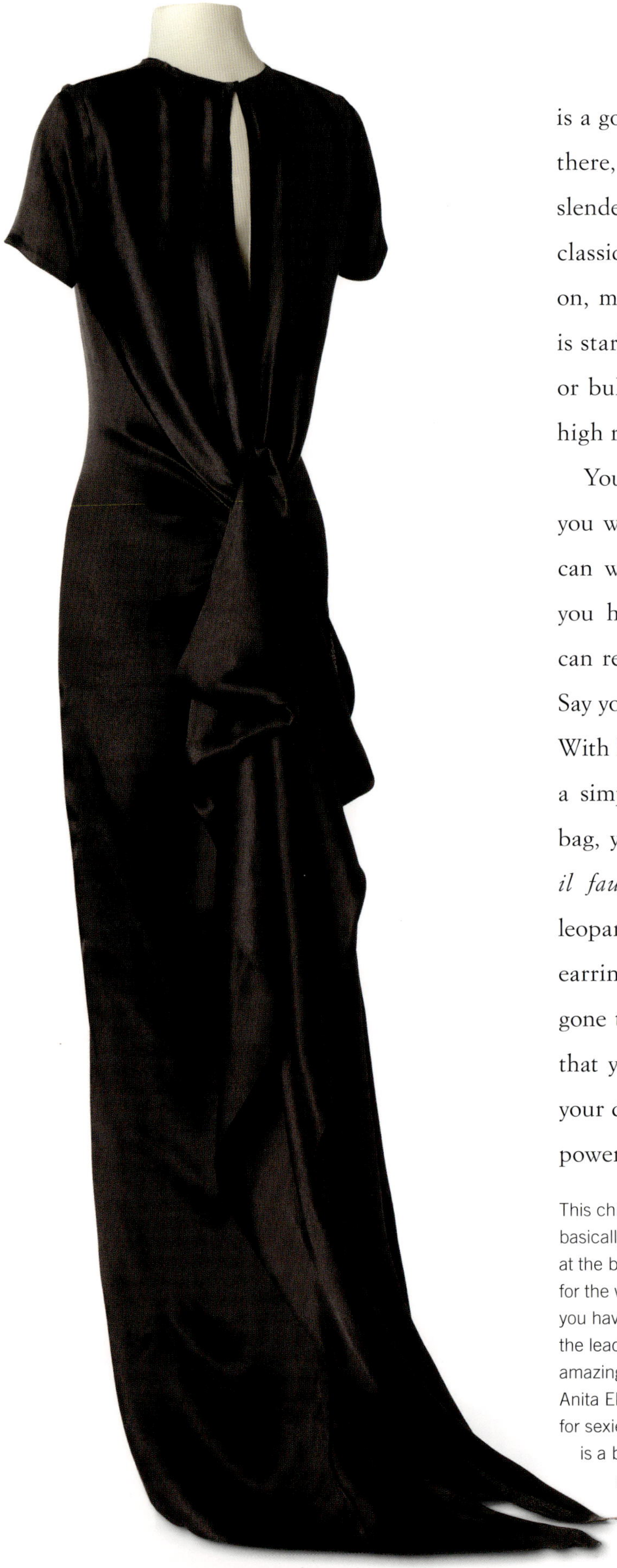

is a good choice. If you have legs up to there, short is the way to go. If you're slender and boyish, a sheath will look classic and chic. Whatever you decide on, make sure the fit is precise. Black is stark next to the skin, and any gapes or bulges are going to be thrown into high relief.

You can play with accessories when you wear a black dress more than you can with any other evening look. But you have to be careful, because they can really change the mood of a dress. Say you're wearing a black crepe sheath. With kitten heels, a pearl necklace, and a simple, Chanel-style quilted evening bag, you're perfectly polite and *comme il faut.* But pair it with superhigh leopard-print platform heels, chandelier earrings, and matching cuffs, and you've gone to a very different place. The fact that you can do this without changing your dress is pretty amazing—that's the power of black.

This chic silk charmeuse dress by Lanvin is basically a T-shirt that's been caught up in a bow at the back. It's classic and beautiful, and perfect for the woman who's understated and elegant. If you have an event where you don't want to steal the leading lady's thunder but still want to look amazing, this is what you wear. *Opposite:* Anita Ekberg's dress in *La Dolce Vita* gets my vote for sexiest dress ever, and the fact that it's black is a big part of that. Black makes the incredibly simple shape work in a way that nothing else could. It's just her and the negative space of the dress—gorgeous.

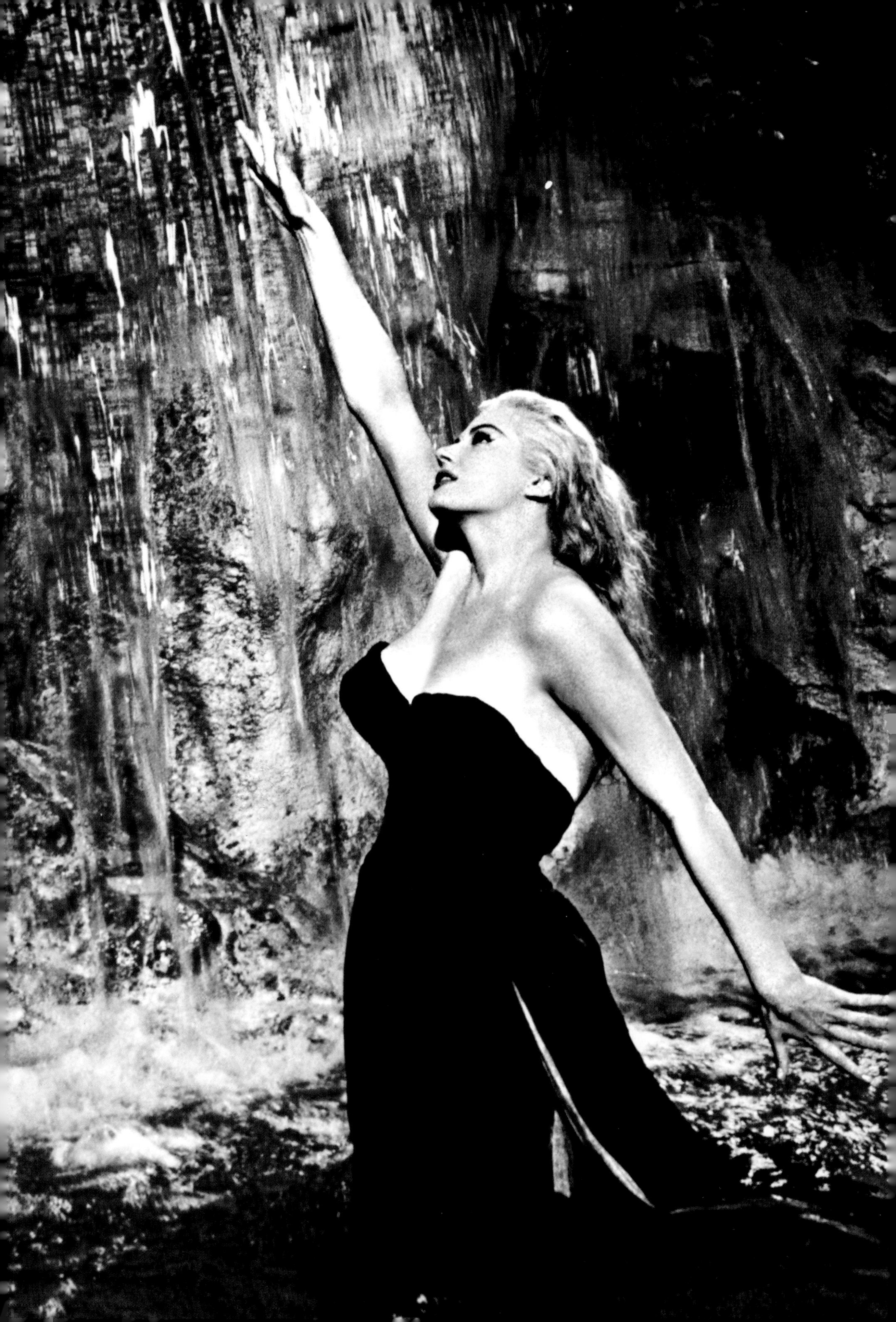

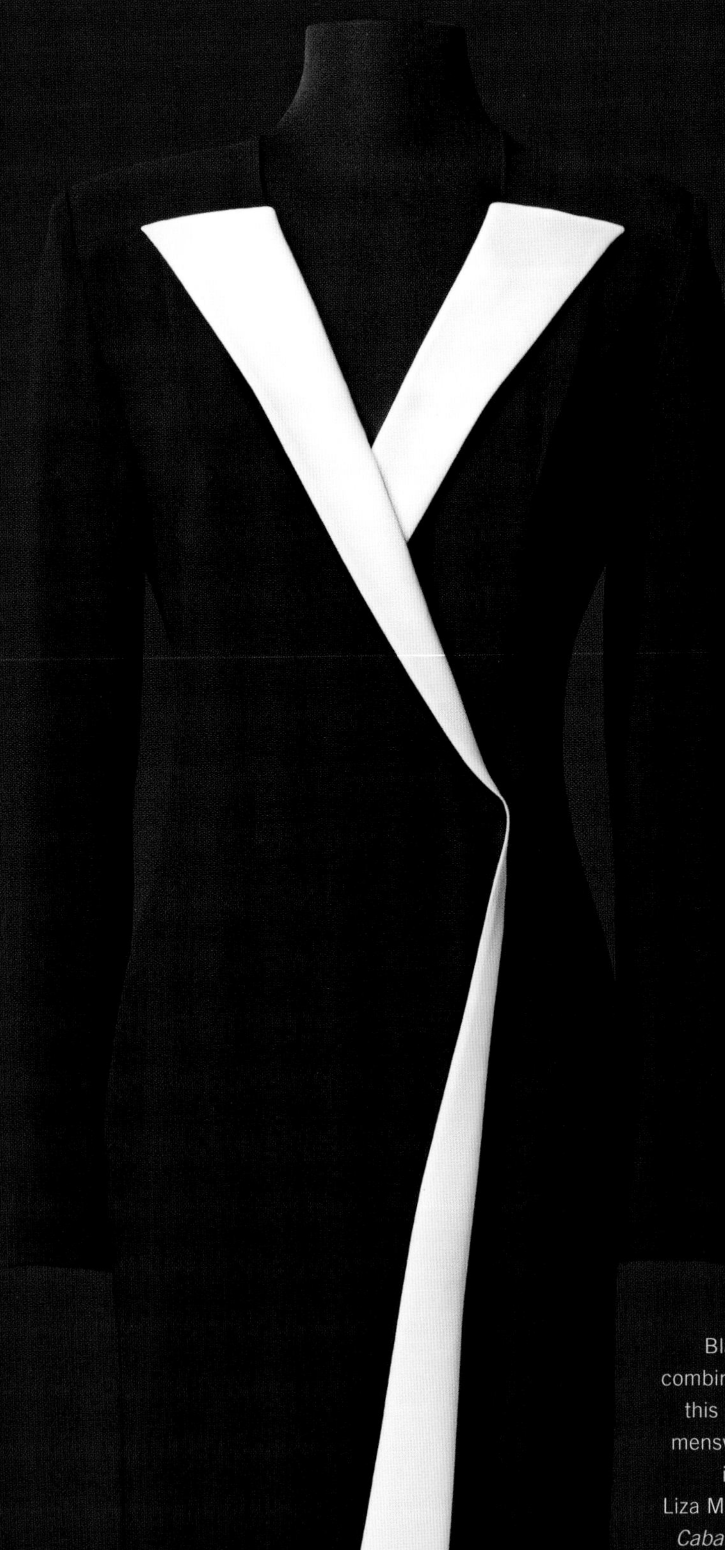

Black and white are a surefire combination. The white facings on this Roland Mouret dress take a menswear-inspired cut and make it totally feminine. *Opposite:* Liza Minnelli's shorts and halter in *Cabaret* is one of the most iconic looks of all time, but I don't think it would be nearly as timeless if it were anything but black, which gives the ensemble a graphic power that never gets old. Imagine it with a short or long skirt, and you could wear it out tonight.

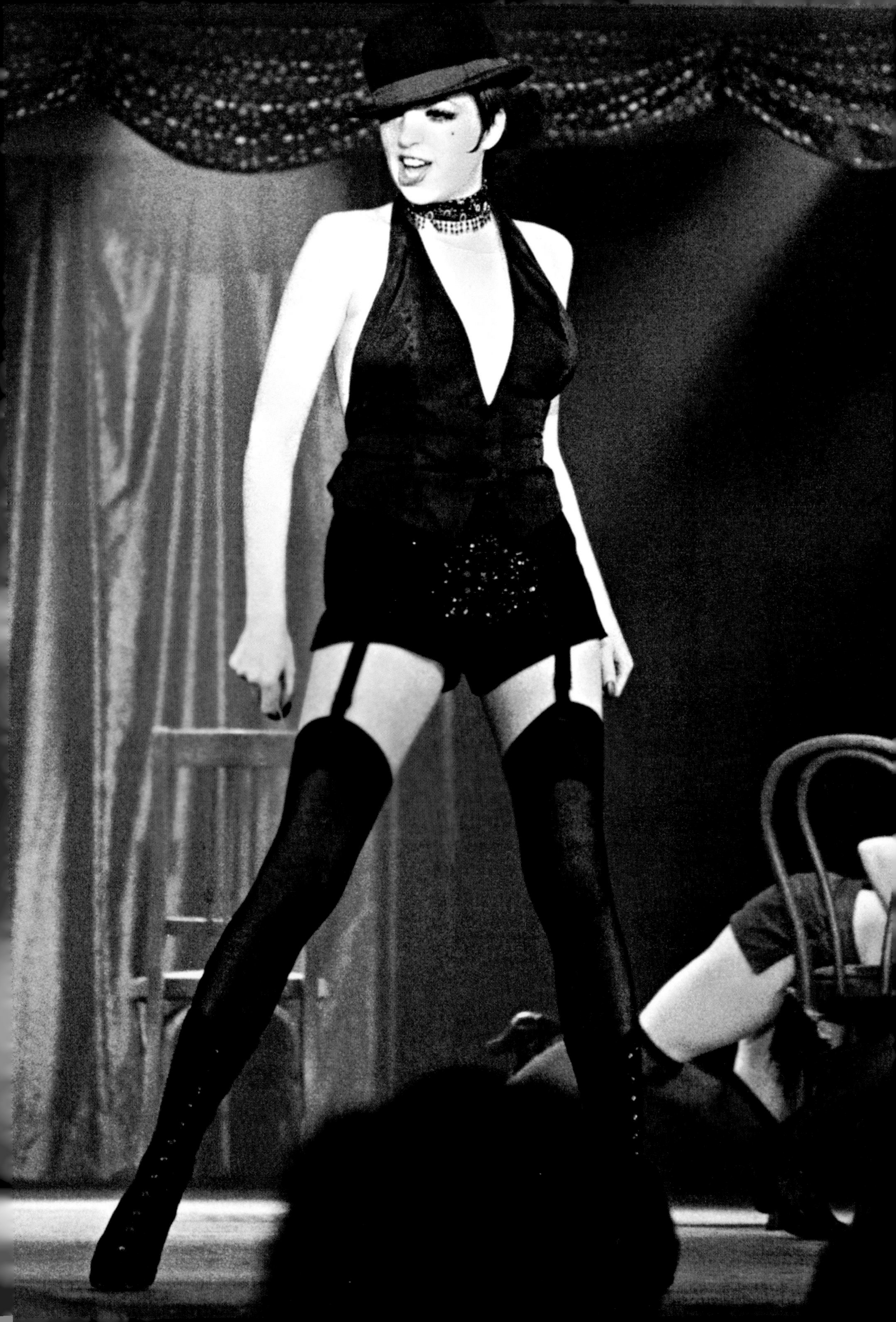

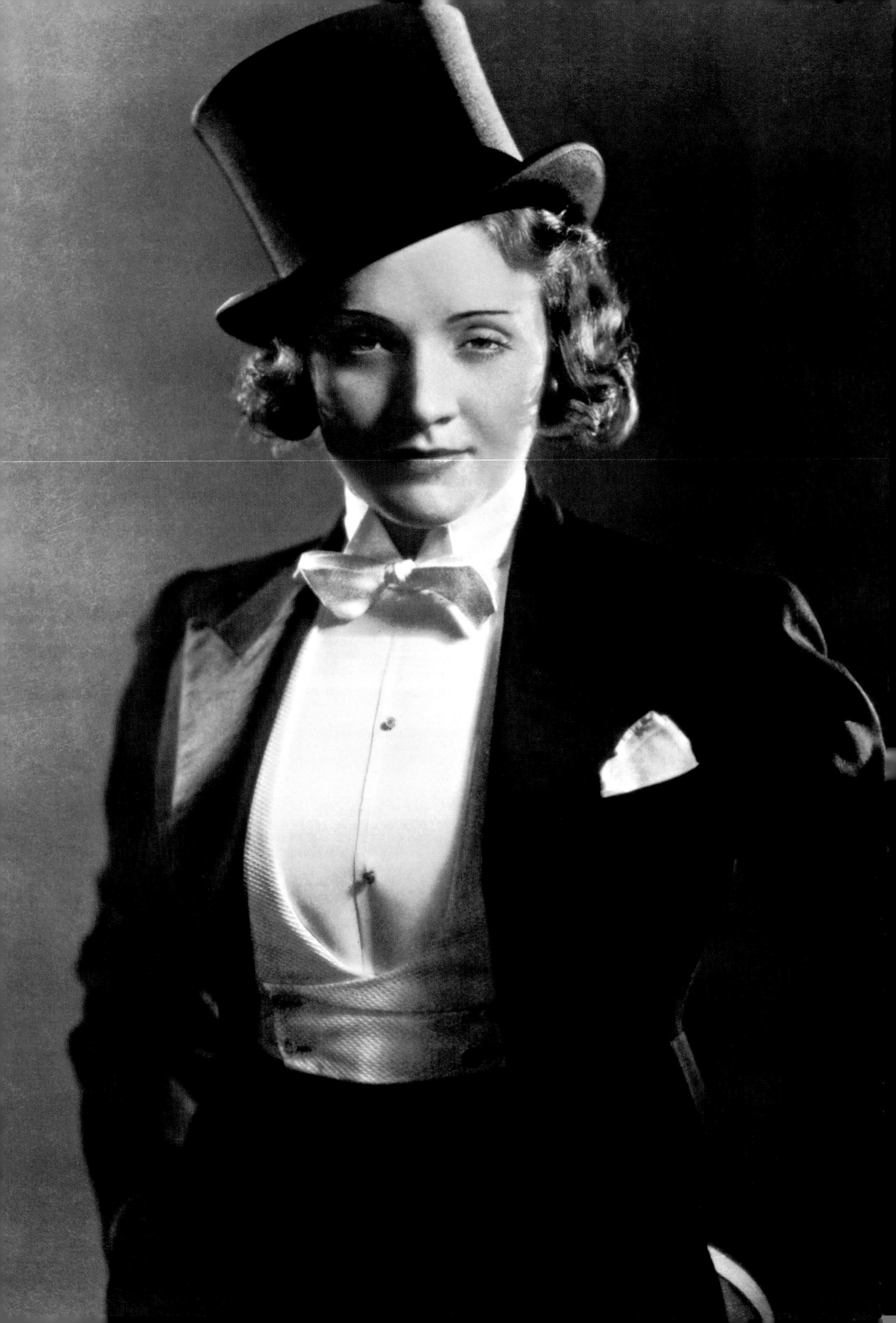

A Formal Affair: The Black-Tie Dress

This chapter is about the fanciest moments in your life: evening weddings, opera openings, awards ceremonies, balls. These are the times when the volume and the tiaras come out, and your dress might be so structured that you'll need help getting into it. I think every woman has an archetype she gravitates to for occasions like these. There are princess women, who want a fitted bodice and a big skirt. There are romantic women, who want a beautifully embellished gown. There are modernist women, who want a clean, architectural look. And there are women who don't like ruffles and are more comfortable in a menswear-inspired look. All of these approaches to black tie are valid; all of them can look stunning, and all of them have plenty of inspirational muses on the silver screen.

Myself, I'm the girl who wants to wear a tuxedo. I've never worn a big dress or been comfortable in a flurry of *flou* (which is what the French call floaty, flirty clothes). I think a woman in a tux is a very modern take on dressing up, with a slightly subversive touch that's still completely acceptable—think of the iconic Helmut Newton photo of a woman standing in a Paris street wearing a smoking by Yves Saint Laurent, looking like the chicest thing ever. I also love how Marlene Dietrich looked in *Morocco,* wearing a top hat and tails as a nightclub singer, and the titillation that goes through the crowd when she plants a kiss on a woman in the audience. (It's even more titillating when you remember that cross-dressing was illegal at the time.) But I don't think you should look like you're in drag. The idea is to *suggest* menswear, not copy it. When Diane Kruger wore a tuxedo during the press run for *Inglourious Basterds,* we chose a Chanel suit that was made for a woman—the key to pulling off this look. The trousers have to be flattering, and that means they need to be cut to accommodate a woman's shape. Also important: The leg should be lean; I don't like that baggy 1980s look. If

Marlene Dietrich, seen here in *Morocco,* pioneered the idea of women in tuxedos. She looks great, but I wouldn't recommend going as far as the top hat—you don't want to look like you're wearing a costume.

> “I like being a woman, even in a man’s world. After all, men can’t wear dresses, but we can wear the pants.”
>
> Whitney Houston

you wear a jacket, make sure the shoulder is trim. You can play around with the size of the lapels and how defined the waist is, but if you’re wearing a suit, the outline has to be sharp. And don’t let the trousers puddle around your shoes. I like to show a little ankle. The fabric choice is important, too. Black needs to be really black—no red or green threads. If you choose a shiny suit, such as a bronze satin, I think it looks better with some contrast trim to keep it graphic. Diane kept her makeup minimal and slicked her hair back to mimic a man’s cut, but I also like this style with siren hair and a red lip to contrast with the masculine influence. And always wear a heel with a tux; flats look too mannish.

There is nothing mannish about the dress Elizabeth Taylor wore in *A Place in the Sun.* From the tight waist to the full tulle skirt, it’s femininity incarnate and the template for every princess fantasy. There’s something delightful about it; she looks like she’s sitting in a cloud. The scale of the dress makes her look tiny by comparison, which is always flattering. The only time this type of dress doesn’t work is if you have a thick waist. In that case, you’re better off with a mermaid version. When a dress has this much of a *ta-da!* factor, you want to keep the accessories clean and modern to avoid looking like a parade float—maybe something small at the ear, possibly a ring or bracelet. Definitely no pearls—that’s too much of a cliché. Like many evening dresses, a princess dress can take a little getting used to, which is why I think that

This cloud of a dress Elizabeth Taylor wears in *A Place in the Sun* was the inspiration for countless prom looks in the 1950s. It’s easy to see why: It’s completely fun and completely flattering, especially when you keep the jewelry small and the focus on that big skirt.

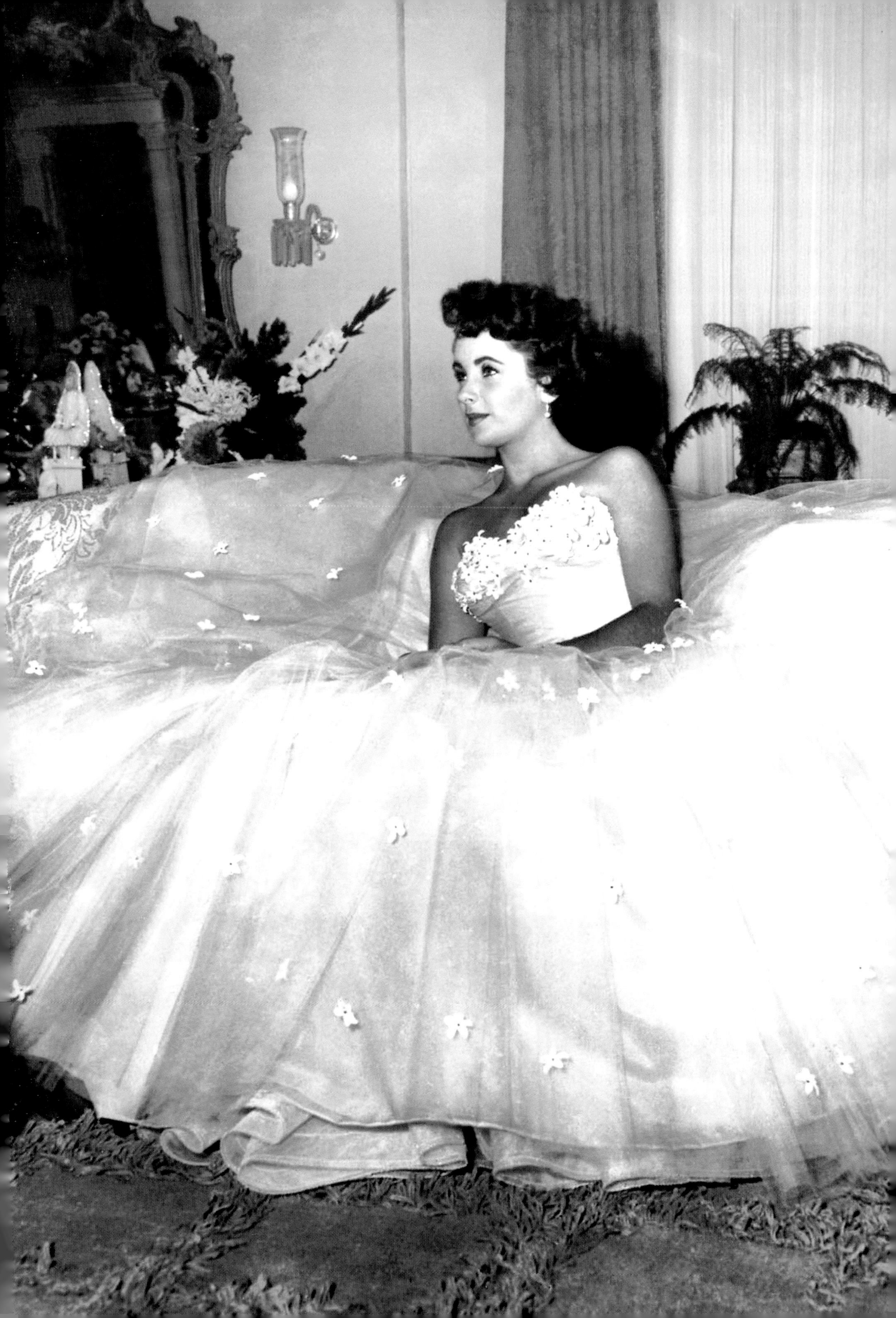

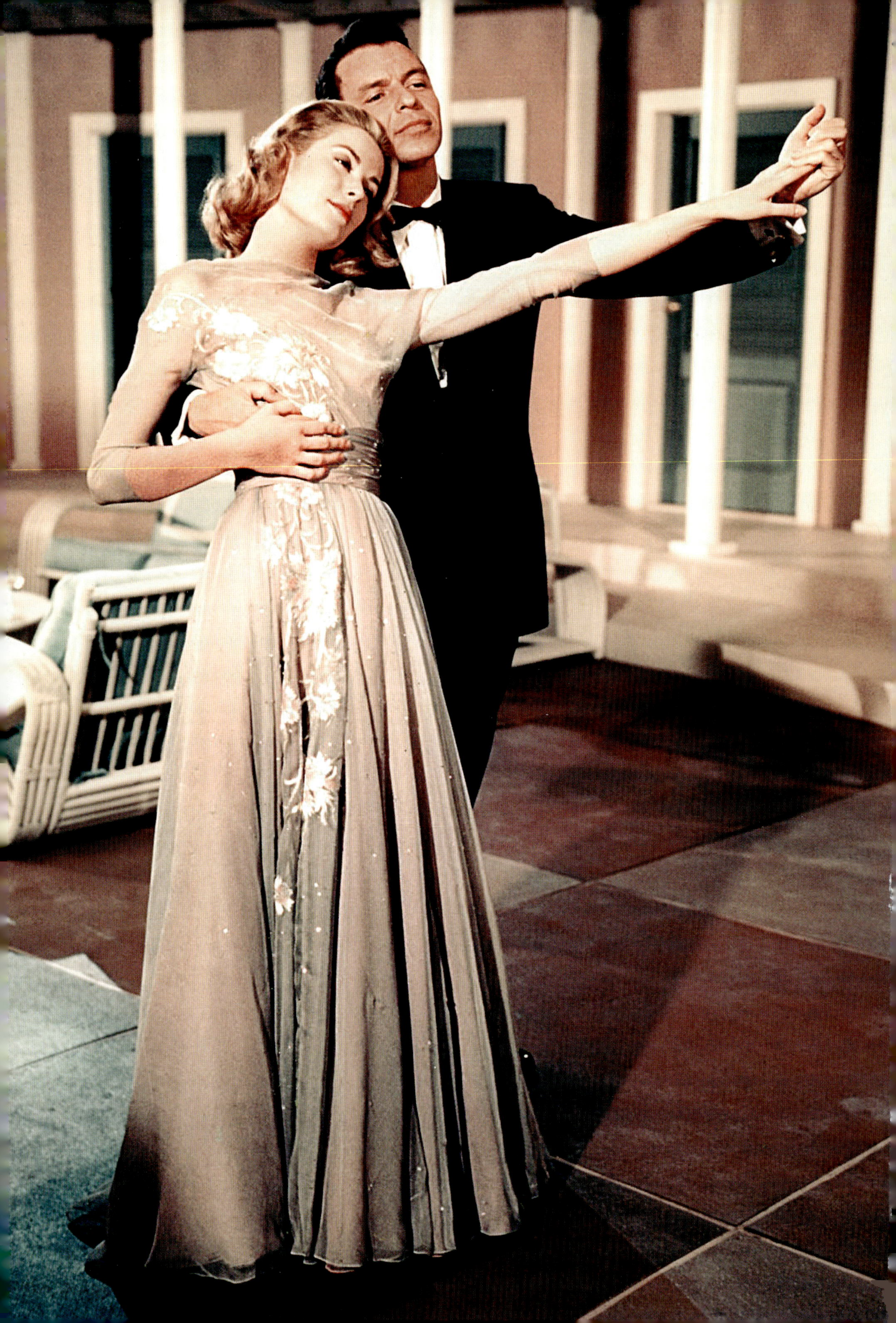

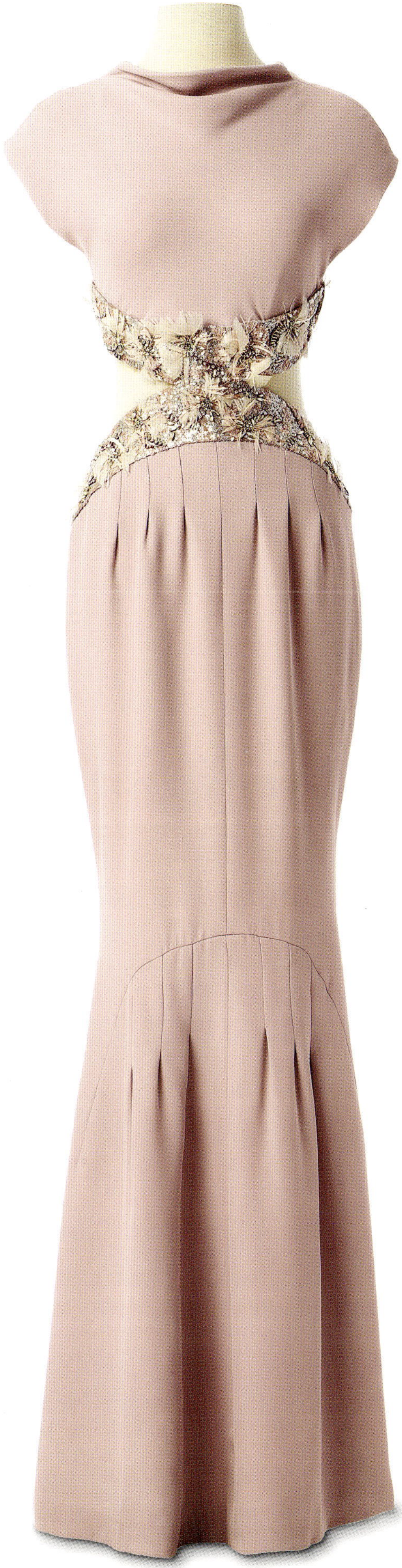

“You can say what you want about long dresses, but they cover a multitude of shins.”

Mae West

This pink Chanel couture gown is a winning combination of conservative and provocative. It's a sweet color, and the neckline is completely covered up—but then you have these beaded cutouts, which, incidentally, draw the eye inward and make the waist look tiny. *Opposite:* A subtly sparkly elegant gown, like this one on Grace Kelly in *High Society,* is what you wear when your guy is in a tuxedo. I love dresses that have simple shapes but intricate handwork. If you're at all self-conscious about your arms, long sleeves are a much better solution than a wrap.

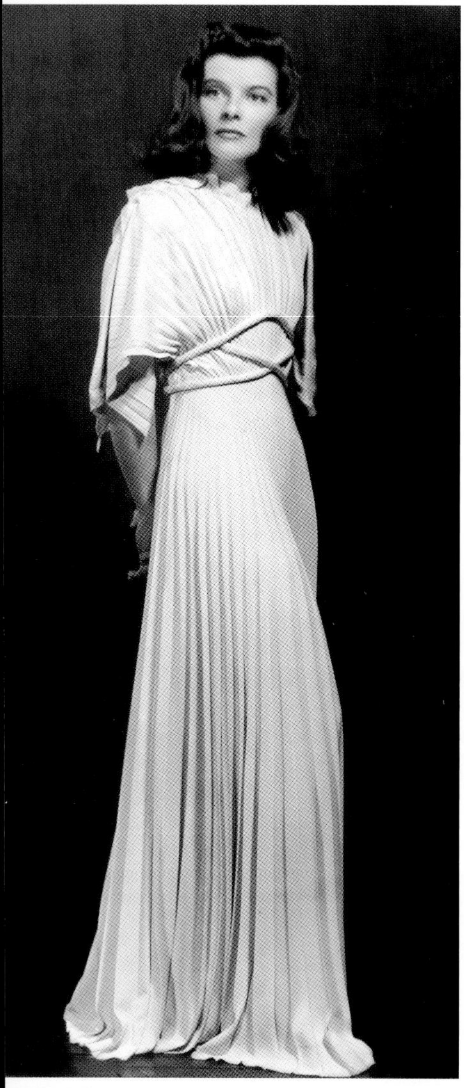

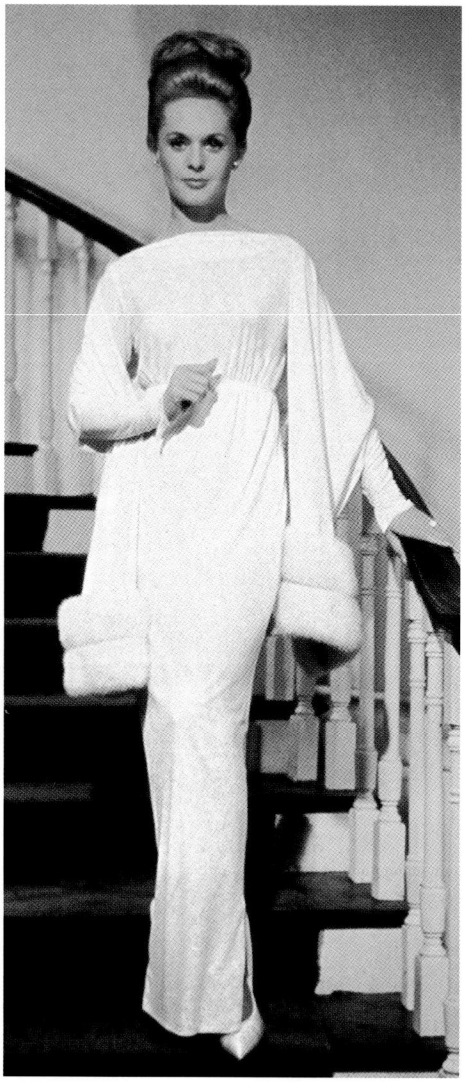

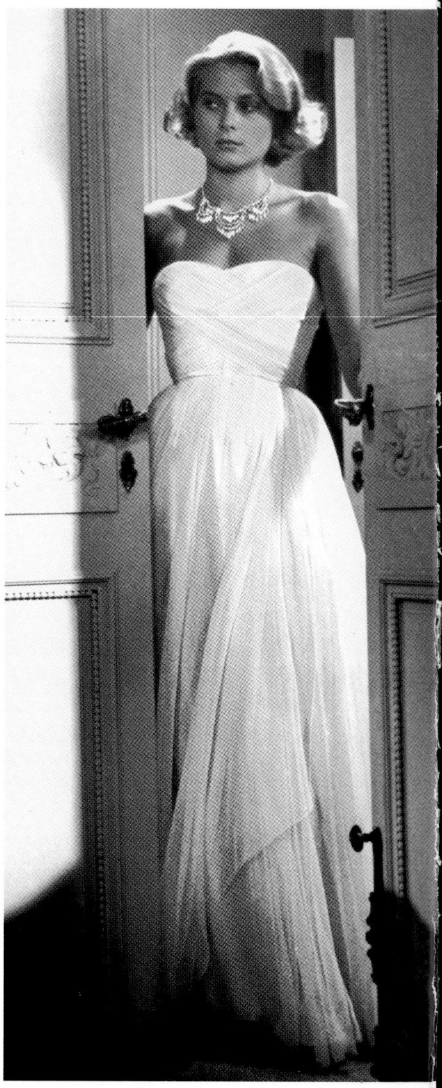

These dresses illustrate how white always works for formal occasions. *From left:* With the Grecian style dress Katharine Hepburn wears in *The Philadelphia Story,* you have to make sure the fabric is heavy enough to fall gracefully, otherwise it blouses and adds bulk; Tippi Hedren in this dress is reason enough to watch *Marnie.* It's supermodern and superflattering. You see a bit of collarbone, a suggestion of the waist. Her hair is part of the line, which is key; messy bedroom hair wouldn't work here. Grace Kelly's chiffon dress from *To Catch a Thief* is the most classic formal gown in the entire world. If you opt for it, make sure the top of the bodice hits at the right place. Too high and you look neckless; too low and your bosom will look like it's sagging. *Opposite:* Joan Crawford's dress from *Letty Lynton* is a textbook illustration of how to make volume work for you; if your shoulders are either wide or weak, this is a way to camouflage them.

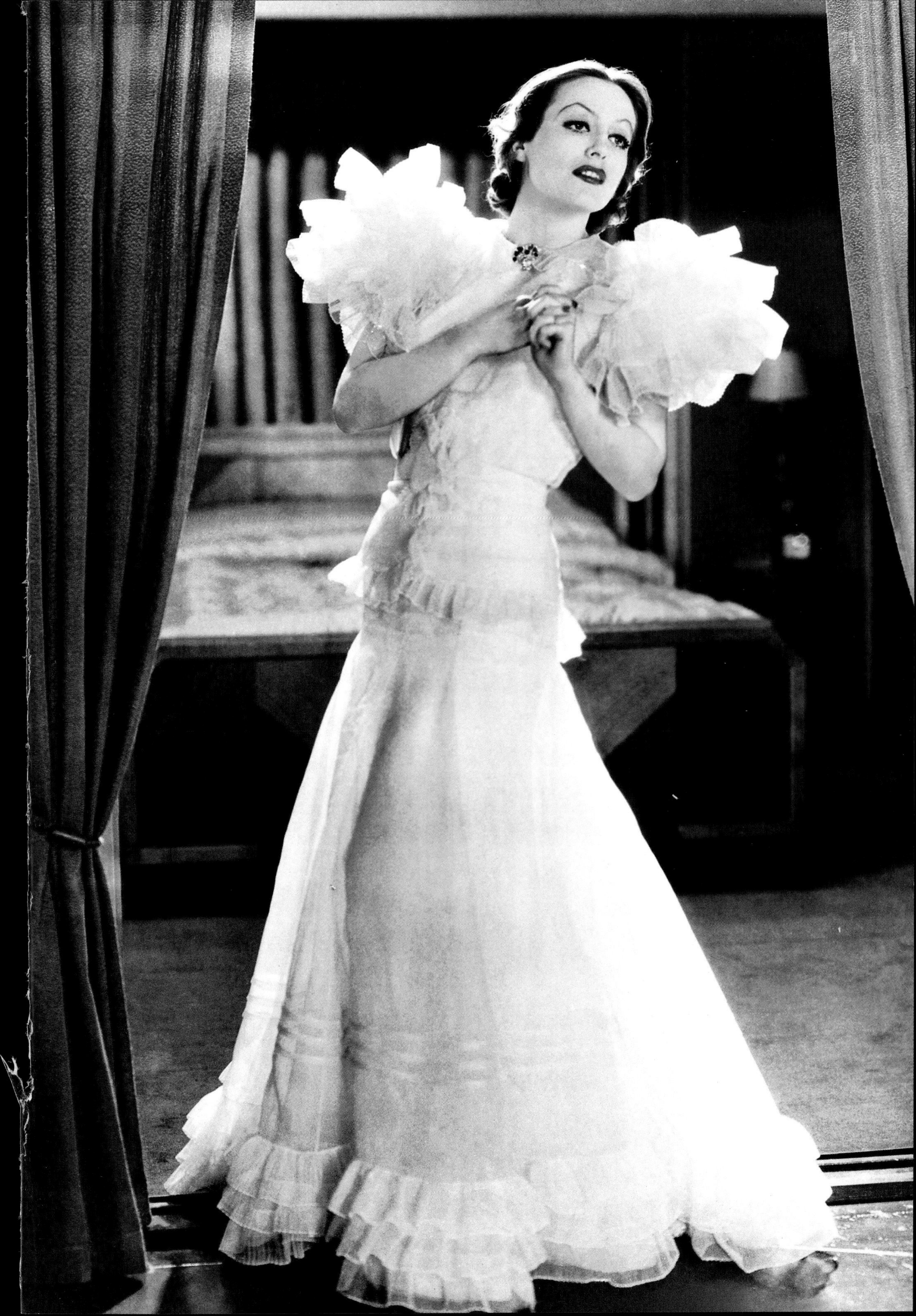

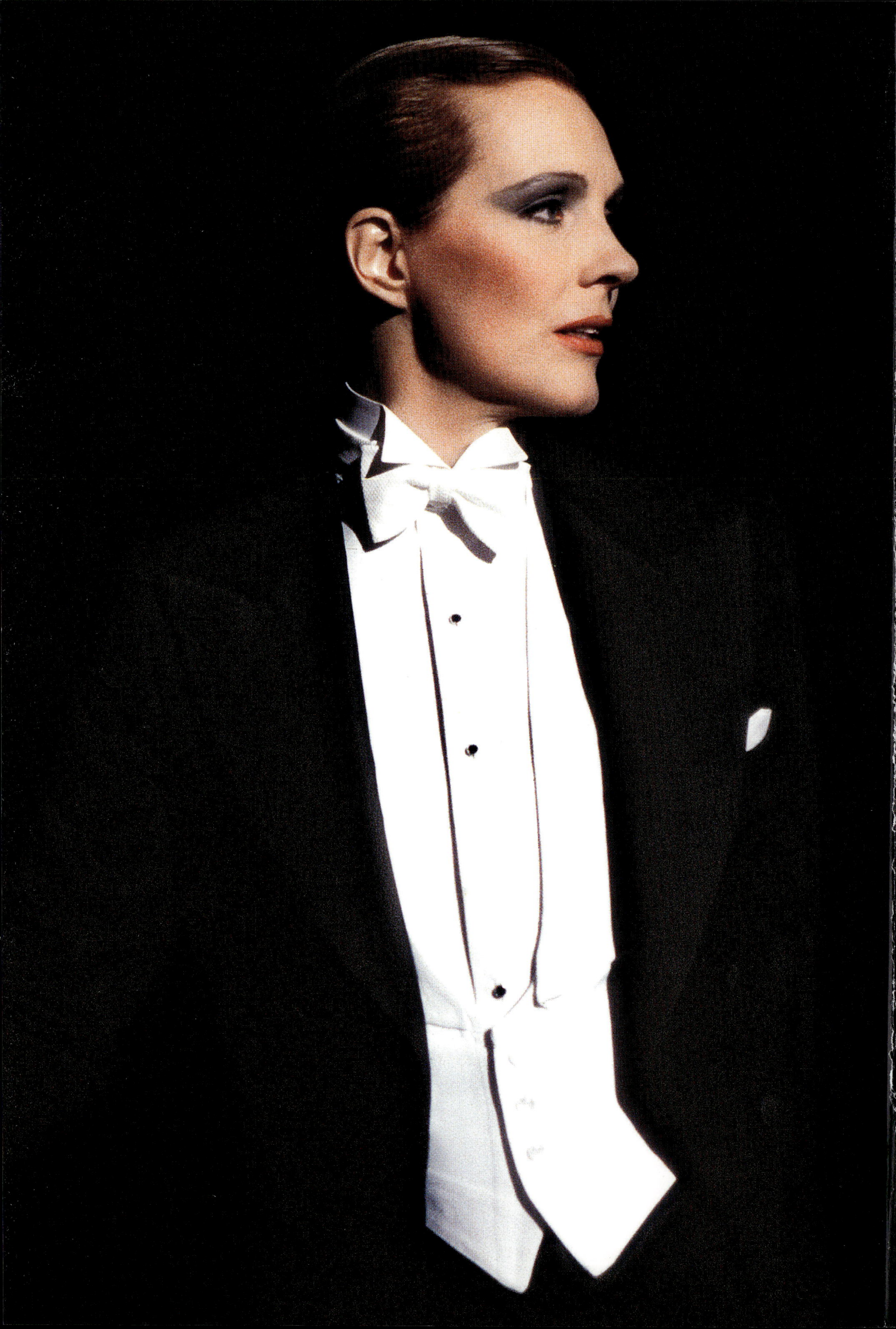

no matter what kind of gown you wear, it's always a good idea to try it on a few days before the event and get your bearings. Then, if you need to take up a hem or tighten a strap, you have time.

One of my favorite on-screen romantic dresses is from a film that no one associates with fashion: *Bride of Frankenstein.* Elsa Lanchester's white net gown (see page 119) has a lovely mix of historical references—puffed sleeves, a square Renaissance neckline, and minutely detailed moon and star embroidery—paired with vintage-y looking jewelry. It's an iconic black-tie look that I could easily see on a fashion-loving girl like Keira Knightley. It's not sexy, but it is very feminine, and that's what you want to emphasize here. Pretty upswept hair, fresh-looking skin, discreet cat's-eye makeup, delicate jewelry—there should be nothing heavy-handed about the grooming or the accessories. When I dressed Rachel Weisz in a platinum

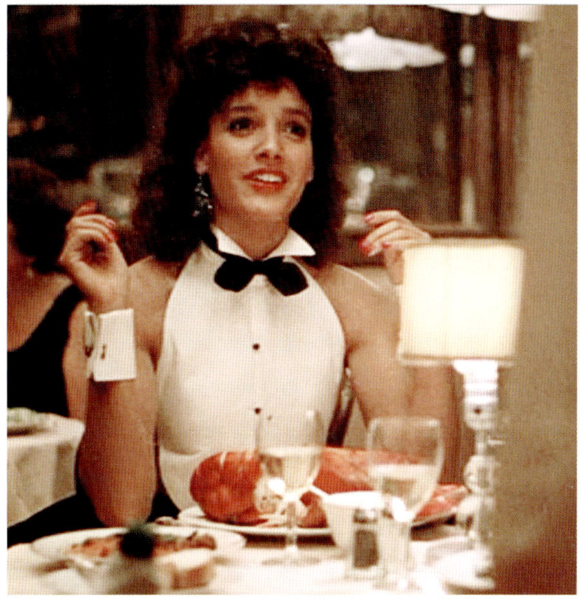

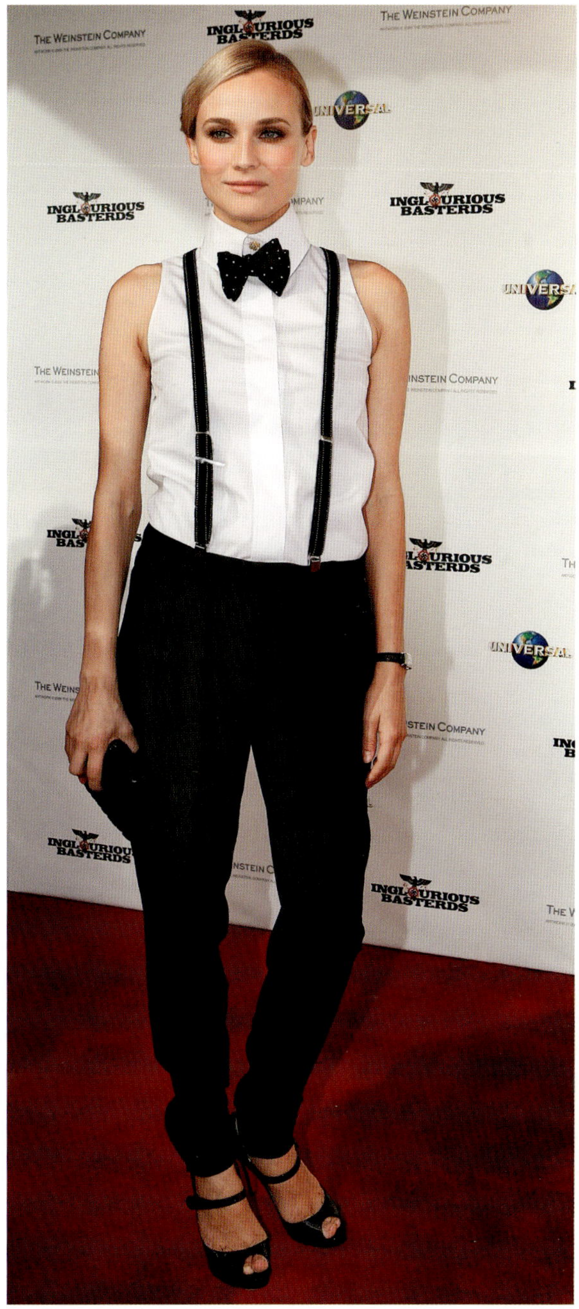

Top: The feminine way to wear a tuxedo is to make it playful and sexy and subversive, like Jennifer Beals does in *Flashdance.* She's made the bib of a man's dress shirt into a halter top and is wearing the cuffs as bracelets, which makes the look supercute and a little naughty. *Bottom:* Take a cue from Diane Kruger, seen here during the press run for *Inglourious Basterds,* and add some feminine details to your tux. Make sure the pants are cut for a woman's figure, and definitely wear heels—flats are too masculine with this look. *Opposite:* Julie Andrews in *Victor Victoria* is one of the original iconic woman-in-a-tuxedo inspirations.

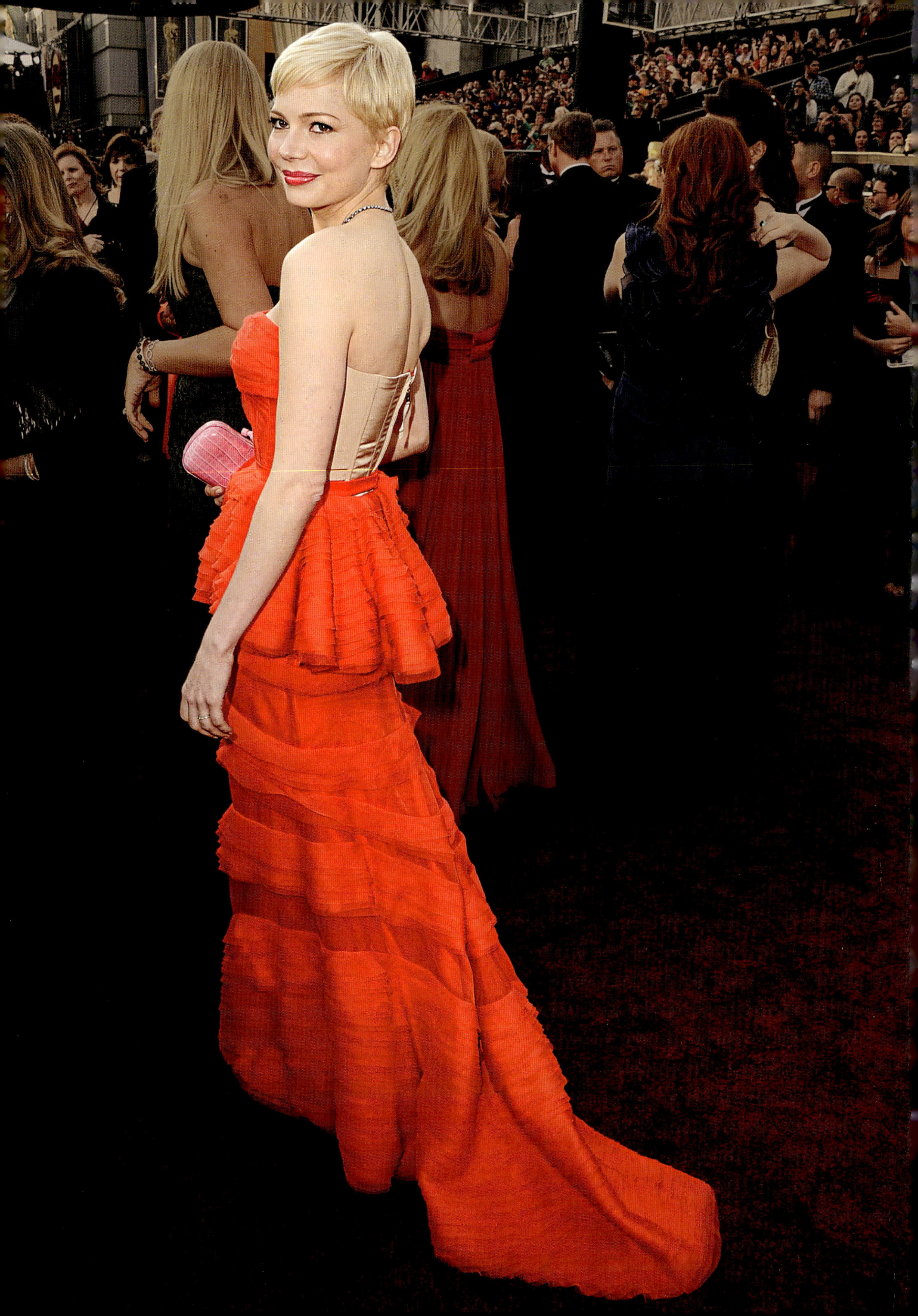

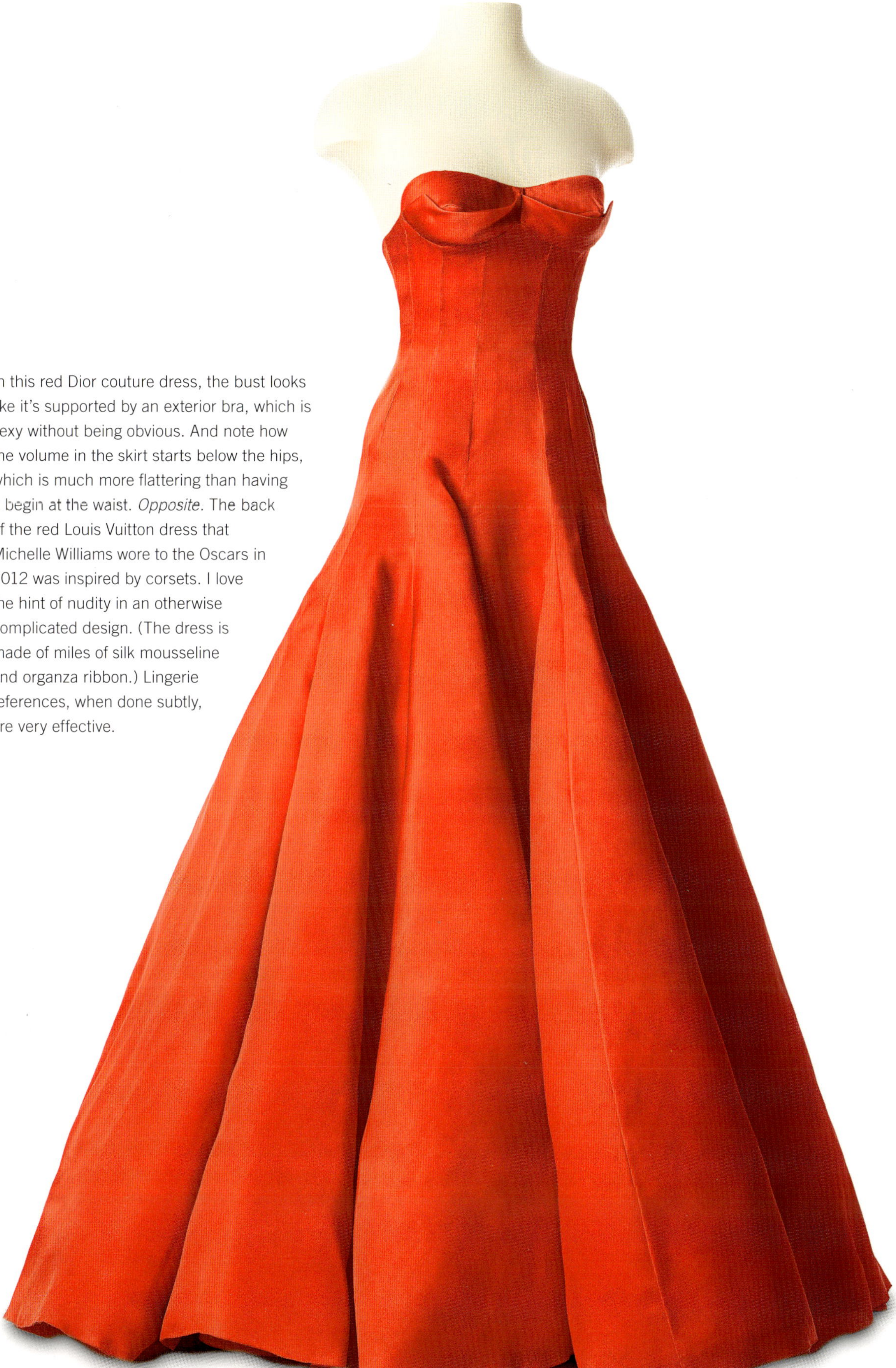

In this red Dior couture dress, the bust looks like it's supported by an exterior bra, which is sexy without being obvious. And note how the volume in the skirt starts below the hips, which is much more flattering than having it begin at the waist. *Opposite.* The back of the red Louis Vuitton dress that Michelle Williams wore to the Oscars in 2012 was inspired by corsets. I love the hint of nudity in an otherwise complicated design. (The dress is made of miles of silk mousseline and organza ribbon.) Lingerie references, when done subtly, are very effective.

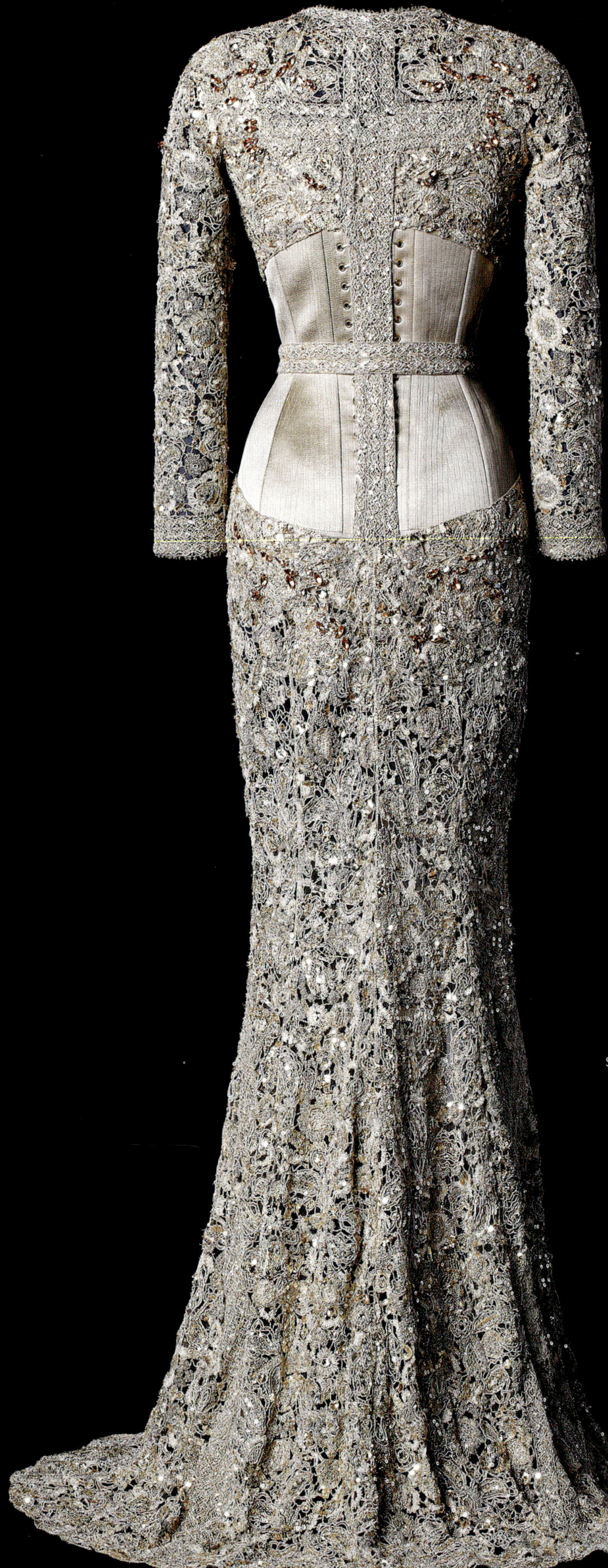

It took hundreds of hours to hand-embroider the gold lace for this Givenchy haute couture gown. Evening is a time when you can indulge in this kind of rarefied detail. Natalie Portman's 2005 Oscar dress (*opposite*), by Lanvin, is subtle but very effective. We wanted her to look fresh, so instead of going for a fitted or trussed-up dress, we went in a metallic tulle that is more of a paint stroke or a wrapping for the body. It's womanly but ethereal, rather than vampy.

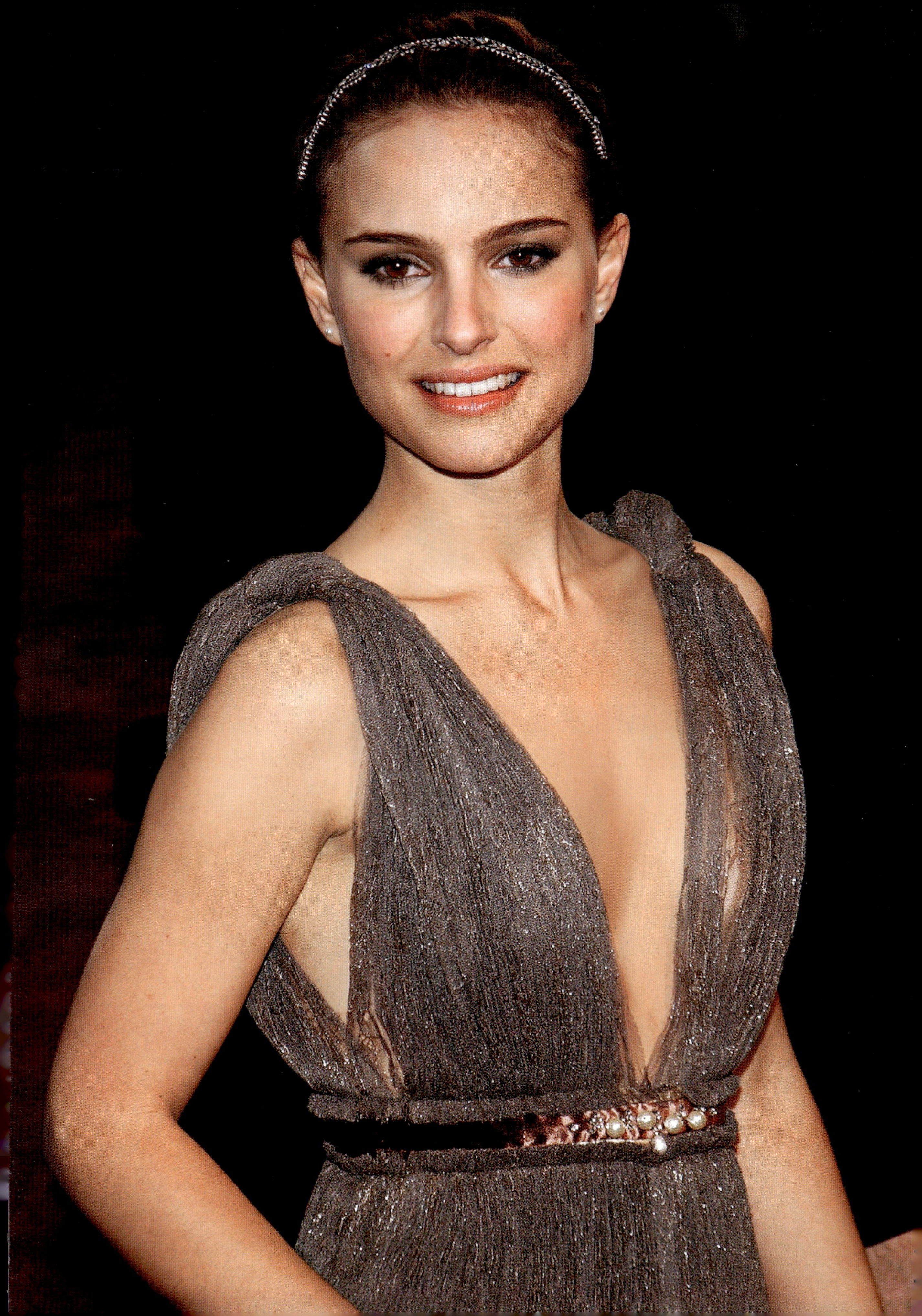

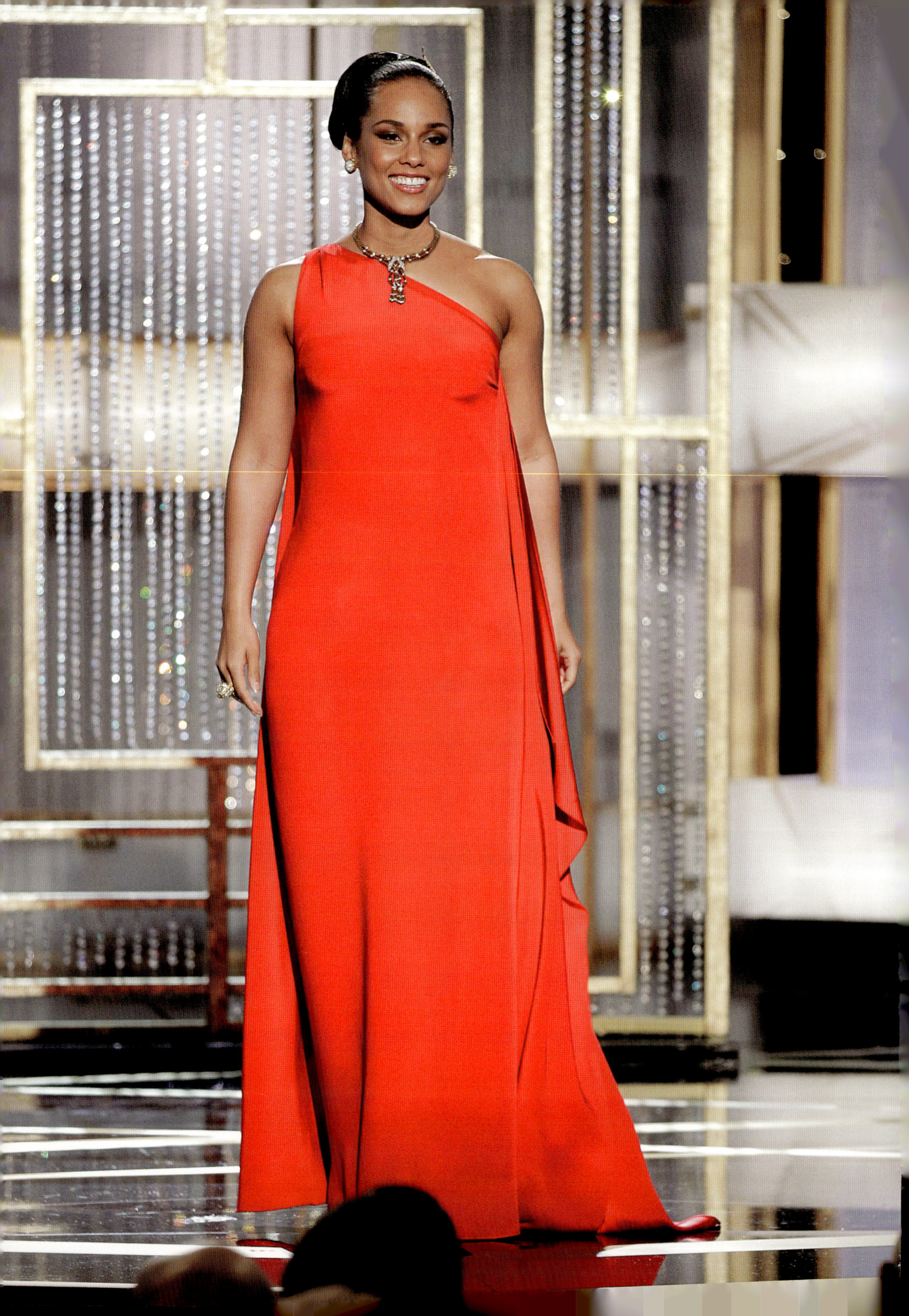

satin Vera Wang for the Oscars (see page 121) in 2007, the look was an homage to *Young Frankenstein.* Rachel is carrying a clutch in this photograph, which brings me to a small but important point. If you're going to carry a clutch, make sure you can easily hold it in one hand so your fingers don't look clawlike.

For women who lean toward an unfussy, modern vibe, the column dress has no peer. The combination of a very simple shape and strong color (including white and black) looks smashing and won't feel like a costume for women who have no patience for frills. When you're wearing a minimal dress, I think hair and makeup should be kept in the background, and you should confine your risks to jewelry à la Audrey Hepburn in *Funny Face* (see page 131). Her hair is slicked back, her shoes—I love that they're no-nonsense low-heeled pumps—match her dress, and then she's wearing this look-at-me green necklace. It keeps the whole thing from feeling trite.

When people refer to statement jewelry, they usually mean a necklace, but I love brooches and don't

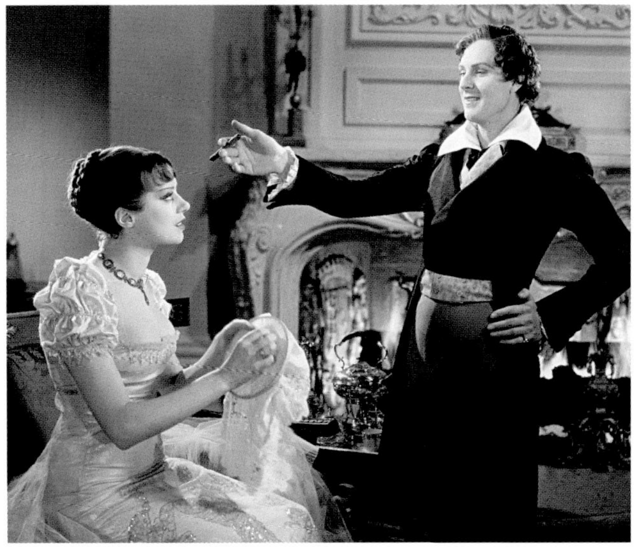

"I've learned to love my curves, my womanliness. I used to hide it, to downplay it. But now I revel in it."

Alicia Keys

Elsa Lanchester's romantic dress in *Bride of Frankenstein* is combined with a simple hairstyle and fresh makeup for a look that's totally modern. It's the details that make it work: the winged eye, the décolletage, the old-fashioned necklace. *Opposite:* My inspiration for Alicia Keys's look at the Golden Globes in 2011 was Maria Callas. We went for a regal 1960s couture look from Michael Kors. A one-shouldered dress is great if you don't want to bare too much skin and for covering up sun damage or crepe-iness.

> "You're considered superficial and silly if you're interested in fashion, but I think you can be substantial and still be interested in frivolity."
>
> Sofia Coppola

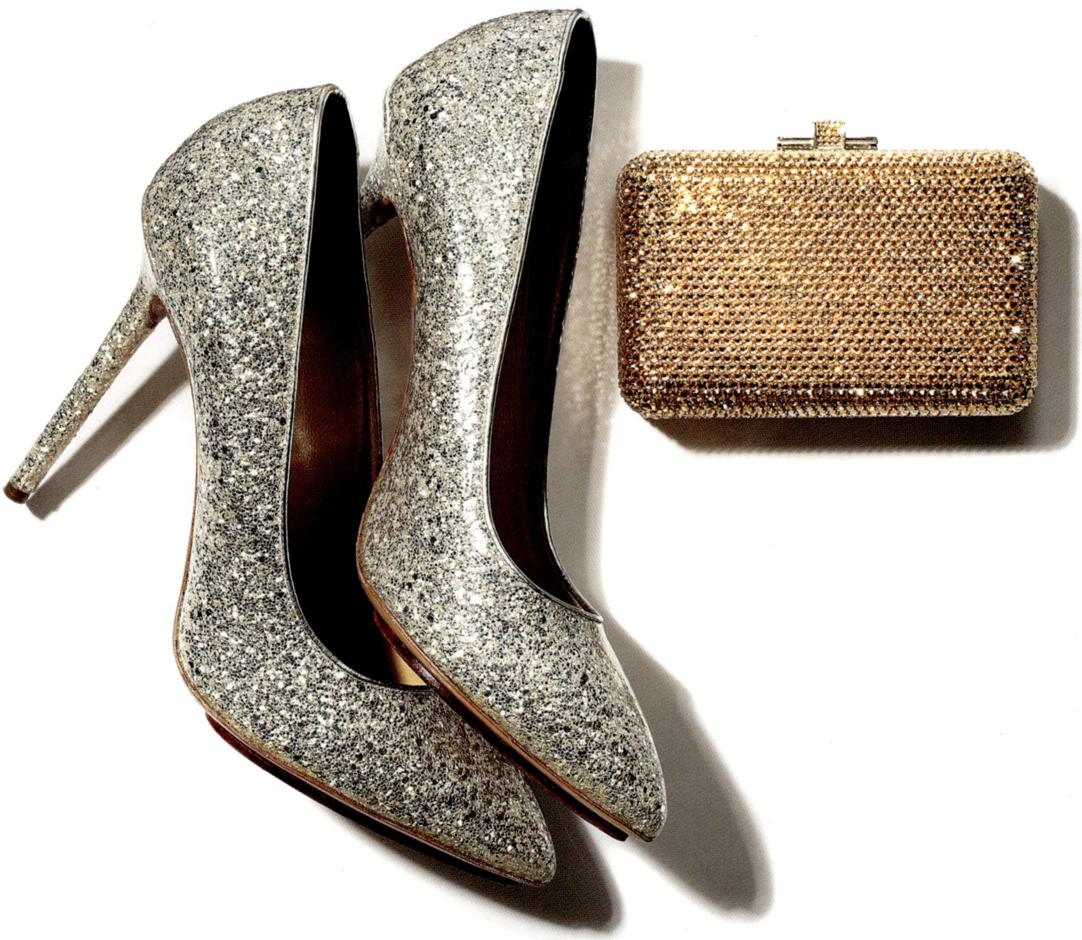

I can never get enough sparkle; it just brings me an enormous amount of pleasure. Plus, I have a three-texture rule that I like to follow and a shiny accessory, such as these pumps by Charlotte Olympia and clutch by Judith Leiber, is a great way to make this look work. Say you have a silk dress with a grosgrain belt—add the sparkly shoes and clutch and you have texture, depth, and interest, all without being overdressed. *Opposite:* Romantic dresses, like this one Rachel Weisz wore for the Oscars in 2007, are generally not sexy. Instead, they're pretty, and that's the quality you want to play up with them. Think touchable, feminine hair and makeup, and delicate accessories.

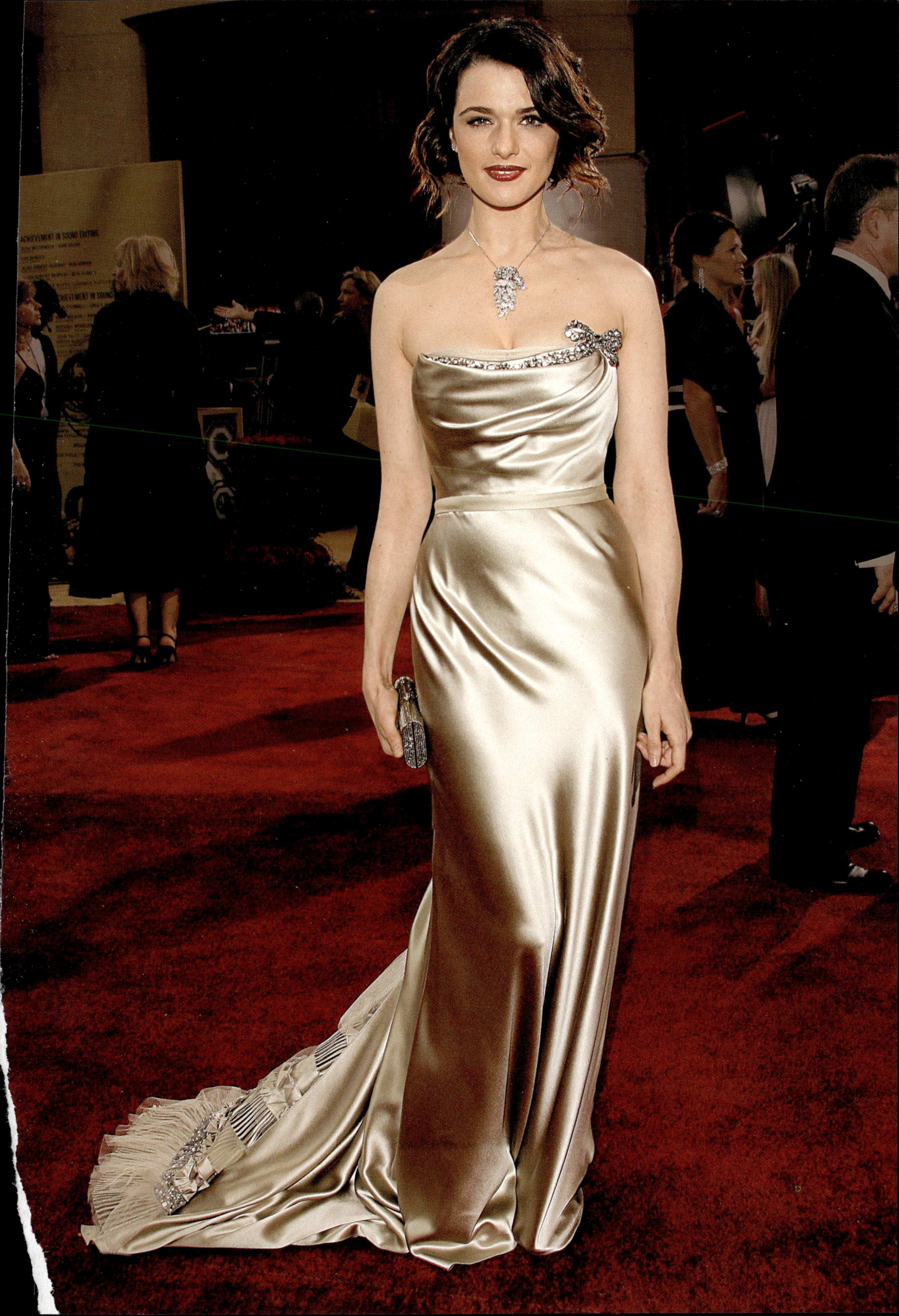

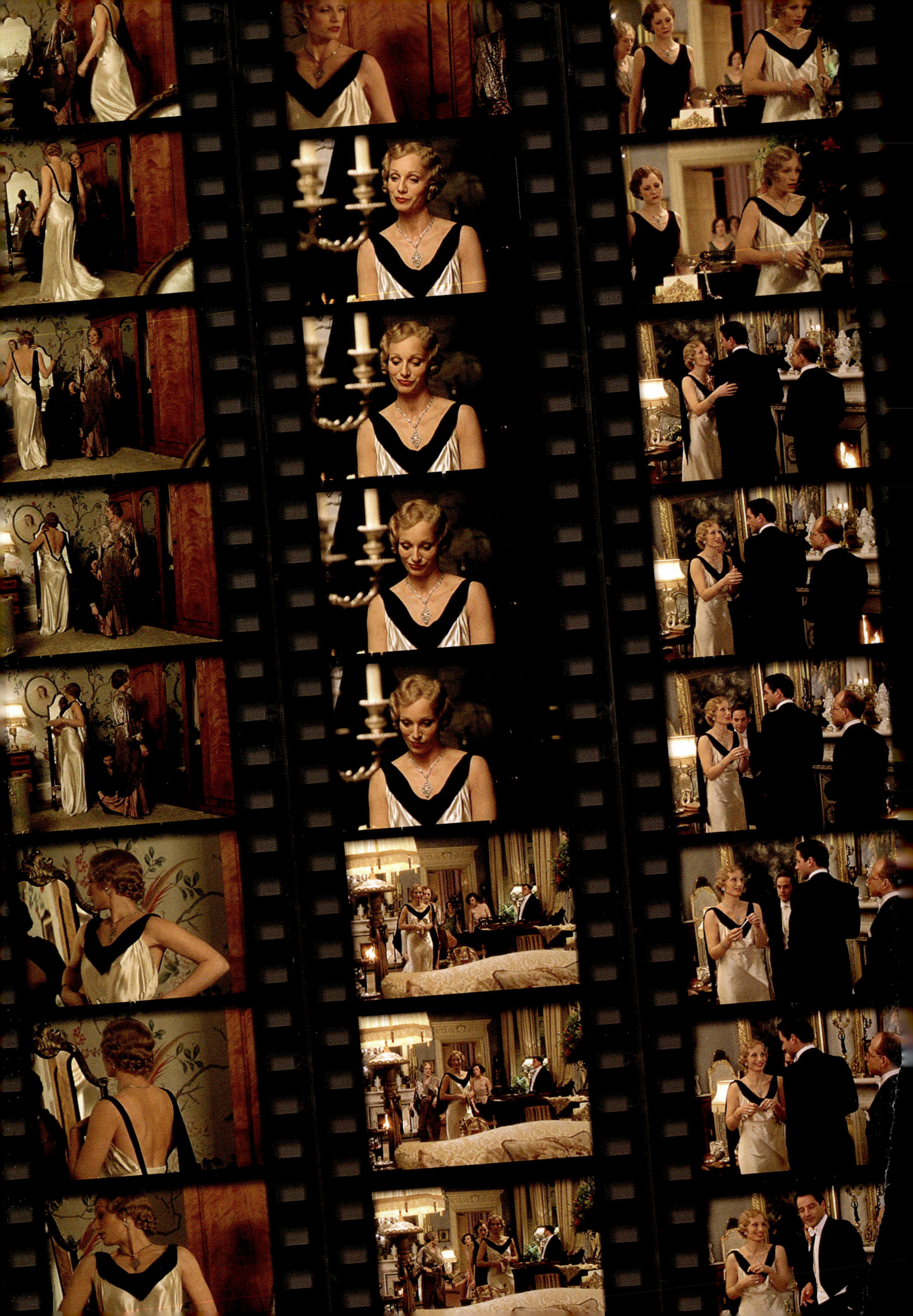

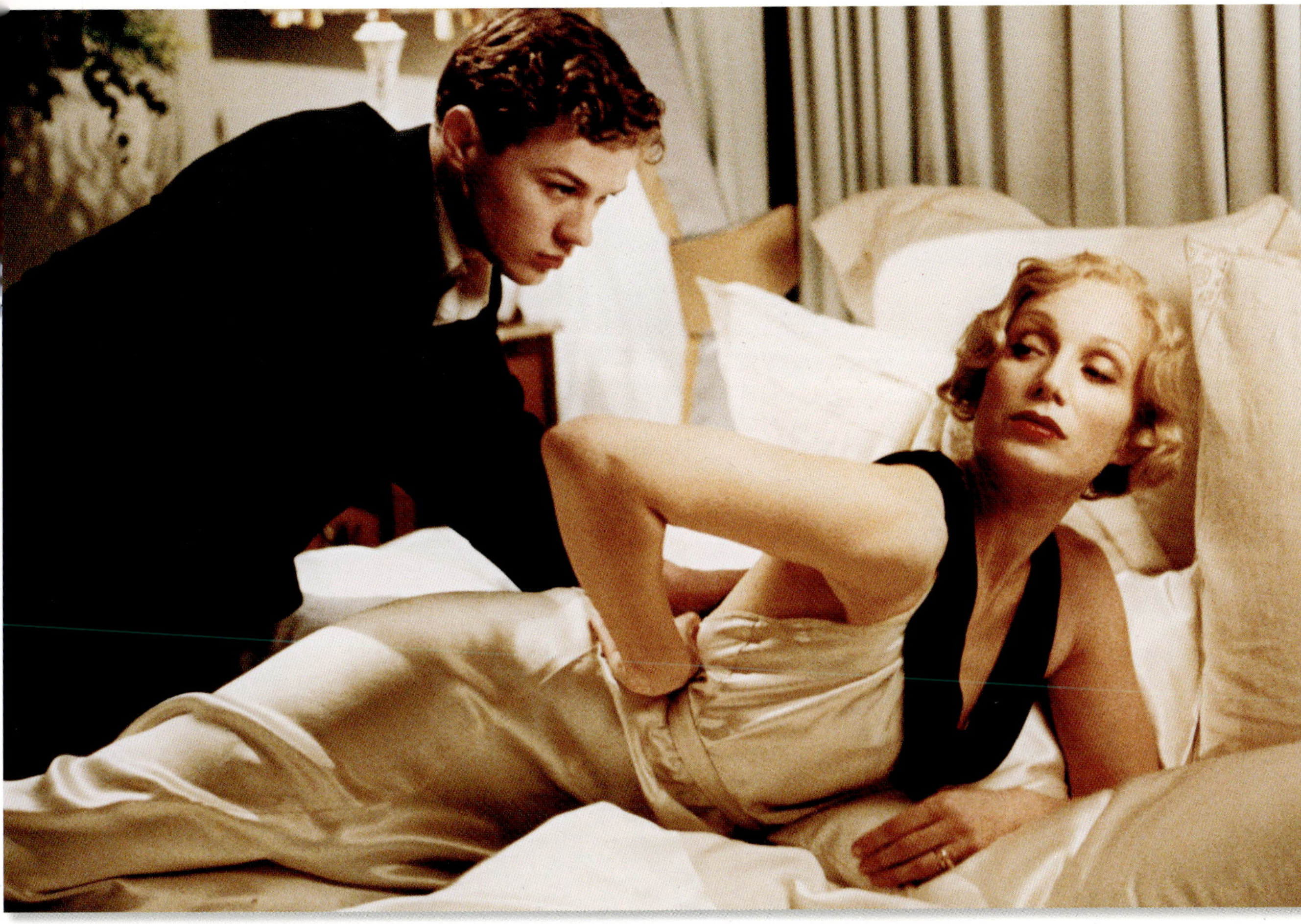

> "Glamour is something you can't bear to be without once you're used to it."
>
> Loretta Young

I have a real thing for 1930s-style satin gowns like the one Kristin Scott Thomas wears in *Gosford Park*. Because they're so light and sensual in the way they move over the body, you need sexier makeup. This kind of dress looks better in a pale color; in a bright one it doesn't look formal enough for black tie. *Following pages:* Julia Roberts in *Pretty Woman* had to be in this book! Her dress is a symbol of her transformation, which is in essence what happens to everyone when they dress for a formal occasion. This kind of corset-style cut with a little drop sleeve to hide the underarm is superflattering on so many women.

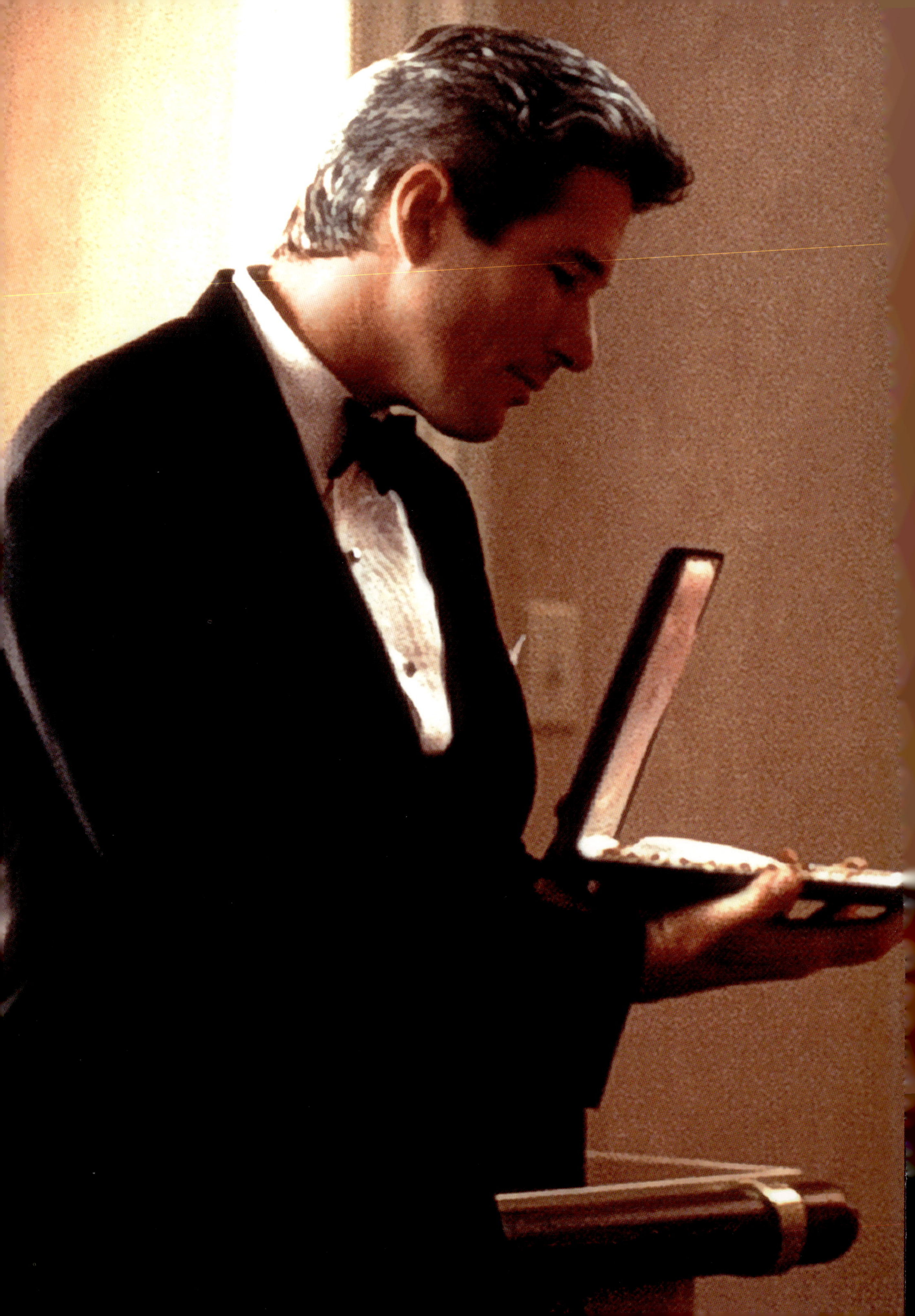

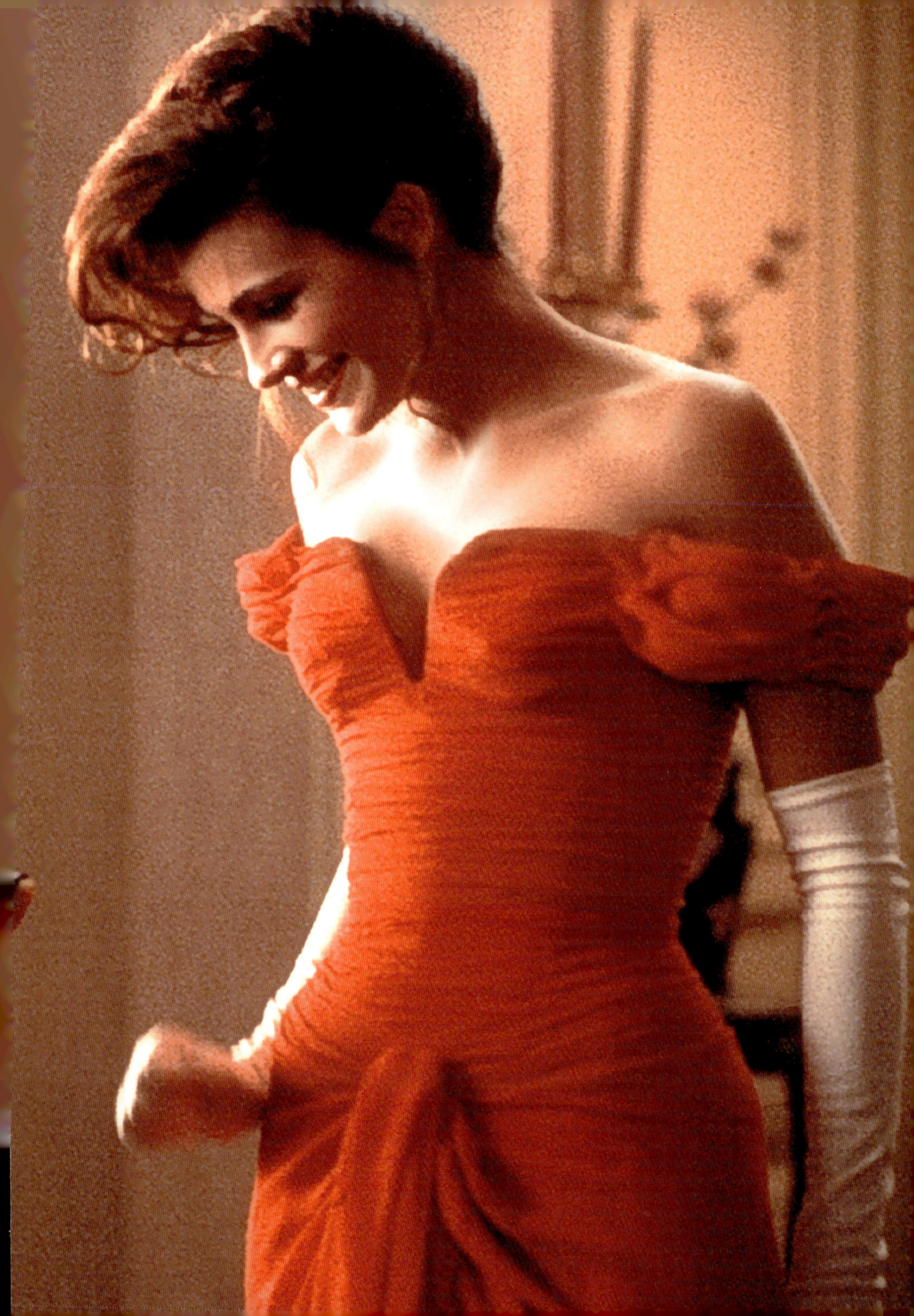

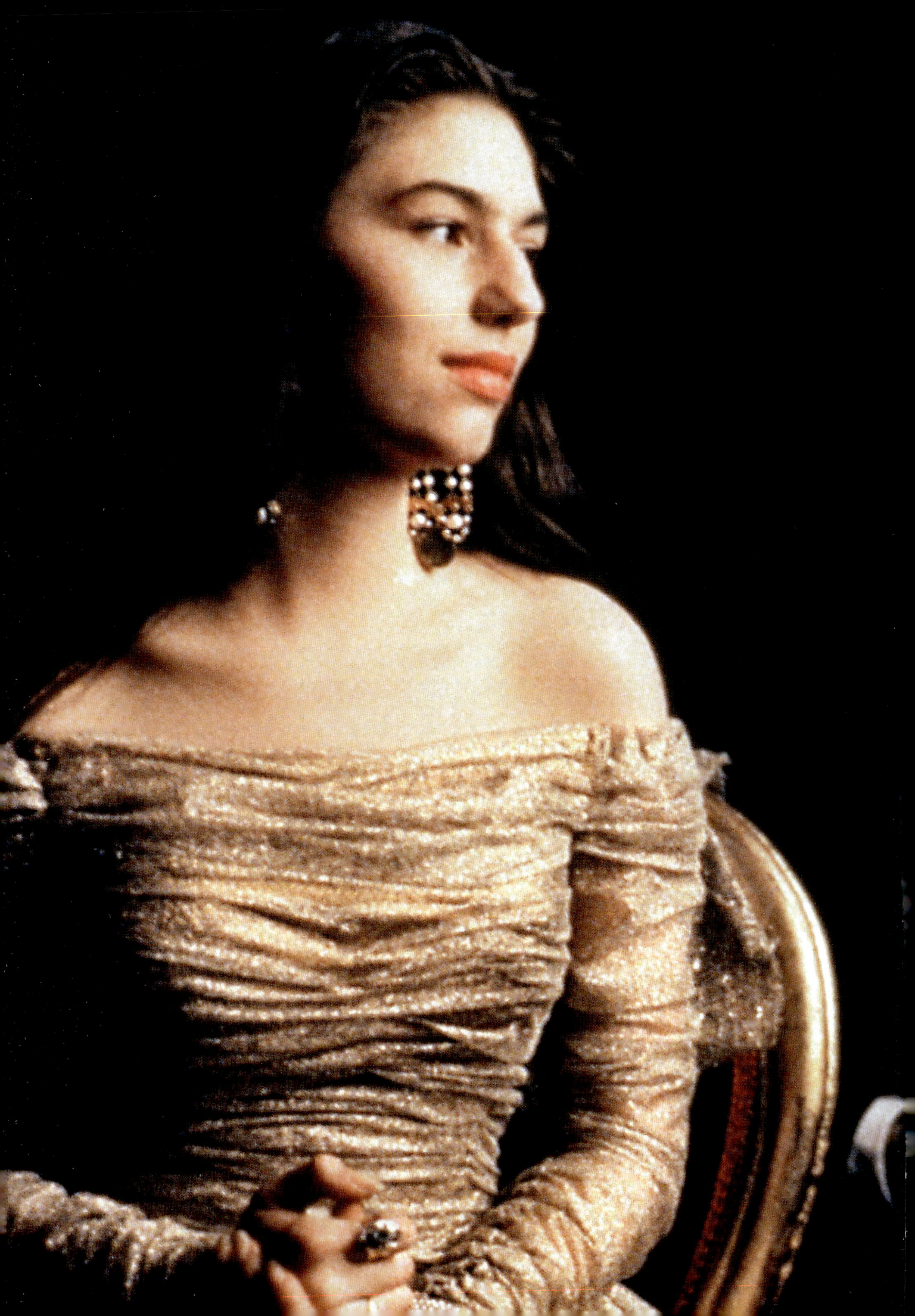

“People tell stories about themselves with their clothing, their hair, with the way they move and the way they present themselves.”

Julianne Moore

understand why everyone else doesn't, too. They're like lost treasures—pretty and sparkly and versatile. I use brooches to emphasize a particular aspect of a look: You can pin one to a hip to draw attention to some draping. You can attach it to a ribbon to make a belt that sets off the waist. You can put one in the hair or on a clutch. Think of your jewelry as a highlighter marker—it draws the eye to wherever you put it. For example, I don't like wide earrings, because they have a way of widening the jawline. Instead, keep your earrings narrow and long to accentuate the

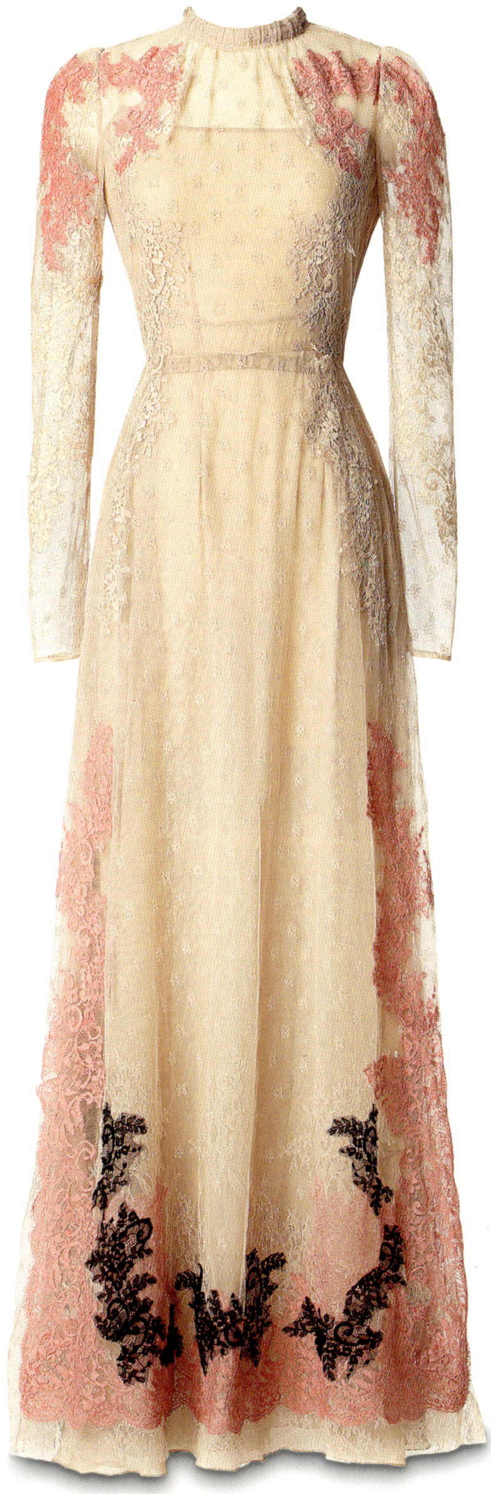

There's a perception that you need to bare a lot of skin in the evening, but I think covered-up dresses, such as this pale-pink lace gown from Valentino, are very chic. The fuchsia-and-black embroidered lace make the dress interesting without weighing it down—the whole thing is light and lovely and youthful. *Opposite*: The metallic gold dress Sofia Coppola wears in *The Godfather: Part III* is delectable in a Renaissance princess way. The jewelry is very important to this look—she's got that bonbon-ish dress, bare shoulders, and then those gypsy earrings that keep the whole thing from getting too sweet.

length of the neck or draw attention to your cheekbones. If you have a beautiful clavicle or attractive wrists, then wear bracelets or rings. I think we spend so much time worrying about our backsides that we forget about things like hands, which can be so expressive and graceful. If you have nice hands, wear a cocktail ring.

What women never seem to be able to forget about are their arms. There's this perception that going to a formal event means baring them, and the woman ends up clutching a wrap around her shoulders all evening, awkwardly fumbling with her drink and clutch every time she needs to shake someone's hand. This drives me crazy! If you're shy about showing your arms—or even if you're not—wear a long-sleeved dress. They work in column (Tippi Hedren in *Marnie*), romantic (Sofia Coppola in *The Godfather III*), and princess (Grace Kelly in *High Society*) silhouettes, are incredibly elegant, and are a little bit unexpected. Plus, it's not a bad idea to be the only girl in the room who isn't showing off a lot of skin. Our everyday clothes can be a bit uniform. In the evening, we get a chance to shine. It would be a shame not to take advantage of that.

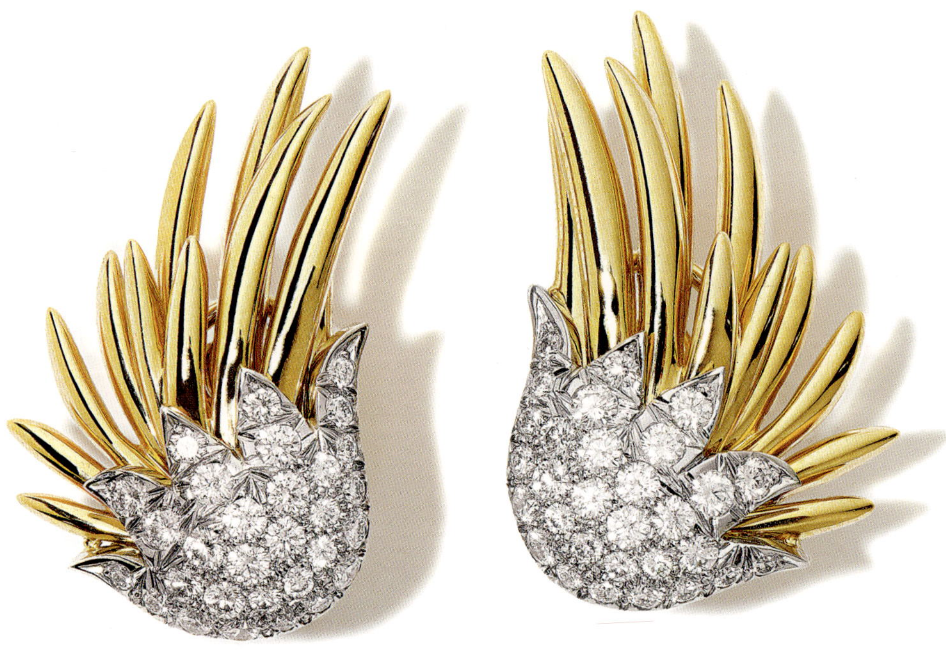

These earrings were designed by Jean Schlumberger, one of the great jewelers of the twentieth century, for Tiffany. You can wear them to point to your cheekbones, as shoe clips, in your hair—the possibilities are endless. *Opposite:* This Audrey Hepburn look from *Funny Face* is a classic modernist dress: a simple shape in a strong color. No embroidery, no fluff. Even her glossed-back hair is sleek and close to the body. *Previous pages*: White is always appropriate for black tie and there's no need for it to look bridal. In *The Tourist,* Angelina Jolie wore a white evening gown with a very Grecian feel, proving once again that you can choose classicism and simplicity and not be boring.

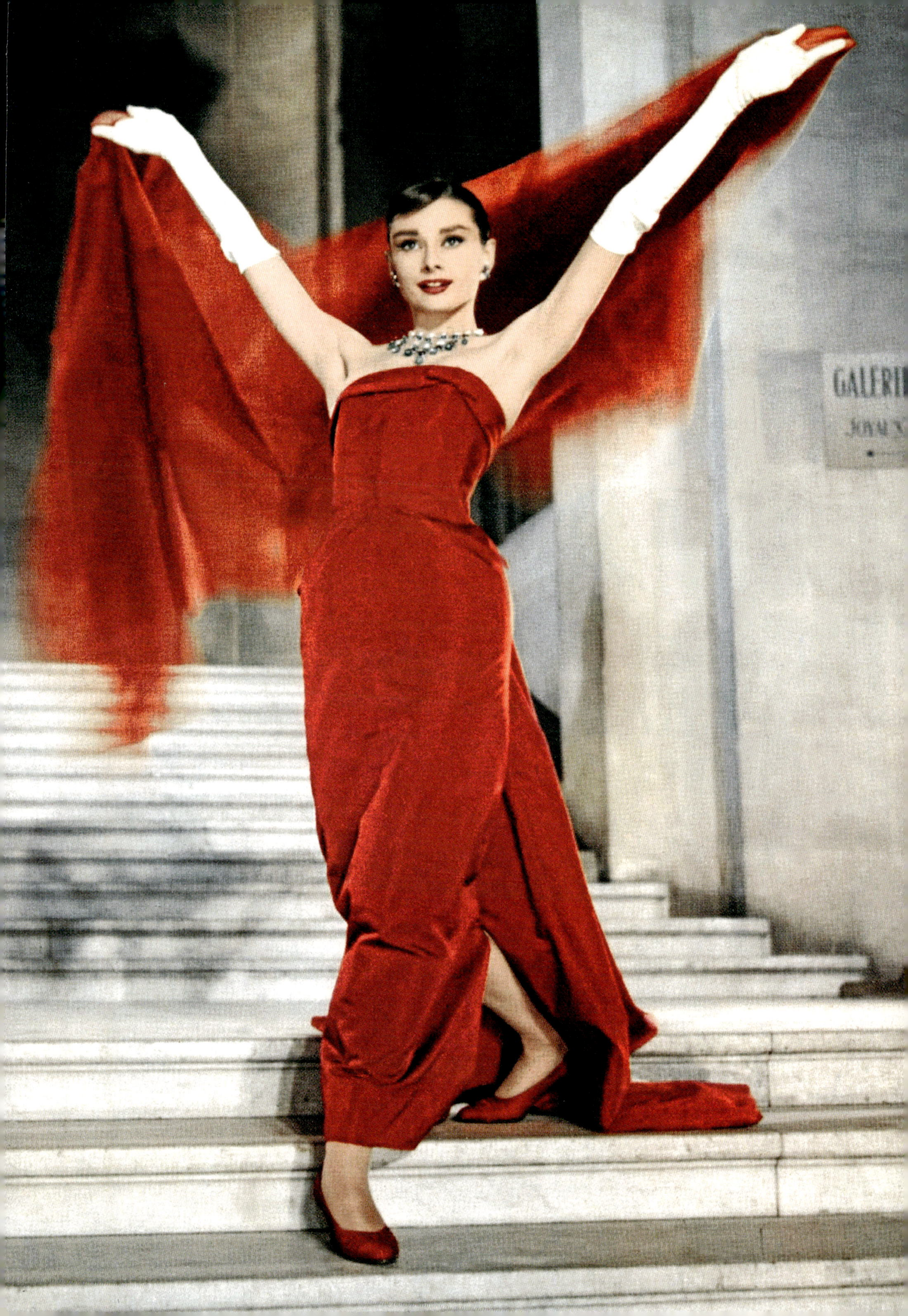
GALERI

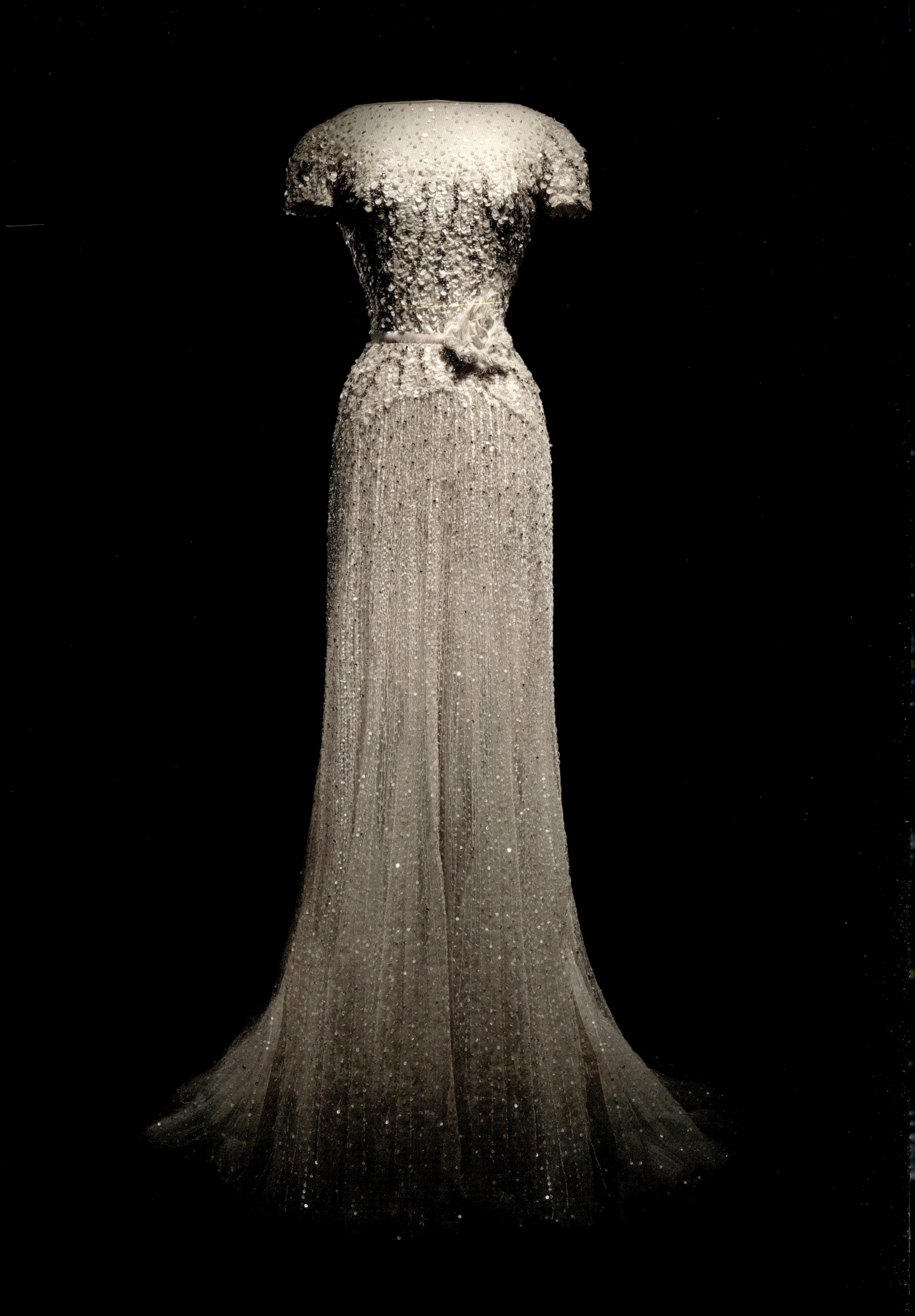

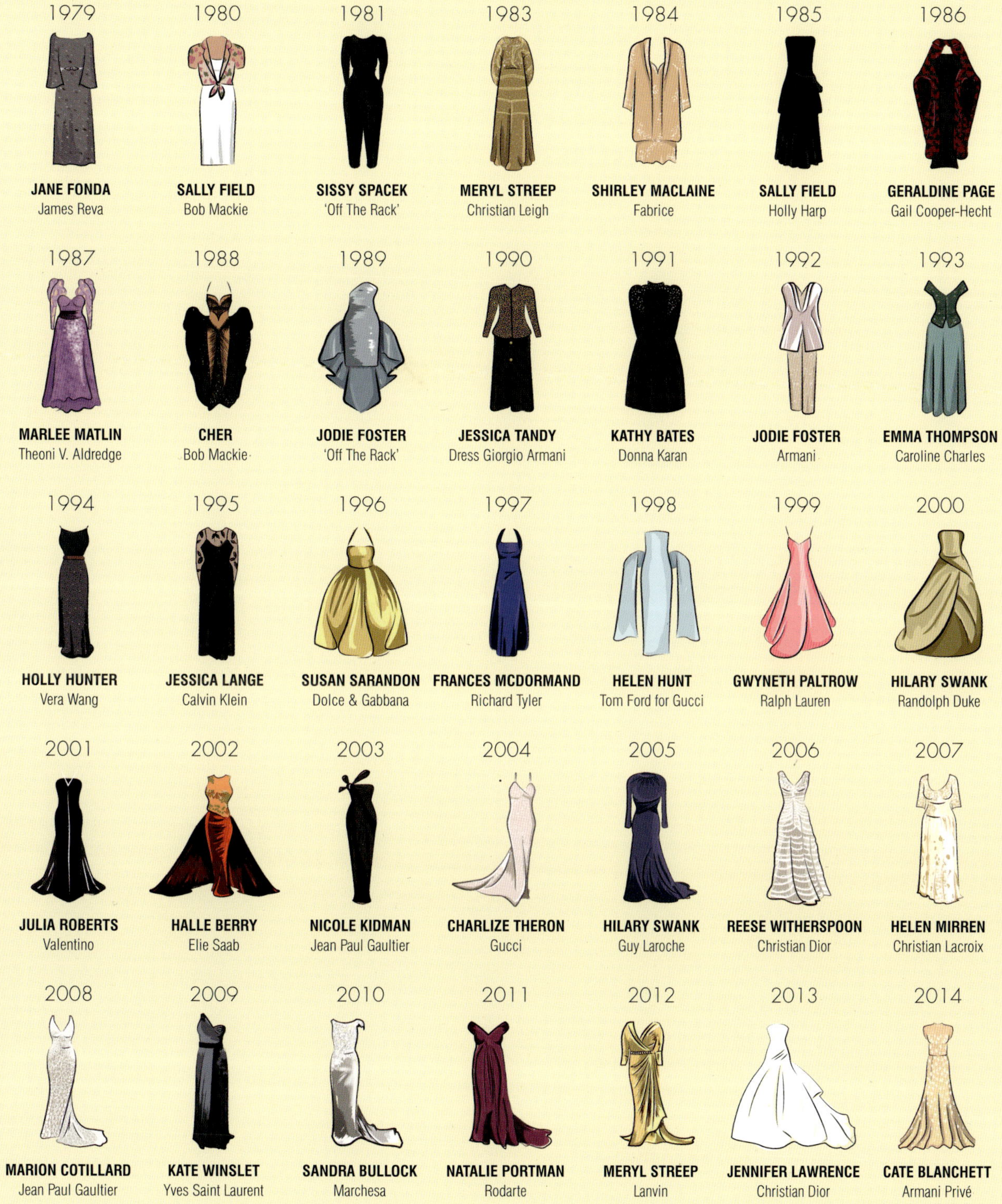

1962 – **SOPHIA LOREN**
1963 – **ANNE BANCROFT**
1964 – **PATRICIA NEAL**
1967 – **ELIZABETH TAYLOR**
1968 – **KATHARINE HEPBURN**
1969 – **KATHARINE HEPBURN**
1970 – **MAGGIE SMITH**
1971 – **GLENDA JACKSON**
1974 – **GLENDA JACKSON**
1975 – **ELLEN BURSTYN**
1982 – **KATHARINE HEPBURN**

An original illustration of the dresses worn by the best actresses at the Academy Awards.

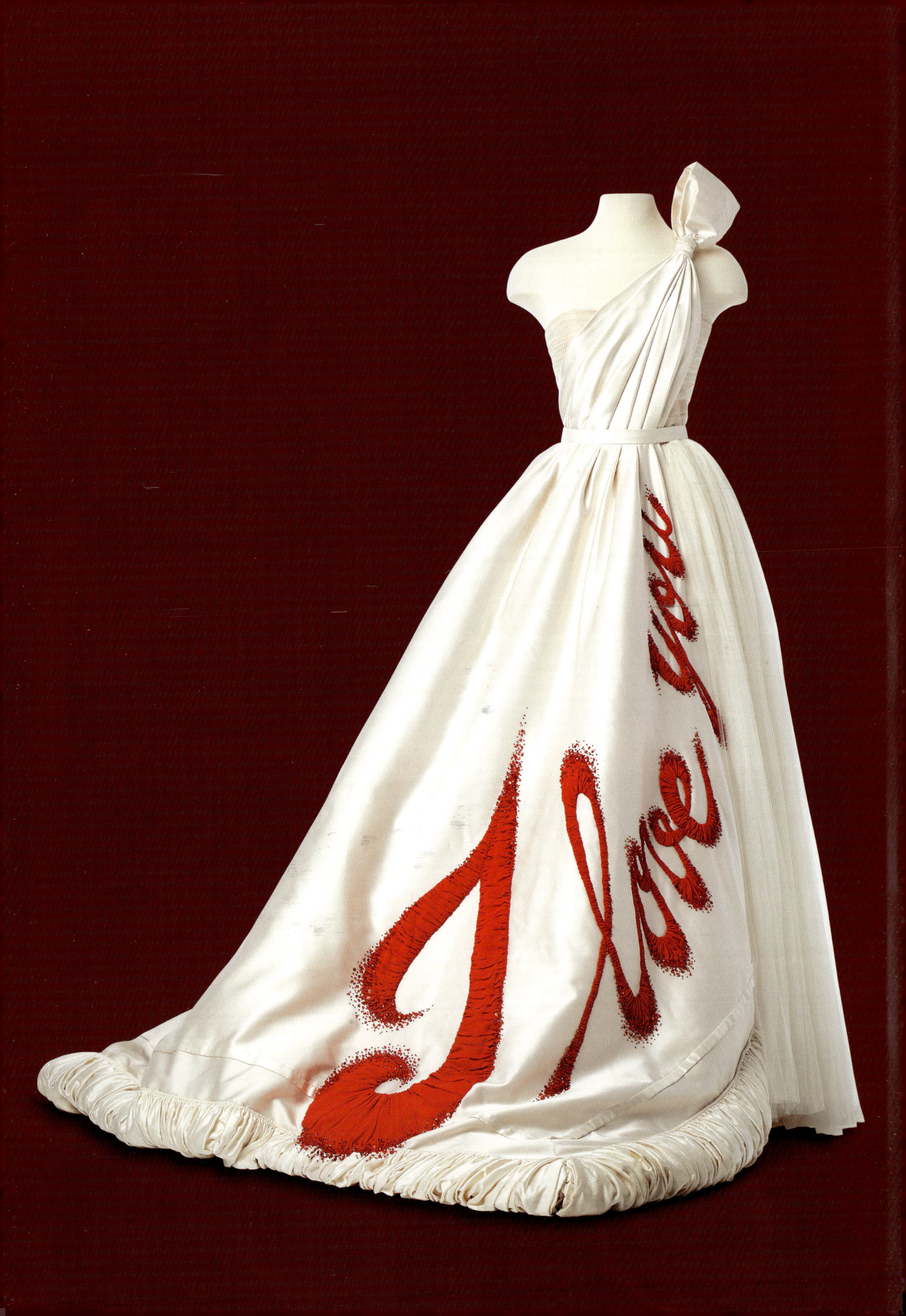
I love you

Acknowledgments

To Martine and Prosper, thank you for getting behind this book! I'm so excited to see my name next to yours! A big thank you to Waris Ahluwalia for introducing us, and thanks to Peter Hess for making the deal. Thank you to Lilli Millhiser for your hard work, grace, and sharp eye. Nancy MacDonell, you make it all sound good! To Tim Hout for taking such gorgeous pictures and really capturing the beauty. Thanks to the team at Assouline for your patience and talent: Esther Kremer, Shoshana Gutmajer, Betsy Mullinix, Jihyun Kim, Camille Dubois, and Lindsey Tulloch. Thank you to Natalie Portman and Troy Nankin for your encyclopedic knowledge of cinema your lists were where the book started. Many, many thanks to the companies and people who lent clothes, jewelry, and accessories: Fred Leighton, Verdura, Albright, Charlotte Olympia, Christian Dior, Dolce & Gabbana, Halston, Givenchy, Jason Wu, Kenneth Jay Lane, Judith Leiber, Christian Louboutin, Manolo Blahnik, Marchesa, Net-a-Porter, Olympia Le-Tan, Oscar de la Renta, Rare Vintage, Saint Laurent, Tiffany & Co., Sydney Garber, Valentino, and Viktor & Rolf. Big couture kisses to Mathilde Meyer, Youssef Marquis, Nancy Walsh, and Kate Walsh. To my clients who inspire me and make work so much fun. To the publicists, tailors, and hair and makeup whose work is what really makes the red carpet sparkle. Thank you to Risa Scobie, Victor Glemaud, Jeanine Lobell, and Hannah Notaro for talking to me about movies, dresses, and life for a zillion hours.

To Mom and Dad, thank you for your endless encouragement and belief in me. And most of all, thank you, Keith, Stellan, and Leif.

Assouline would like to thank: Oren B. Silverstein/Alamy Inc.; Jennifer Belt/Art Resource; Jamie Vuignier/The Kobal Collection at Art Resource; Toni Campo; Elisabetta Catalano; Caroline Chabidon; Serge Darmon/Collection Christophel; Oscar Espaillat/Corbis; Caroline Sturgess/Everett Collection; Sarah Zimmer/Getty Images; Carlo Giusti; Barbara Gogan; Laziz Hamani; Robert Kot; Bill Laughlin; Michelle Wright/Library of Congress; Sophia Loren; Beatrix Mahd Soltani; Paul North and William Hughes/Mediarun Digital; Andy Howick/mptvimages; Neal Peters and David Smith/The Neal Peters Collection; Derek Davidson/Photofest; Cheryl Della Pietra; Andrea Rincon Ray; Jasmine Habeler/Valentino Garavani Virtual Museum; Maria Fitzsimons/WENN.

This Viktor & Rolf dress is pure fantasy: The I-love-you embroidered front panel is actually a warm lap robe that comes off and can be wrapped around you, should you be riding in a horse-drawn carriage. Underneath is the most perfect, light-as-air haute couture ball gown.